D1029351

Freedom of Speech and
Press in America

Freedom of Speech and Press in America

By Edward G. Hudon

FOREWORD BY JUSTICE WILLIAM O. DOUGLAS

INTRODUCTION BY MORRIS L. ERNST

Public Affairs Press, Washington, D. C.

About the Author

With the exception of three and a half years of military service during World War II, Edward G. Hudon has been an employee of the Supreme Court of the United States since July, 1942. He has been an Assistant Librarian at the Court since 1947. A lawyer by training, he is a member of the bars of Maine, the District of Columbia, and of the Supreme Court of the United States.

Dr. Hudon holds five academic degrees (B.S., LL.B., LL.M., M.S. in L.S., S.J.D.). He has been a frequent contributor to legal periodicals.

Published by Public Affairs Press
419 New Jersey Ave., S.E., Washington 3, D. C.
Copyright, 1963, by Edward G. Hudon
Printed in the United States of America
Library of Congress Catalog Card No. 62-22380

FOREWORD

Dr. Hudon's book on free speech and free press is in the tradition of the late Zechariah Chafee. His book is in many respects the best analysis in English of the anatomy of our First Amendment rights. He gives an overall account—historic and contemporary—that is most revealing to those who seek understanding. This work is indeed a mosaic designed with meticulous care and precision. Honesty with details as well as with substance makes the final product impressive and enduring

Among those who on one hand proclaim liberty or on the other urge that it be curtailed, there are few who know the heritage they seek to exploit or curtail. Rare indeed are those who have the insight which this book provides. Freedom of press is largely in the hands of money-makers who either editorialize the news to fit the prejudices of one segment of society or who keep their pages free of contentious issues that might alienate some.

Free speech and free press—not space ships or automobiles—are the important symbols of western civilization. In material things the communist world will in time catch up. But no totalitarian regime can afford free speech and a free press. Ideas are dangerous—the most dangerous in the world because they are haunting and enduring. Those committed to democracy live dangerously for they stand committed never to still a voice in protest or a pen in rebellion.

In some ways we retreated from that ideal since World War II. This text gives an account of the important events that mark that decline in freedom. But those events are only isolated ones, like peaks in a long range of mountains. Equally important are the community attitudes that acquiesced in these retreats from our constitutional ideal —the default of the pulpit, the spiritual bankruptcy of the press, the ideological shiftlessness of school boards, the disappearance of the adventuresome attitudes of the universities.

It is good that this book is available. To those who read carefully, the highroads as well as the lowroads are made clear. There will be in the next decade no more important subject facing Americans.

WILLIAM O. DOUGLAS

Washington, D. C.

v

INTRODUCTION

This volume by Edward G. Hudon, a distinguished student of the law, will, I trust, meet with wide interest. Even though most members of the Bar seldom in their practice have the joyous experience of trying to ambush the Great Concern of our Republic over our First Amendment in the Bill of Rights, I have the fond hope that they will want to read this book carefully.

The author stresses, from his point of view, the early British and colonial attitudes toward freedom of thought and expression and is clearly mindful of the scar given to freedom of the mind in 1798, when the Alien and Sedition Laws were enacted with support from some of the very same Founding Fathers.

Dr. Hudon's discussion of the clear and present danger rule I found valuable, particularly because I am by no means in agreement with his historic interpretations. I, for one, never like subjective words such as "clear and present danger." I am not easily scared, so seldom if ever in life has a danger been clear or present to me. Holmes was a slogan maker while Brandeis played with the slide rule of law. The latter urged for "freedom" as long as there is time to make answer or, in the alternative, time to call the police.

Nor do I believe that our judicial system has lacked consistency. It has been as consistent as life itself. The Bill of Rights and particularly the great First Amendment guaranteeing freedom of press was written when our government was run by superior people—that is, when less than 25% were literate, when women, by and large, were deemed unfit for education other than the spinet and the needle. It was designed as a vague ideal when our population was only around four million and when mail was sent from Boston to Atlanta by sailing vessel via England because this was quicker than overland by our so-called roads in the winter months. The Founding Fathers could not foresee the advent of the telephone, the typewriter, the photographs of Daguerre, motion pictures, radio, television and, of course, Telstar. It was with a quill pen that our rule of freedom of thought was expressed as an ideal.

In the author's terms, the law is volatile. I disagree. But I enjoyed the quiet, speechless debate I had with this volume because I believe, happily, life is volatile, if the word means constantly changing its stance.

People of our Republic increasingly are avoiding courts. They shy away from quiet rooms where truth is sought by a matching of wits through skilled advocates. Rather are we increasingly using power—sit-down, sit-in, sit-on, anything rather than rational thought.

The author traces in brief compass the story of the major Supreme Court decisions regarding freedom of speech, press and movies. He sees a new approach developing in this 1960 decade. I think his volume makes a contribution not only for those who agree with the reasoning and the historical interpretations, but probably to a greater degree for those who, like me, are in substantial disagreement.

Dr. Hudon believes in "natural law," and, for a nonworshipper like me, this approach seems to be nothing but a bit of metaphysics. What looks to him like variableness to me seems to be little more than prudent refinement. I have never known a law of nature applicable to man. Certainly, among the bees the murder by the queen of her male mates is condoned just as the law of nature that applies to the sex habits of rabbits has no applicable use in man's handling of the law of population explosion.

I enjoyed the book probably and particularly because the author pressed my mind to defend my own position. I suggest man seldom learns from agreement. The great mental fertilizer of civilized man is disgreement proffered with good will. On these terms I thank the author.

MORRIS L. ERNST

New York City

PREFACE

Freedom of speech and press depends on more than declarations of rights, proclamations, and constitutional provisions forbidding its infringement. It depends on courage, personal convictions, and the realization that a right which is so essential to a democratic society cannot be taken for granted, but must ever be a matter of vigilant concern, even as it was in 1788 when the question was asked: "The liberty of the press was the tyrant's scourge—it was the true friend and the firmest supporter of civil liberty; therefore why pass it by in silence?"[1]

In 1789 freedom of speech and press in America merely involved the relatively simple interests of a few million persons. Moreover, when the First Congress endeavored to satisfy widespread popular demand for a bill of rights, the means of communication that existed were almost rudimentary and the nature and structure of society was relatively uncomplicated. Today freedom of speech and press profoundly affects a nation with a population fast approaching 200 million persons living in an era dependent upon communication by telephone, radio, television, and even telstar. Now governmental, economic, and social activity has become so complex that it inevitably impinges upon the freedom of every American citizen. Manifestly, it is more important today than in 1789 "that in a community where men's minds are free, all shades of opinion must be immune from governmental inquiry lest we end with regimentation."[2]

The speech and press guarantees of the First Amendment were intended as more than instruments of political expediency. Their purpose was to protect the rights of the minority from any whims of the majority. But in spite of the express nature of the words of the Amendment, freedom of speech and press has frequently been subjected to severe strain. It has been so because, from the advent, there has existed a constant search for a principle, a theory, or even a phrase with which to interpret the words: "Congress shall make no law . . . abridging the freedom of speech or of the press."

Intermittently one theory, principle, or phrase has been predominant and then another, but never one that has persisted for much more

ix

than a decade. To no small measure that has been due to the neglect, if not actually the brushing to one side, of the "harmonizing sentiments of the day" which Thomas Jefferson referred to in his letter to Henry Lee in 1825. With reference to the Declaration of Independence he wrote: "Neither aiming at originality of principle or sentiment, nor yet copied from any particular and previous writing, it was intended to be an expression of the American mind, and to give to that expression the proper tone and spirit called for by the occasion. All its authority rests then on the harmonizing sentiments of the day, whether expressed in conversation, in letters, printed essays, or in the elementary books of public right, as Aristotle, Cicero, Locke, Sidney, etc."[3]

This study presumes that Jefferson's statement holds true for the First Amendment as well as for the Declaration of Independence. It theorizes that recourse to contemporary thought and principle, as well as to the events that provoked men to act as they did when the Amendment was adopted, could place it in its proper environment and setting for a more stabilized interpretation. For that reason, the study delves into the British law of speech and press as it existed in England and Colonial America prior to the Revolution, and also into the theories of law and sovereignty which permitted this English and Colonial law to follow the course that it did. In setting forth that argument, however, care has been exercised in the arrangement of the material to the benefit of any who will disagree.

The objective of this book is to present the American panorama of freedom of speech and press. It is fitting that this should be done now when this country not only stands as the forerunner for the rights of the individual, but also serves as the model for many of the emerging countries of the world. It is even more fitting that this should be done at this time when freedom of expression is forbidden to countless millions by a totalitarianism that threatens civilization itself. But whatever may be the merits of this book, the late Zechariah Chafee's *Free Speech in the United States* will long continue as the classic on the subject. His was—and remains—the pioneer work.

* * *

The author wishes to acknowledge his debt to Professors James Forrester Davison and Robert Galloway Dixon, Jr., both of The George Washington Law School faculty, for the wise counsel and constructive criticism that they gave during the research that led to his book. He also wishes to express his gratitude to Paul P. Harbrecht, S. J., a friend of many years now serving as a project director for the Twentieth Century Fund's study of capitalism, who gave valuable advice on some phases of Chapter III.

EDWARD G. HUDON

Washington, D. C.

1. See proceedings of the South Carolina Convention that met in 1788 to consider the adoption of the Constitution. Elliot, *The Debates in the Several State Conventions on the Adoption of the Federal Constitution, as Recommended by the General Convention at Philadelphia in 1787* (1876), v. 4, p. 314.

2. Mr. Justice Douglas dissenting in *Russell* v. *United States*, 369 U.S. 749, 776 (1962).

3. *The Writings of Thomas Jefferson*, Memorial Edition (1904), v. 16, pp. 118, 119.

GENERAL BIBLIOGRAPHY

Chafee, Zechariah, Jr. *Free Speech in the United States* (Cambridge, Mass., Harvard University Press, 1954).

Douglas, William O. "The Right to be Let Alone," *The Right of the People,* Lecture II (Garden City, N. Y., Doubleday & Co., Inc., 1958).

Downs, Robert B., ed. *The First Freedom; Liberty and Justice in the World of Reading* (Chicago, American Library Association, 1960).

Emerson, Thomas I., and Haber, David. *Political and Civil Rights in the United States; A Collection of Legal and Related Materials*, 2nd ed., 2 v. (Buffalo, N. Y., Dennis & Co., Inc., 1958).

Griswold, Erwin N. "The Right to be Let Alone," 55 *Northwestern University Law Review* 216 (1960).

Konvitz, Milton R. *Fundamental Liberties of a Free People: Religion, Speech Press, Assembly* (Ithaca, N. Y., Cornell University Press, 1957).

Levy, Leonard W. *Legacy of Suppression; Freedom of Speech and Press in Early American History* (Cambridge, Mass., The Belknap Press, 1960).

MacIver, Robert N. *Academic Freedom in Our Times* (New York, Columbia University Press, 1955).

Padover, Saul K. *The World of the Founding Fathers; Their Basic Ideas on Freedom and Self-Government* (New York, Thomas Yoseloff, 1960).

University of Chicago. *The People Shall Judge; Readings in the Formation of American Policy*, 2 v. (Chicago, University of Chicago Press, 1949).

Warren, Samuel D., Jr., and Brandeis, Louis D. "The Right of Privacy," 4 *Harvard Law Review* 193 (1890).

CONTENTS

xiii

CHAPTER I

ADOPTION OF THE CONSTITUTION AND THE FIRST AMENDMENT

FREEDOM OF SPEECH AND PRESS AND THE FEDERAL CONVENTION

"By this Constitution, some of the best barriers of human rights are thrown away."[1] These were the words with which Patrick Henry expressed his bitterness and dissatisfaction with the document that emerged from the Federal Convention of 1787. He, and many others like him, were unhappy because the Constitution as it was presented to the states for ratification contained no guarantee of individual liberties. This omission was contrary to sentiment throughout the states that favored such a guarantee and which had already caused eight states to adopt written bills of rights.[2] Moreover, those states without specific provisions of this nature in their constitutions had inserted in them other restrictions on their legislative bodies.

The excuse given for the omission was that the idea for a bill of rights had not been thought of until three days before the end of the Convention, and that it had then been dismissed in a short conversation without formal debate or a definite proposal.[3] An examination of the *Records of the Federal Convention* reveals that on September 12, 1787, after the Committee of Revision reported the Constitution as revised and arrranged, a motion was made and seconded to appoint a committee to prepare a bill of rights, but this was defeated by a vote of 10 to 0.[4] Later this same day another motion for such a committee was made by Elbridge Gerry and seconded by George Mason.[5] Roger Sherman objected that the state declarations of rights were sufficient; they were already in force and would not be repealed by the new Federal Constitution. Mason argued for the motion on the basis that the laws of the United States would supercede the state bills of rights.[6] Again the vote was 10 to 0 against.

A further examination of the *Records of the Federal Convention* reveals that among the propositions referred to the Committee of Five

1

on August 20, 1787, one provided that "the liberty of the Press shall be inviolably preserved."[7] The *Records* also indicate that on September 14, Mr. Pinkney and Mr. Gerry moved to insert a declaration "that the liberty of the Press should be Inviolably observed."[8] Mr. Sherman objected again: "It is unnecessary—the power of Congress does not extend to the press."[9] The matter was finally rejected by a vote of 7 to 4.[10]

When the work of the Convention was finished, Elbridge Gerry refused to sign the proposed Constitution because of its lack of a bill of rights. George Mason, who was largely responsible for the Virginia Declaration of Rights, also refused to sign; he returned to Virginia intending to prevent the adoption of the Constitution because of this same defect.[11] On his copy of one of the drafts he had written: "There is no Declaration of Rights, and the laws of the general government being paramount to the laws and constitutions of the Several States, the Declaration of Rights in the separate states are no security.[12]

DISSATISFACTION WITH THE ABSENCE OF A BILL OF RIGHTS

No sooner had the proposed Constitution been published than a clamor for a national bill of rights arose. It was strongest among the more radical and democratic elements including Jefferson, Monroe, Gerry, and Patrick Henry, but it also came from the farmers and the country people, the professional and the mercantile classes. They were familiar with the history of personal rights in England, and the recollection of experiences under English rule were still vivid. Although the law of seditious libel had been repudiated by a New York jury in the case of Peter Zenger,[13] there was general knowledge of the numerous English prosecutions since 1760 of which fifty had ended in convictions under the common law rule. As a consequence, immediately after separation from England most of the former colonies had enacted bills of rights and other barriers against similar despotism by their state legislatures. Now they demanded the same protection from the new national government.

The debate over a federal bill of rights was carried on in print, in the various conventions that met to consider the adoption of the proposed constitution, and by private correspondence. The subject of the debate was not whether man does or does not have rights that are natural, inherent, and inalienable. It was generally agreed that he did. To deny this would have meant not only to repudiate the very principles over which the Revolution had been fought, but also to reduce the Revolution to the level of successful banditry. Instead, the subject of the debate was what measures were necessary to preserve the natural, inherent and inalienable rights of man from being infringed upon in the future. Some felt reassured that the Constitution as proposed to the states was adequate, others feared that it was not. The former favored its adoption without modification; the latter insisted on a bill of rights.

The Federalist, letters written by Madison, Jay, and Hamilton under the name of Publius for publication in New York newspapers, presented the most forceful arguments in favor of the adoption of the Constitution as it was proposed. In one of these, No. 84, which was written on the subject of alleged defects in the Constitution, Hamilton contended that bills of rights historically had no place in constitutions which recognize sovereignty in the people. The people, he argued, surrendered nothing to the government organized under such a constitution; therefore, they need not reserve to themselves anything in particular. Not only, he contended, was a bill of rights not necessary under such circumstances, but it was dangerous. It could but contain reservations to powers not granted in the first place and, in consequence, it might provide a pretense to any desirous of usurping power later. Against the ambitious of these, it would be inconsistent to argue that a power was not surrendered by the Constitution when safeguards were included in it to guard against the abuse of that power. It mattered not, he continued, in what manner the rights of the people were declared, so long as they existed in the instrument which established the government. He proclaimed the Constitution as a better recognition of popular rights than any of the several state bills of rights. It was itself a bill of rights: " 'We, the people of the United States, to secure the blessings of liberty to ourselves and our posterity, do *ordain* and *establish* this Constitution for the United States of America.' Here is a better recognition of popular rights, than volumes of those aphorisms which make the principal figure in several of our State bills of rights, and which would sound much better in a treatise of ethics than in a constitution of government."[14]

On the subject of liberty of the press, Publius asked, "What signifies a declaration, that 'the liberty of the press shall be inviolably preserved?' What is the liberty of the press? Who can give it any definition which would not leave the utmost latitude for evasion?" To which he answered, "I hold it to be impracticable; and from this I infer, that its security, whatever fine declarations may be inserted in any constitution respecting it, must altogether depend on public opinion, and on the general spirit of the people and of the government. And here, after all, as is intimated upon another occasion, must we seek for the only solid basis of all our rights."[15]

In his speech before the Pennsylvania convention in which he defended the absence of a bill of rights, James Wilson probably best summarized the arguments of those who claimed that a bill of rights was not necessary. Although he admitted that he might be mistaken in the matter, he stated that he did not remember having heard the subject mentioned until about three days before the end of the convention, and then not by direct motion.[16] He believed that in a government of enumerated powers not only is a bill of rights not necessary but imprudent. Should an attempt at enumeration be made, everything not included would be presumed to be given. Therefore, he considered the omission of a bill of rights itself neither so dangerous nor as important as some omission in such a bill should one be included.[17]

From Paris Jefferson took issue with those who argued that a bill of rights was not necessary. In his correspondence with Madison he wrote: "a bill of rights is what the people are entitled to against every government on earth, general or particular; and what no just government should refuse, or rest on inference."[18] He stated his dislike for the lack of a declaration in a letter to Washington and added, "I am in hopes that the opposition of Virginia will remedy this, & produce such a declaration."[19] Jefferson mistrusted the majority and he feared for the rights of the minority: "The executive, in our government, is not the sole, it is scarcely the principal object of my jealousy," he argued. "The tyranny of the legislatures is the most formidable dread at the present, and will be for many years."[20] In this fear he was not alone. Madison had expressed similar concern during the Federal Convention when he had asked, "how is the danger, in all cases of interested coalitions, to oppress the minority, to be guarded against?"[21] Now Publius recognized the problem even as he defended the Constitution.[22] But perhaps no one put it more cogently than did James Iredell. He exclaimed: "The pleasure of a majority of the Assembly? God forbid! How many things have been done by majorities of a large body in *heat* and *passion*, that they themselves afterwards have repented of!" [23]

In the Virginia convention, James Monroe and Patrick Henry

probably best summarized the arguments of the proponents of a bill of rights.

Monroe, the more moderate of the two, feared the necessary and proper clause which granted to Congress the power "to make all Laws which shall be necessary and proper for carrying into Execution the foregoing Powers, and all other Powers vested by this Constitution in the Government of the United States, or in any Department or Officer thereof."[24] He believed that because of the general and unqualified powers that this clause granted, not only could the right to trial by jury be infringed but also "the liberty of the press, and every right that is not expressly secured and excepted from the general power."[25] Without an express provision that would secure inalienable rights he saw the Constitution as a dangerous instrument calculated to secure neither the interests nor the rights of anyone.

Patrick Henry advocated rejection of the Constitution by Virginia because by its action that state was strong enough to secure the adoption of a bill of rights. He cited the history of civil rights in England to refute the argument that all powers not granted are reserved; concerning the argument that several states had not included bills of rights in their constitutions he asserted that the substance of bills of rights were otherwise contained in them. If the reservation of inalienable rights was intended, he advocated an express stipulation to that effect. Moreover, even if its necessity should be doubted, a bill of rights would exclude the possibility of dispute.[26]

Mason withheld his support until the proposed Constitution should "have such amendments as will secure the liberties and happiness of the people on a plain, simple construction, not a doubtful ground."[27]

Notwithstanding controversies in the state conventions, by the end of May, 1790, the Constitution had been adopted by thirteen states. But even in adopting it five states expressed dissatisfaction over the absence of a bill of rights. Thus, Virginia, New York and Rhode Island included proposed bills of rights in their ratifications; during the Maryland deliberations such a bill was drafted but not included in the notice of adoption;[28] North Carolina at first voted down ratification until a bill of rights should be included, but later repented and ratified.[29]

THE FIRST AMENDMENT

When the First Congress met, James Madison offered amendments embodying the state recommendations for a bill of rights. He deemed it "a desirable thing to extinguish from the bosom of every member of the community, any apprehensions that there are those among his countrymen who wish to deprive them of the liberty for which they valiantly fought and honorably bled."[30]

Madison's original recommendation provided not only that "the people shall not be deprived or abridged of their right to speak, to write, or to publish their sentiments; and the freedom of the press, as one of the great bulwarks of liberty, shall be inviolable,"[31] but also that "No state shall violate equal rights of conscience, or the freedom of the press, or the trial by jury in criminal cases."[32] The select committee of the House of Representatives to which this was referred added freedom of speech. As it was adopted by the House it read, "the equal rights of conscience, the freedom of speech or of the press, and the right of trial by jury in criminal cases, shall not be infringed by any state."[33] This action was taken in spite of Thomas Rucker of North Carolina's motion to strike it out because, in his opinion, it would interfere with the state governments.[34]

Madison had supported this amendment as the most valuable of the list. He had asserted that it was as important to secure essential rights against state action as against action by the central government, but much to his disappointment the Senate struck out the provision restricting the powers of the states, a move in which the House later concurred.[35] Of the twelve amendments submitted to the states, the third provided: "Congress shall make no law respecting an establishment of religion, or prohibiting the free exercise thereof, or abridging the freedom of speech, or of the press, or the right of the people peaceably to assemble and to petition the government for a redress of grievances."[36] Ten of the proposed amendments were adopted and this one became the First Amendment to the Constitution of the United States.

Many passions had been aroused to produce a result which sought to secure freedom of expression, a right considered fundamental to the preservation of liberty. But why should this have provoked so much fuss? Certainly those who objected to, as well as those who favored, a specific guarantee believed that speech and press should be free. To find an answer it is necessary to do two things: first, to review the history of speech and press in England and Colonial America to determine what it was that one group was more apprehensive of than the other; second, to review the concepts of law and sovereignty, and the theories of politics and government that were known at the time of the American Revolution—to establish what it was that was adopted and what it was that was sought to be left behind. It is only then that it can be understood what the evils were that the Constitution of the United States and its First Article of Amendment sought to eliminate and guard against.

CHAPTER II

ENGLISH AND COLONIAL BACKGROUND

HISTORICAL TRENDS

The law of speech and press as it existed in England and America at the time of the American Revolution was the result of a historical development of long duration. From the beginning concern for the security of the state and the preservation of the public peace motivated whatever measures were adopted, whether by legislative enactment or by judicial interpretation, however oppressive the measures happened to be. Any self-expression, even though honest and sincere, which expressed dissatisfaction with the government or with the conduct of its affairs by its officials was considered a threat to law and order and therefore intolerable. Such self-expression was presumed to harbor a malicious intent which did not necessarily mean an evil or spiteful intent, but rather a foreseeable tendency to create public mischief that was translated into constructive or presumptive intent. In his discussion of criminal libel Sir William Russell illustrated the temper of the body of law which ensued: "The ground of the criminal proceedings is the *public mischief,* which libels are calculated to create in alienating the minds of the people from religion and good morals, rendering them hostile to the government and magistry of the country; and, where particular individuals are attacked, in causing such irritation in their minds as may induce them to commit a breach of the public peace."[1]

The era in which this development took place was turbulent. During much of it neither organized police nor standing armies existed and private war was not unknown. To a considerable extent, severity of law and of punishment were relied on for the preservation of the public peace.

FREEDOM OF THE PRESS IN ENGLAND

To trace the history of this body of law in England the starting point is the statute *De Scandalis Magnatum* enacted in 1275[2] which was

8

political in nature and had as its object the preservation of the realm rather than the redress of private wrong. It provided for imprisonment of anyone who should disseminate false news or "tales" from which discord might result between the king and his people. The statute was re-enacted in 1378 to include peers, prelates, justices, and various other officials,[3] and again in 1388 with the provision for the punishment of offenders "by the advice of the said council."[4] The re-enactments of 1554,[5] and 1559,[6] added "seditious words" to the statute. With this new provision, vague or general words that could not support an action at common law could support such an action under the statute if spoken of a "magnate." The truth could not be pleaded as a defense.

The statute *De Scandalis Magnatum* is significant. It was a criminal law which punished political scandal. It was administered by the Court of Star Chamber once its administration by the Common Law Courts was considered ineffectual.

The Court of Star Chamber was originally that part of the King's Council which sat in the "starred chambre" at Westminster to handle administrative and judicial matters, as distinguished from that part of the Council which followed the King, the "Council at Court" that later became the Privy Council. Henry VII included in its jurisdiction wrongs not immediately within the reach of the Common Law Courts.[7] Prior to the time of Elizabeth the Common Law Courts provided practically no remedy for defamation.

To a great extent the Star Chamber was responsible for the evolution of censorship and the law of seditious libel. Its intervention was largely due to the invention of printing, and it was to preserve order that it undertook to suppress defamation likely to endanger the safety of the government. Furthermore, it was well suited to cope with the increasing prominence of the press as a means of expressing public opinion which had its start during the reign of Henry VIII. As a royal court that enjoyed the royal prerogative it was unhampered by rules of evidence and it had no regard for form; it heard only its own counsel and it sat whenever it desired.

To supplement the statute *De Scandalis Magnatum* the Star Chamber incorporated into English law the the Roman law of *injuria* and *libellus famosus*. The latter treated verbal insults as criminal or quasi criminal,[3] and it provided an additional basis for the jurisdiction exercised by the Star Chamber.

During the reign of Elizabeth the Star Chamber effectively controlled printing and publishing by censorship, a measure that was

9

thought essential for the peace and security of the state. Its ordinance of 1585 required a special license to print a book and it established a monopoly of printing in the Stationers' Company composed of ninety-seven London stationers. This company was empowered to seize all publications by outsiders; offenders were brought before the Star Chamber. In 1637 printing was further regulated by another ordinance which limited the number of printers, presses, and apprentices. This one required a fresh license to reprint a book once examined and licensed, and it regulated the importation of books from abroad.

As the law was administered by the Court of Star Chamber the security of the state was regarded as imperilled by seditious libel against the rulers of the state. Moreover, the maintenance of peace was considered threatened by libels on individuals, especially if they were influential. Furthermore, the Star Chamber sought to put down duelling, generally provoked by libels. Some measure of control was necessary: *"If it be against a private man it deserves a severe punishment,* for although the libel be made against one, yet it incites all those of the same family, kindred, or society to revenge, and so tends *per consequens* to quarrels and breach of the peace, and may be the cause of shedding of blood, and of great inconvenience: *if it be against a magistrate, or other public person, it is a greater offence;* for it concerns not only the breach of the peace, but also the scandal of government; for what greater scandal of government can there be than to have corrupt or wicked magistrates to be appointed and constituted by the King to govern his subjects under him? And greater imputation to the state cannot be, than to suffer such corrupt men to sit in the sacred seat of justice, or to have any meddling in or concerning the administration of justice."[9]

A libel was punishable although it pertained to a dead person. If it was of a dead private individual revenge was still possible by his family and that could cause a breach of the peace; if it was of a dead magistrate or public person it was a scandal on the government which does not die. Furthermore, it did not matter whether the libel was true or false, whether it was of a person of good or of ill repute. A libel might take the form of an epigram or rhyme in writing or sung and repeated in the presence of others; it might also take the form of an ignominious or shameful painting or sign. If it was against a private person a finder might either destroy it or deliver it to a magistrate; but if it was against a magistrate or public person the finder was admonished to deliver it to a magistrate so that its author might be found and punished.

The Star Chamber was so efficient in its prosecution of libels that in one case an author was fined £10,000, given a sentence of life imprisonment, branded on the forehead, his nose slit and his ears cut off. His crime consisted of having expressed a dislike for actors and acting in a book. This was looked upon as directed against the Queen who had recently taken part in a play, and therefore against the government.[10]

Although the Long Parliament abolished the Star Chamber in 1641 it continued the licensing system by its orders of 1642 and 1643. After the Restoration the licensing statute was revived by the Licensing Act of 1662, a temporary statute which was kept in force until 1679. In 1685, during the reign of James II, the act was renewed; it did not finally lapse until ten years later. But even during the interim from 1679 to 1685 licensing was no less effective. When Chief Justice Scroggs was summoned by the King to render an opinion on what could be done to regulate the press, he announced the opinion of the court that it was criminal to publish any public news without first having obtained a license. Whether the news was true or false, of praise or censure, was immaterial.

While the licensing system was in force, "authors and printers of obnoxious works were hung, quartered, mutilated, exposed in the pillory, flogged, or simply fined and imprisoned, according to the temper of the judges; and the works themselves were burned by the common hangman."[11] With its expiration in 1695, newspapers multiplied and immediately became an instrument for party warfare. As a result strong opposition to the press developed among governing classes. A revival of the licensing act was suggested but rejected. Instead in 1711, during the reign of Queen Anne, a Stamp Act was enacted that levied a duty on all newspapers and advertisement.[12] The objective was to restrain the press and crush small newspapers.

Although it was partially taken care of by the Stamp Act, the vacuum left in 1695 by the expiration of the licensing act was largely filled by the Common Law Courts. Not to be outdone by the Star Chamber, these had already incorporated within their jurisdiction the principles developed by the latter, and as early as 1606 the case *De Libellis Famosis*[13] had established that seditious writing was punishable either by indictment at common law or by the Star Chamber. With the abolition of the Star Chamber in 1641 the Common Law

11

Courts assumed or inherited the position of *custos moram* of the realm and absorbed the entire jurisdiction over defamation. At first, these courts were hampered by the necessity of establishing a malicious intent, a finding of fact by a jury. But seditious libels affected the state and it became accepted that the intentional publication of a document, seditious or defamatory in character, constituted the offense. The jury merely determined the fact of intentional publication, the court decided as a question of law whether or not the publication was seditious or defamatory.[14]

When it is realized that during this era it was treason to so much as imagine the King's death,[15] it can readily be understood why political libels were the order of the day. And these were carried to such limits that in 1684 Sir Samuel Barnardiston was tried, convicted, and fined for expressing political opinions in a private letter written to a friend.[16] He had done no more than repeat the current political rumors, some of which favored the Whigs. One of his remarks was directed at Sir George Jeffreys who presided over the trial and charged the jury.

On another occasion the jury that tried John Tutchin was told in part by the presiding judge: "To say that corrupt officers are appointed to administer affairs, is certainly a reflection on the government. If people should not be called to account for possessing the people with an ill opinion of the government, no government can subsist. For it is very necessary for all governments that the people should have a good opinion of it. And nothing can be worse to any government, than to endeavor to procure animosities, as to the management of it; this has always been looked upon as a crime, and no government can be safe without it be punished."[17] Tutchin had published articles in which he had alleged mismanagement of the navy and corruption in the ministry. The seditious character of the matter printed having been determined as a matter of law, he was found guilty of composing and publishing.

In 1731 Richard Francklin was tried for publishing "A letter from the Hague" in his newspaper, *The Craftsman*.[18]. This was an opposition paper and the letter was critical of the government's foreign policy. An offer to prove the truth of the matter published was rejected by Lord Chief Justice Raymond. He said, "It is my opinion, that it is not material whether the facts charged in a libel be true or false, if the prosecution is by indictment or information." The Chief Justice then pointed out the serious nature of libels against private individuals, and the even more serious nature of libels against public officials. These were said "to sow sedition, and disturb the peace of the Kingdom."

Any who thought this wrong were advised to "apply to the Court, and they will do you justice." The jury was instructed to determine the question of publication and also to determine if the letter referred to the ministers of Great Britain. Whether or not the matter published was a libel was reserved for the court. The usual conviction together with punishment by fine and imprisonment followed.

The law of the press as it existed in England at the end of the eighteenth century was probably best summarized by Blackstone as follows: "The liberty of the press is indeed essential to the nature of a free state; but this consists in laying no *previous* restraints upon publications, and not in freedom from censure for criminal matter when published. Every freeman has an undoubted right to lay what sentiments he pleases before the public; to forbid this, is to destroy the freedom of the press: but if he publishes what is improper, mischievous, or illegal, he must take the consequences of his own temerity."[19]

Although Blackstone's *Commentaries* has been dismissed by an English court as "an elementary text book for students and must be judged as such," ample judicial support for Blackstone's view is found in Lord Mansfield's instructions to the jury in the case of *H. S. Woodfall:* "As for the liberty of the press, I will tell you what it is; the liberty of the press is, that a man may print what he pleases without a licenser: so long as it remains so, the liberty of the press is not restrained."[21]

In the denial of the motion for a new trial in the *Dean of St. Asaph's Case,* Mansfield again defined liberty of the press. This time as follows: "To be free, is to live under a government by law. The *liberty of the press* consists in printing without any previous license, subject to the consequences of law. The *licentiousness* of the press is *Pandora's* box, the source of every evil."[22]

At common law, unfavorable criticism of the King's conduct, the constitution, the laws, or of men in public office was absolutely forbidden. Such criticism was considered to bring disrepute on the government and to weaken its authority. It was no defense to show that the purpose of the criticism was to bring about orderly reform in government and not to stir up disorder. It was according to this principle of law that John Wilkes, a member of the House of Commons, was convicted. He had published an attack on the King's message to Parliament in his newspaper.[23]

The criminality of an act in an indictment for libel was a question of law for the court and not for the jury to decide. Truth or falsity was immaterial and again not for the jury to decide; the crime consisted merely of publishing a libel. Criminal intent charged to the defendant was merely a matter of form. It was not a part of the definition of libel, it required no proof on the part of the prosecutor, and it admitted no proof in rebuttal on the part of the defendant.[24] This was the unanimous answer of the judges on the occasion of the consideration of the Fox Libel Act[25] when seven questions were submitted to them by the House of Lords to determine the state of the law as to the function of juries in cases of libel.[26] That was the law as it had already been expounded in the *Trial of Woodfall*[27] and the *Dean of St. Asaph.*[28]

Only after the Constitution of the United States and its First Amendment had been adopted did the Fox Libel Act[29] become law in England. Based largely on Erskine's argument for a general verdict in the defense of the Dean of St. Asaph,[30] this act of 1792 enlarged the scope of the jury's function in libel cases and authorized a general verdict of guilty or not guilty upon the whole matter put in issue. The jury could no longer be directed by the presiding judge to find the defendant guilty merely upon proof of publication.[31]

But even after the passage of the Fox Libel Act, trials for political and seditious libel continued. Indeed, they were as common as before, if not more so. In fact, on December 18, 1792, subsequent to the passage of the act, the prosecution of Thomas Paine for publishing *The Rights of Man* took place.[32] As soon as the defense had been presented in the case, Paine was convicted by a jury that expressed the desire to hear neither reply nor summing-up. In effect, the Fox Libel Act substituted the jury for the judge and as late as 1914 Dicey could assert that "Freedom of discussion is then, in England, little else than the right to write or say anything which a jury, consisting of twelve shopkeepers, think it expedient should be said or written."[33]

In 1843, fifty years after the Constitution of the United States had been adopted, freedom of the press became a reality in England. The event which brought this about was the enactment of Lord Campbell's Act, a law which made truth a defense to an indictment for libel.[34] But it was not until 1855 that the Stamp and Advertising Tax was finally rejected.

FREEDOM OF SPEECH IN ENGLAND

At the time of the adoption of the American Constitution, the only guarantee of freedom of speech that existed in England was that of

14

freedom of speech and debate in Parliament. But even this was established only after a long struggle between the Crown and Parliament which culminated in the Bill of Rights, a condition imposed on William and Mary when they accepted the crown after the banishment of the Stuarts in 1688.

During the middle ages the Speaker of the House of Commons claimed freedom of speech alone as Prolocutor of the House. However, as early as 1523 a claim was made by Sir Thomas More, the Speaker, for this freedom for all of the members of Commons. The claim was made again in 1541, and it has since become an established practice but not without a struggle. The need for such freedom is illustrated by the conviction of Haxey, a member of Commons, as a traitor in 1396 because he had submitted a bill to reduce the excessive charges of the Royal household. It is also illustrated by the imprisonment of Richard Strode in 1512, also a member of Commons, because he had proposed a bill for the regulation of tin-mining. Haxey's conviction was later reversed as "against the law and custom which had been before in Parliament."

In her speech at the dissolution of Parliament in 1566, Queen Elizabeth expressed her resentment at the discussions in Parliament and at the petition that had been presented to her on the question of succession. In 1571, in reply to the Speaker's petition for privileges at the opening of the Parliament, the Queen warned Commons "to meddle with no matters of state, but such as should be propounded unto them."[35] At the opening of the Parliament of 1593 the request for liberty of speech met with an even cooler reception. This time the Queen asserted that the "Privilege of speech is granted, but you must know what privilege you have; not to speak every one what he listeth, or what cometh in his brain to utter that; but your privilege is *Aye* or *No*."[36] In 1576 and 1587 Peter Wentworth was bold enough to speak in resistance to the Queen's interference with liberty of speech in Parliament. His efforts in both instances were rewarded with imprisonment.

James I got along no better with his Parliaments than did Elizabeth when the question was freedom of speech. His answer to a petition which expressed hope for a marriage of the Prince of Wales to a Protestant princess, instead of the Infanta of Catholic Spain, was a letter to the Speaker forbidding Commons from meddling with the mysteries of state. They were told not to speak of the proposed match.[37] Although Commons considered this a threat to freedom of speech, an "ancient and undoubted right, and an inheritance received from [their] ancestors,"[38] the King did not see it that way. By way of reply he remarked, "Although we cannot allow of the style, calling it your ancient and undoubted right and inheritance; but would rather have wished, that ye had said, that your privileges were derived from the grace and permission of our ancestors and us; (for most of them grow from precedents, which shews rather a toleration than inheritance) yet we are pleased to give you our royal assurance, that so long as you contain yourself within the limits of your duty, we will be as careful to maintain and preserve your lawful liberties and privileges as ever any of our predecessors were, nay, as to preserve our own royal prerogative. So as your house shall only have need to beware to trench upon the prerogative of the crown; which would enforce us, or any just king, to retrench them of their privileges, that would pare his prerogative and the flowers of the crown: but of this, we hope, there shall never be cause given."[39]

Charles I followed the example of his predecessors. During his second Parliament, he committed to the Tower two of the members for alleged insolent speech. They were not released until the King had been assured that the two had not spoken the words imputed to them. Following the dissolution of his third Parliament (1629), the King proceeded against those who had been active against him. Some were committed to the Tower and others were prosecuted before the King's Bench where judgment was rendered against them. The convicted were fined and ordered imprisoned during the King's pleasure, not to be released until they had given surety of good behavior. One, Sir John Elliot, refused to give surety and he died in prison.[40]

The question was resolved with the banishment of the Stuarts in 1688. William and Mary took the throne, but only after they had agreed to the conditions under which they could reign. They had to subscribe to the Bill of Rights which declared "that the freedom of speech and debate or proceedings in Parliament ought not to be impeached or questioned in any court or place out of Parliament."[41]

FREEDOM OF PRESS IN THE AMERICAN COLONIES

In the colonies, as in England, licensing and censorship followed very close the introduction of printing.[42]

The first book to be published in the colonies was one published by Steevan Days in Massachusetts in 1639; in 1656 Samuel Green established a press in Massachusetts, the second in the colonies. The efforts

16

of both were rewarded by the General Court with 300-acre land grants, but this tolerance was short-lived. It seems that religious books which were thought to be dangerous had appeared and in 1662 two licensors were appointed without whose permission nothing could be published. Early in 1663 the General Court repealed the licensing act, only to reimpose a similar one the following year. The act of 1664 followed the pattern set in England: no printing press could be established elsewhere than in Cambridge and nothing could be printed without the permission of the licensors. Violations were punished by forfeiture of equipment and the right to engage in the occupation. In one instance, in 1668, approval already granted by the licensors was revoked by the General Court. The author of the book questioned was thought to be a "popish minister."

From this early beginning, a license continued to be a prerequisite to publication in Massachusetts until 1719, twenty-four years later than in England. As in the mother country after the expiration of the licensing act, freedom of the press meant nothing more in this colony than freedom from prior restraint. In 1768 the Chief Justice of the colony probably best summarized the colonial law of the press in an instruction to a grand jury as follows: "Formerly, no Man could print his Thoughts, ever so modestly and calmly, or with ever so much Candour and Ingenuousness, upon any subject whatever, without a License. When this restraint was taken off, then was the true Liberty of the Press. Every Man who prints, prints at his Peril; as every Man who speaks, speaks at his Peril. It was in this Manner I treated this Subject at the last Term, yet the Liberty of the Press and the Danger of an *Imprimatur* was canted about, as if the Press was going under some new and illegal Restraint. No Gentlemen of the Bar, I am sure, could have so misunderstood me. This Restraint of the Press, in the Prevention of Libels, is the only Thing which will preserve your Liberty. To suffer the licentious Abuse of Government is the most likely Way to destroy its Freedom."[43]

The story was repeated in Pennsylvania. At the solicitation of William Penn, William Bradford brought a press to that colony in 1682. No sooner had the advance sheets to his first publication been seen by the Secretary of the Council than Bradford was in trouble. He was ordered not to print anything without a license from the Council. To add to his troubles, Bradford was ordered by the Society of Friends to submit to censorship by four of its members. Finally, in 1691 he was prosecuted for seditious libel. At his trial he argued that it was for the jury to decide the seditious character of the publication as well as the fact of printing. This argument was rejected then as it was one hundred years later when it was again advanced by Thomas Erskine in England. Bradford was released when the jury disagreed. He then moved his establishment to New York City where his talents were better appreciated. The Council of that city provided an inducement of a yearly salary of £40 and a promise of the public printing.

The southern colonies lagged behind those of the north in the development of printing. However, this did not displease the authorities. Indeed, in 1671 Governor Berkeley expressed his pleasure at this lack of progress in Virginia in the following manner: "But, I thank God, we have no free schools nor printing; and I hope we shall not have these hundred years; for learning has brought disobedience and heresy and sects into the world; and printing has devulged them, and libels against the government. God keep us from both."[44]

Even the laws of the colony could not be printed without a license. John Bucknew was made aware of this in 1682 when he was arrested for printing the laws of Virginia without one. The advice of the King was sought in the matter and his instructions were quite simple: no printing press on any occasion whatever. Thereafter printing was not allowed in Virginia from 1683 to 1729. From 1729 until 1765, one press which was largely controlled by the governor existed in the colony.

The first newspaper to be published in the American colonies did not survive its first issue. Known as "Public Occurrences" from the words that appeared on its first page, it was published in Boston by Richard Pierce in 1690 but it was immediately suppressed because it mentioned the Indian Wars and commented on local affairs.[45]

In Pennsylvania James Franklin was imprisoned in 1722 because of a letter in the form of a satire which appeared in his newspaper, the *New England Courant*. The letter criticised the government of the colony for its lack of promptness in dealing with pirates off the coast. Because of his efforts at public discussion, Franklin was ordered to submit to censorship. When he did not do so and the next issue of the newspaper appeared with another satire on the government, he was ordered to cease publication. But this proved not to be too great an obstacle. Publication was continued in the name of Benjamin Franklin. Even earlier, James Franklin had encountered another type of difficulty when his newspaper had been condemned as an "inspiration of the devil" by the clergy.[46]

The first newspaper to be published in Virginia, the *Virginia Gazette*, appeared in 1736. It expired with its owner in 1750, but in 1751 it was revived and it continued until 1778. The value of this enterprise is reported to have been described by Jefferson as follows: "Till the beginning of our revolutionary disputes we had but one press; and that having the whole business of the government, and no competition for public favor, nothing disagreeable to the governor could find its way into it."[47]

Of all the prosecutions against newspapers and their publishers that took place in colonial America, without a doubt the most celebrated was that of Peter Zenger in New York.[48] This arose from satirical ballads reflecting on the Governor and his Council which Zenger published in his newspaper, *The New York Weekly Journal*. The issues objected to were described "as having in them many things tending to raise factions and tumults among the people of this province, inflaming their minds with contempt for his majesty's government, and greatly disturbing the peace thereof." 17 Howell's State Trials 675,682 (1735). These particular issues were ordered by the Council to be publicly burned by the common hangman, but when this officer refused to carry out the order they were burned by the sheriff's negro slave. The Grand Jury failed to indict Zenger and the General Assembly refused to take action. Therefore, an information was filed by the Attorney General who acted under the orders of the Governor.

To add to Zenger's dilemma, counsel retained by him were disbarred from practice when they had the temerity to question the right of the Chief Justice of the colony to sit at the trial. However, Andrew Hamilton, a Quaker lawyer from Philadelphia who was Speaker of the Pennsylvania Assembly, appeared unsolicited and defended Zenger. At the trial, Hamilton admitted publication by Zenger, but he offered to prove that the matter published was true. This was rejected as follows: "You cannot be admitted, Mr. Hamilton, to give the truth of a libel in evidence. A libel is not to be justified; for it is nevertheless a libel that it is true."[49]

When Hamilton pressed for a general verdict he was told: "No, Mr. Hamilton; the jury may find that Mr. Zenger printed and published these papers, and leave it to the Court to judge whether they are libellous. You know this is very common: it is in the nature of a Special Verdict where the jury leave the matter of law to the court."[50] Hamilton appealed to the personal knowledge of the jury and won an acquittal. His feat was without fee or reward other than to be awarded the freedom of the City of New York. It was, however, acclaimed as a "generous defense of the rights of mankind, and the liberty of the press."[51] Furthermore, it provided excellent script for present-day radio and television writers.

19

CHAPTER III

BRITISH CONCEPTS OF LAW AND SOVEREIGNTY: THEIR REJECTION IN COLONIAL AMERICA

SOVEREIGNTY AND ITS EFFECT ON SPEECH AND PRESS

The law of speech and press that prevailed in England and in the American colonies at the time of the American Revolution was formulated during an era when the ruling authority was believed to have absolute, uncontrolled sovereignty. At the start, the Salisbury Oath of 1066 and its national act of homage and allegiance to William vested sovereignty in the king; later, the Petition of Right forced on Charles I by the Parliament of 1628,[1] and the Bill of Rights agreed to by William and Mary at the conclusion of the Revolution of 1688,[2] firmly established the rule of Parliament and vested sovereignty in that body. Coke wrote of the latter, the sovereignty of Parliament: "Of the power and jurisdiction of the Parliament, for making of laws in proceedings by bill, it is so transcendent and absolute, as it cannot be confined either for causes or persons within any bounds."[3]

In 1765, a year after the passage of the Stamp Act, Blackstone subscribed to this theory when he asserted that with all forms of government, "However they began, or by what soever they subsist, there is and must be in all of them a supreme, irresistible, absolute, uncontrolled authority, in which the *jura summi imperii*, or the rights of sovereignty reside."[4] He concluded: "So long therefore as the English constitution lasts, we may venture to affirm, that the power of parliament is absolute and without control."[5] Although the power is not used today, it apparently continues to exist and it can still be written: "The Constitution has assigned no limits to the authority of Parliament over all matters and persons within its jurisdiction. A law may be unjust and contrary to sound principles of government; but Parliament is not controlled in its discretion, and when it errs, its errors can only be corrected by itself. To adopt the words of Sir Edward Coke, the power of Parliament 'is so transcendent and absolute, as it cannot be confined either for causes or persons within any bounds.' "[6]

So long as this philosophy was subscribed to and given effect any censure or criticism of the ruling authority, public officials, or of the laws and institutions of the country was inevitably considered libelous, public mischief, and even thought to create a danger to the government which had to be suppressed.

Perhaps this was in temper with the period during which it originated because of the lack of adequate police authority and even of standing armies, but as time went by it became outmoded and not in harmony with public opinion. For instance, as early as 1644 John Milton protested the licensing acts and wrote: "Give me the liberty to know, to utter, and to argue freely according to conscience, above all liberties."[7]

Erskine was no less eloquent when he argued in the defense of Thomas Paine more than a century later: "Other liberties are held under governments, but liberty of opinion keeps governments themselves in due subjection to their duties. This has produced the martyrdom of truth in every age, and the world has been only purged from ignorance with the innocent blood of those who have enlightened it."[8]

But as is so often the case, even Milton and Erskine would have deprived some from enjoying the fruits of the liberty which they so valiantly sought. Milton would have excluded "tolerated popery, and open superstition;"[9] Erskine has been said to have objected to religious heretics.[10]

It was, however, generally accepted that there was one limit to this doctrine of "a supreme, irresistible, absolute, uncontrolled" authority. This stemmed from the belief that there is a body of law which is superior to man-made law—that all earthly authority and all men, however exalted or however humble, are subject to natural law, natural right and justice, the supreme law which determines even the validity of man-made law. This belief served as the fighting faith of the American Revolution in the form of a Declaration of Independence, and later as the basis for the Constitution of the United States. But even earlier, as friction between the American colonists and England developed and progressed to a breaking point, natural law provided a foundation for American resistance. The colonists reached deep into the eighteenth century law of nature, the post-Reformation successor to scholastic natural law. To understand this doctrine as the American colonists knew it, an understanding of its origin and a study of its evolution is necessary.

THE HERITAGE OF GREECE AND ROME

The earliest traces of natural law can be found in Greece as early as 300 B.C. in the tenets of the Stoic School founded by Zeno. These were tenets that placed a strong belief in an overriding power of divine providence. They imposed on every man the duty to play his allotted part, whatever that was or however trifling and miserable it might be; they gave to man a special position among creatures since they gave him reason, a sense of right and wrong as opposed to the mere instincts and impulses of animals. Man was fitted to a social life. Thus, Stoicism taught right reason; it imposed a universal, unchangeable standard of what was right and just. This was the law of nature which was binding on ruler and subject alike. Customs could vary from place to place, but behind these variations there had to be a unity of purpose which the Stoic looked on as a world-wide system of law with endless local branches. That meant a dual system of law, i.e., customary law and a more perfect overriding law of nature existing side by side, with the latter tending to keep the former from becoming unreasonable.

The importance of Stoicism is that it provided a ready-made philosophy for Rome, a city that could grow in power and wealth through conquest but could not develop a philosophy of its own. With it Rome could shake itself loose from the confines of a system of law that was adequate to serve the needs of the city-state, but not adequate to serve the city that dominated the known world. The law of Rome the city-state—the *ius civile*—was religious and ceremonial in character, and its application was limited to those who were born to it as Roman citizens. But as the city grew in power and influence, its alien population increased and that gave rise not only to the question of legal protection for alien dealing with alien, but also for alien dealing with Roman. The solution was a practical application of the Stoic idea of two systems of law existing side by side. Parallel to the *ius civile* there developed the *ius gentium,* the law common to all people which was based solely on equity, fair dealing, common sense, and with what was considered good business practice.

Although in itself, *ius gentium* had no particular philosophical meaning, *ius naturale,* the latin translation of the Stoic Greek philosophical term, did and as these two together, the rule of reason of Stoic origin and the positive law of the state, were made to cooperate

22

they tended to generate substantial justice, to promote equality before the law and even to break down the ceremonial character of the *ius civile*. In the hands of Cicero who sought throughout his professional life to restore the Roman Republic and its Constitution to the positions they formerly occupied, this was given statement which was passed on to the Roman lawyers, and by them to the Fathers of the Church to provide the basis for christian natural law. As it traveled this route it was universally known throughout the Western World. An interesting feature of its journey is the fact that the text of Cicero's *De Re Publica* (with the exception of the *Somnium Scipionis)* was lost to the world from the twelfth to the nineteenth century, and its most striking passages were preserved for these centuries only because they appeared in the books of St. Augustine and Lactanicus.[11]

Although Cicero did not draw a clear distinction between *ius naturale* and *ius gentium* as the later Roman lawyers did, he nevertheless presented a well-developed conception of organized society in relation to nature. He believed in the existence of a supreme being and consequently in a constant, eternal law which he defined as "right reason in agreement with nature."[12] that which should and that which should not be done.[13] He was familiar with the two opposing theories that again reasserted themselves in the classic struggle of the latter part of the seventeenth century in England: one that man was originally a solitary creature without inclination to society, but was driven to it for mutual defense; the other, that man has a natural inclination for society.[14] He repudiated the former and accepted the latter when he viewed the commonwealth as a natural association and an expression of common will and consent which he called the *res publica* or *res populi*, "an assemblage of people in large numbers associated in an agreement with respect to justice and a partnership for the common good."[15] The commonwealth was the property of the people from whom even the authority of the ruler had to be derived.[16]

As time went on, Roman lawyers came to distinguish *ius gentium* from *ius naturale* as Cicero had not, but like him they never doubted the existence of a higher law to which positive law had to measure up if it was to be law at all. As the Republic became an Empire, of necessity there were changes in the idea of the state. Moreover, there were deviations or even additions as Seneca's idea of a primitive state of innocence, a golden age of happiness which was more the result of ignorance than of virtue from which man passed because of vice, corruption and avarice. But although these adjustments, deviations

23

and even additions were made, the Stoic idea of life and society as it had been made popular by Cicero continued to prevail down to modern times. It provided the legacy of Greece and Rome upon which the way was paved for christian natural law. Just as it had served the needs of Cicero and the Roman lawyers, so Stoic philosophy played a part in the formulation of christian dogmas and in the interpretation of the teachings of Christ.

SCHOLASTICISM AND NATURAL LAW

In the hands of St. Augustine and the other fathers of the church, scholastic natural law took shape, was passed on to the middle ages and the golden age of scholasticism which is best represented by the *Summa Theologia,* the great synthesis of St. Thomas Aquinas, and then to the late scholastics represented by Suarez.[17]

As with its predecessors, scholastic natural law continued the theory of an overriding law which, in the christian era, became the wisdom of God, the revelation of things according to divine reason, to which all creatures, both animate and inanimate, are subject and in which they all participate. Among these creatures man alone has understanding and free will, and he alone possesses the imprint of divine light. As a rational creature he can distinguish right from wrong, good from evil, and participate in eternal and divine law according to his own capacity and inclination. Being social by nature he has a natural inclination to live in society, and this presupposes a ruling authority or government. However, by the nature of things he is born independent and free, and no man has political jurisdiction over another without the other's consent. In the words of St. Augustine, "This is prescribed by the order of nature: it is thus that God has created man. For 'let them,' He says, 'have dominion over the fish of the sea, and over the fowl of the air, and over every creeping thing which creepeth on the earth.' He did not intend that His rational creature, who was made in His own image, should have dominion over anything but the irrational creature—not man over man, but man over the beasts."[18]

Nevertheless, government there must be, but as a part of the natural order it represents the transfer of authority which, although it is derived immediately from man, is derived mediately from God. Its function is the well-being of society and the common good of the state. It must strive for a perfect society—for peace, justice, and right order. By law—government established law which St. Thomas called "a rule and measure of acts, whereby man is induced to act or is restricted from acting"[19]—it sets the standard. This law must, continued St.

24

Thomas, "be just, possible to nature, according to the customs of the country, adapted to place and time."[20] It must will what is good and impel all men to peace and virtue. Insofar as it accomplishes these ends, law partakes of right reason and it must be obeyed. On the other hand, there is no duty to obey the commands of one who oversteps his authority and there is a duty to resist that which is evil. For, in the transfer of God-given authority man retains rights that are transcendent, i.e., natural to him and permit him to comply with his obligations to God so that he can achieve his ultimate goal, eternal salvation. Thus, he has a right to live as a human person, to perfect his moral nature, and to live as a free intelligent individual. These are rights that permit him to participate in eternal or divine law and their existence does not depend on the authority of human government. Moreover, any law that is destructive of these or of the common good denies natural justice. Therefore, it is in violation of the fundamental rights of mankind, is contrary to natural law, and therefore not law at all.

In essence, these principles set forth a claim of superiority of the spiritual over the temporal power, and this, in turn, produced the conflicts that took place between the two during the middle ages.[21] But even these conflicts had a salutary effect in the sense that they paved the way for the recognition of the freedom of the individual as against the coercive power of the state. This recognition as we know it is a direct result of the early assertion of the spiritual power that there is a freedom of moral and spiritual elements as against temporal power. On the other hand, as one considers the principles of freedom and equality of scholastic natural law one is faced with the anomaly that from the beginning slavery was not condemned as contrary to Christianity. Instead, it was viewed as a form of divine punishment and a remedy for sin. Slavery had existed earlier among the Greeks, it was prevalent throughout the Roman world, and Christianity did not seek to establish itself by revolution but accepted society as it found it. Moreover, the church did not take social condition into account; it accepted master and slave alike, and its levelling influence was such that former slaves could and did accede to the Chair first occupied by St. Peter.[22] However, from the start the church exerted its influence to ameliorate the condition of the individual slave and, among other things, it restored the family to him.

APPEAL TO NATURAL LAW DURING THE MIDDLE AGES

During the middle ages scholastic natural law was generally accepted as the reasonable basis for all law. Bracton recognized its existence when he wrote of God as the author of justice, and when he wrote of jurisprudence as "the knowledge of divine human things, the science of what is just and unjust."[23] To right, Bracton ascribed three precepts: "to live honestly, to do no harm to another, to award to each his right."[24] Later, Christopher St. Germain wrote of this same body of law as a part of the law of England in his celebrated *Dialogue in English, betweene a Doctor of Divinitie, and a Student in the Lawes of England.*

During the middle ages all authority of government, and that included the king, was thought subject to, and limited by, the natural law. Of the authority of the king as subject to God, Bracton wrote: "There are also under the king the freemen and serfs subject to his power, and every person is under him, and he is under no person but is only under God . . . But the king himself ought not to be subject to man, but subject to God and to the law, for the law makes the king."[25]

The limitation on the king even extended to his dispensing authority. For instance, although he could dispense with an offense that was *malum prohibitum*, he could not dispense with one that was *malum per se*. The law of nature was, however, a rather tenuous basis on which to oppose established authority unless one was on the winning side. It was in vain that Sir Thomas More protested that the indictment brought against him "was grounded upon an act of Parliament, directly repugnant to the laws of God and his Holy Church, the supreme government of which, or any part thereof, no temporal person may by any law presume to take upon him . . . it is therefore, among Catholic Christians, insufficient in law, to charge any Christian to obey it."[26] He paid with his head for his refusal to subscribe to the Oath of Succession.

In actual practice, the natural law, the supreme law and the ultimate source of all lawful authority, appears to have served more as a means with which to extend than to limit authority. It served to create new legal remedies where none existed at common law and to extend existing jurisdictions. That was possible because of a residium of power which the king was thought to possess over and above his actual defined powers. In turn, this residium had a limitation; it was limited by the law of nature and right reason which even the king could not suspend or dispense with. Later, in a like manner the law-making power of Parliament was thought limited by the same fundamental law.[27] Still later, this same limitation was appealed to by the American revolutionists.[28]

Meanwhile, through the exercise of this residium of power, many of the principles of natural law were incorporated into English law. That was done to fill the deficiencies of existing common and statutory law, and to bring about right and justice. To a great extent the guiding hands were those of the Chancellors of which the earliest, until the fall of Wolsey in 1529, were Catholic ecclesiastics. It was to the law of God, of nature and of right reason that these men turned when, as keepers of the king's conscience, they sought to remedy the defects and the injustices of existing law.[29] They looked to natural law identified with the law of God for the solution of problems to which no provision of positive law applied. This was equity which Bracton defined as "the suitable adjustment of things, which in like causes seeks to administer like rights, and adjusts all things well on an equal platform, and it is termed equity, as being as it were equality, and it is employed in things, that is, in the sayings and actions of men."[30] It had been established by the ecclesiastic Chancellors as a separate system of law with its own procedure derived from the canon law, and it continued its own separate way even after the ecclesiastics had been replaced by men trained in the law.

TRANSITION FROM SCHOLASTICISM TO DEISM

After the rise of Protestantism the spiritual as well as the temporal authority of the Pope had to give way in the Protestant state that England became; scholastic natural law had to be replaced by something that was disconnected from the theology of the church. The answer was found in impersonal human reason which was made to replace God and divine reason. The accent was placed on the individual with an original state of nature as a starting point. Men were not so much looked upon as equal in the eyes of God as equal in the eyes of each other; a supreme authority was still recognized, but nature had intervened between God and man; belief in God was still admitted, but everything came to be based on reason and impersonal nature.

This divorce of natural law from theology was not something which took place overnight. It was, instead, the result of a slow process of transition that occupied the better part of a century. The first trace of headway is found in Grotius who wrote during the first quarter of the seventeenth century. But even Grotius, a Protestant, borrowed heavily from the scholastics—so much so that his natural law has been referred

27

to as a continuation of the tradition of Suarez and St. Augustine.[31] Thus, he attributed to man an impelling desire for society and a power of discrimination.[32] He described man as "endowed with the faculty of knowing and of acting in accordance with general principles,"[33] something peculiar to the nature of man and not common to all animals. He believed that "we must without exception render obedience to God as our Creator, to Whom we owe all that we are and have; especially since, in manifold ways, He has shown Himself supremely good and supremely powerful, so that to those who obey Him He is able to give supremely great rewards, even rewards that are eternal, since He Himself is eternal."[34] The sources of law he enumerated as "the maintenance of social order . . . consonant with human intelligence,"[35] and "the free will of God, to which beyond all cavil our reason tells us we must render obedience."[36]

Grotius had indeed drunk deep at the fountain of scholasticism up to this point, but it was when he went further and sought to construct a theory of law independent of God and theology that he broke away, emphasizing his concern "to refer the proofs of things touching the law of nature to certain fundamental conceptions which are beyond question, so that no one can deny them without doing violence to himself. For the principles of that law, if only you pay strict heed to them, are in themselves manifest and clear, almost as evident as are those things which we perceive by the eternal senses; and the senses do not err if the organs of perception are properly formed and if the other conditions requisite of perception are present."[37]

"Measureless as is the power of God," wrote Grotius, "nevertheless it can be said that there are certain things over which that power does not extend; for things of which this is said are spoken only, having no sense corresponding with the reality and being mutually contradictory. Just as even God, then, cannot cause that two times two should not make four, so He cannot cause that which is intrinsically evil be not evil."[38] Here was the start of the road to deism.

Grotius' statement was fragmentary. It came early and there was still much to be done before a break with scholasticism could be a matter of accomplishment. Nevertheless, it provided a beginning to which the Protestant philosophers of the seventeenth century added and on which they expounded.

A more decisive step was provided by Samuel Pufendorf when he questioned "whether it can be said on any useful sense that *God set before himself and man* a common *end,* or that the order constituted for man, that is, the observance of the law of nature, produces the end of creation as set down by God."[39] The reason of man himself was the mechanism with which to deduce the law of nature. He believed that this could be accomplished without divine revelation. "[I]t can," he wrote, "still be investigated and definitely proved, even without such aid, by the power of reason as it has been given man by his Creator and still persists."[40] Among other things, the nature, condition and desires of man himself were to be observed and considered—his self-love, his desire to preserve himself, and his dependence on his fellow-creatures.

An even more decisive step, one that was perhaps not even intended, was that provided by Newton. In its inception this one had nothing to do with philosophy. Instead, it was a contribution to science, the result of discoveries in the field of astrology from which Newton formulated the law of universal gravitation. But when, in 1688, he published his *Principia* and announced his discoveries to the world a new weapon was placed in the hands of the deists. From that point on how could it be denied that man could dispense with divine inspiration? Man had only to observe the world about him to discover inevitable truths and guiding principles. Moreover, Newton's *Principia* was an immediate success and within a century it had gone through no less than eighteen editions or reprints. For the non-scientific it was explained and popularized not only in English, but also in French, German, Latin, Portuguese and Italian.

Perhaps the most decisive, if not the last, step in the transition from scholasticism to deism was John Locke's denial that there is an innate notion of God. He dismissed as a mistake the thought that there are "innate principles," "primae notiones," stamped upon the mind of man, which it receives in its very first being, and comes into the world with.[41] To Locke these were doctrines taught children as soon as they are capable of apprehension, but before their memories have developed to the point that they are able to register actions and the dates new things appear to them. God had created all things in perfect wisdom and he had "furnished man with such faculties that would serve him to all ends requisite to such a being"—he had fitted man with the faculty to discover and retain truth. Therefore, the sensation of external things and reflections were all that man needed to get along. Unassisted, the application of these to man's experiences would produce the right answers.

The transition from scholasticism to deism was now complete. New frills were to be added, it is true, but a basic philosophy divorced from God and God's law was available to all who wished to invoke it. But even so, theology was still relied on by all who advanced new ideas as history was read, reread, and even misread for religious and moral support. Moreover, this new rational construction of the law of nature was susceptible to more than one interpretation in an era that witnessed the rise of the modern independent state as well as the transition from scholasticism to deism. Opposing parties could bring forth their own particular interpretations with which to prove their own particular theses. From a common starting point such widely separated theories of government as those of Thomas Hobbes and John Locke could emerge. Both are important because the first advocated a creed which was rejected by the American Constitution, the second a creed upon which, to a large extent, the American Constitution was founded.

OPPOSING THEORIES OF GOVERNMENT OF LOCKE AND HOBBES

In his *Leviathan* first published in 1651, Thomas Hobbes expounded a political philosophy which was a justification of absolute authority. The way for this had been paved earlier during the sixteenth century by Jean Bodin, a Frenchman, in his celebrated *De Republica* published in 1586. Bodin attributed sovereignty *(Majestas)* to the state and he defined it as the "highest power over citizens and subjects, unrestrained by laws."[42] Although he subscribed to Christian doctrine and admitted that the sovereign was subject to the law of God and to the law of nature, in Bodin's scheme of things there was no one around to impose these limits. There were earlier manifestations of this idea, but Bodin was the first to exactly define it.

Hobbes built on the foundation laid by Bodin, but in order to do so he used the prevailing idea of an original state of nature as his starting point. He envisaged man in his original state as a miserable, solitary creature in a lawless society in which only the fittest survived, forever at war with his fellow man and forever seeking to deprive him of life and liberty. There were no notions of right and wrong, and the only recognized right to property was what man could grab and hold by force.[43].

According to Hobbes, to relieve himself of this unhappy state of affairs, by an original covenant man created a common power in which each surrendered his entire right of self-government. A commonwealth was formed in which indivisible authority was vested in the sovereign. No member could justly dissent and he who did was subject to destruction. The sovereign could be guilty of no injustice or injury because, by his original consent given willingly or because of the fear of destruction, every member was the author of every action taken by the sovereign. The latter had the right to determine what was or was not for the public good. He was charged with the ends, for that reason he could choose the means and this included the power of life and death.

Liberty and freedom meant nothing more to Hobbes than the absence of opposition. He defined a freeman as "he, that in those things, which by his strength and wit he is able to do, is not hindered to what he has a will to."[44] The will of the subject depended on the will of the sovereign and consisted in nothing more than that to which the sovereign did not object. By such liberty even the sovereign's power over life and death was not limited, much less abolished, for the sovereign could do neither injury nor injustice to the subject.

Opposed to this was the philosophy of government of Locke who, like Hobbes, used the existence of an original state of nature as a starting point, but that is the extent to which the two agreed. Unlike Hobbes', Locke's original state of nature was idyllic and peaceful. It was a state in which all men had absolute independence, freedom and equality, and in which all men were subject to no authority other than that of the law of nature[45] which Locke identified with the law of reason, a law which "teaches all mankind who will but consult it, that being all equal and independent, no one ought to harm another in his life, health, liberty or possessions."[46] By nature he gave to every man the power to preserve his life, liberty and estate against all; also the power to judge and to punish anyone who would deprive him of these in violation of the law of reason. The power to judge and punish was, however, not arbitrary and absolute. Instead, it was limited to the need for restraint or reparation with "God and nature never allowing a man so to abandon himself as to neglect his own preservation."[47]

In effect, what Locke was writing about here was a right of revolution. He considered it tyranny to use power to one's own private advantage and beyond right, instead of for the good of those under it. Whosoever exceeded authority given to him and made his will, not the law, the rule ceased to be a magistrate and could be opposed. The reason men entered into society was, wrote Locke, for the preservation of their property. When an opposite result was reached—when the legislators endeavored "to take away and destroy the property of the people, or to reduce them to slavery under arbitrary power"[48]—then Locke considered that these put themselves at war with the people and the latter were absolved from further obedience. The objection that such a philosophy would lay the foundation for rebellion he answered as follows: "The end of government is the good of mankind. And which is best for mankind? That the people should be always exposed to the boundless will of tyranny, or that the rulers should be sometimes liable to be opposed when they grow exorbitant in the use of their power and employ it for the destruction and not the preservation of the properties of their people."[49]

There was enough similarity between Locke and the scholastic doctrine of the Church to enable the followers of Hobbes to characterize Locke's theories as "popish doctrine."[50] Nevertheless, Locke had secularized scholastic natural law and made it acceptable to an era when canonists were not particularly popular. Further expounded by Algernon Sidney, [51] Pufendorf[52] and Burlamaqui,[53] it was this secularized version that was accepted in America and became the creed of the American Revolutionists of 1776.[54] By then it had become a political force that was so dynamic that it shook the world.

It is important to note that with this new dynamic political force, the accent was placed on rights rather than purely on law. The natural law was no longer thought of solely as a body of precepts that made up the supreme law to which the order of the world must conform to be according to the will and wisdom of God. Instead, it was the source of rights to which the individual was entitled and of which he could not be deprived. Moreover, it was no longer a question of living by God's law in order to achieve eternal salvation, the ultimate goal, but rather a question of providing the individual with the means whereby he could assert rights that were considered inalienable.[55]

This was a natural consequence of the transition from scholasticism to deism which had found its fruition in the works of Locke. With the shift in emphasis from the will of God to the importance of the individual, it was only logical that natural law should sooner or later be synonymous with natural right. Hobbes had rebelled against this when he had insisted that a distinction existed between the two.[56] Locke, however, had likened the natural freedom of man to the liberty of Englishmen to dispose of actions and possessions according to the laws of England,[57] and it was this latter brand natural law that prevailed. In a like manner Pufendorf had written of the "rights attendant to man in his natural state,"[58] Burlamaqui that "[t]he idea of Right, and much more that of Natural Right are undoubtedly relative to the nature of man."[59] Vattel had entitled his work, *Le Droit des Gens ou Principes de la Loi Naturelle*.[60]

32

It was not from Hobbes but from these that the leaders of the American Revolution gleaned their concepts.[61] In fact, on at least two occasions Jefferson lamented Destutt Tracy's apparent adoption of "the principles of Hobbes, or humiliation to human nature; that the sense of justice and injustice is not derived from our natural organization, but founded on convention only."[62] He also wrote of Tracy: "I gather from his other works that he adopts the principles of Hobbes, that Justice is founded in contract solely, and does not result from a construction of man."[63] This was contrary to Jefferson's belief "that it is instinct and innate, that the moral sense is as much a part of our constitution as that of feeling, seeing and hearing."[64] James Wilson and Alexander Hamilton were no less ardent in their dislike of Hobbes.[65]

In all of this there was ample precedent for a Virginia Declaration of Rights, a Declaration of Independence that proclaimed the "unalienable rights" of man, and later a Bill of Rights appended to the Constitution of the United States which assures the continued existence of these "unalienable rights." But the question was, and still is, what these "rights" mean and how far they extend.

ACCEPTANCE OF NATURAL LAW AND LOCKE BY THE AMERICAN COLONIES

For a variety of reasons it was only logical that the American colonists should turn to natural law, the secularized version with the accent on rights, in their conflict with the mother country. From the beginning of the colonial period trained lawyers were not always available to cope with the technical procedure of the English common law. Furthermore, until the middle of the eighteenth century the legal profession was viewed with suspicion and courts were often made up of laymen. Existing statutes frequently were not applicable to local conditions which were often primitive on an everchanging frontier. Law books and reports of decided cases were rare; so few statutes were printed that it was uncommon for a lawyer to possess even a full set of the laws of his own colony. Self-reliant lawyers and judges developed their own law. They turned to the Bible, concepts of natural law and justice, and to what was accepted as just and right in the community.

Added to this there was the strong religious sentiment that prevailed among the colonists, many of whom were not long removed from Europe which they had left behind so that they might live by God's law as they undestood it. From their pulpits preachers and theologians expounded theories of natural law as the only just law. In Massachusetts Jonathan Mayhew preached that "Government is both the ordinance of God, and the ordinance of man: of God, in respect to his original plan, and universal Providence; of man, as it is immediately the result of human prudence, wisdom concert."[66] In South Carolina the Reverend Samuel Quincy preached that the knowledge of God by light and nature taught that God "has endowed us with Reason and Understanding (Faculties which Brutes have not) on purpose to contemplate his Beauty and Glory, and to keep our inferior Appetites in due Subjection to his Laws, written in our Hearts."[67]

It was not thought uncommon for a judge in Massachusetts to declare in the decision of a case that "the fundamental law which God and nature has given to people cannot be infringed."[68] In 1649, when a court of that colony could not decide what kind of a sin the rape of a small child was, the court "sought to know the mind of God by the help of all the elders of the country."[69] This was supported by good authority. The general laws of Massachusetts colony provided for resort to the word of God "in the case of the defect of a law, in any particular case."[70] In a similar manner the first constitution of Connecticut provided that "where a people are gathered together the word of God requires that to maintain the peace and union of such a people there should be an orderly and decent Government established according to God, to order and dispose of the affairs of the people at all seasons as occasion shall require; do therefore associate and conjoin ourselves to be as one Public State or Commonwealth; and do for ourselves and our Successors and such as shall be adjoined to us at any time hereafter, enter into Combination and Confederation together, to maintain and preserve the liberty and purity of the Gospel of our Lord Jesus which we now profess, as also the discipline of the Churches, which according to the truth of the said Gospel is now practiced amongst us; as also in our Civil Affairs to be guided and governed according to such Laws, Rules, Orders, and Decrees as shall be made, ordained and decreed."[71]

Magistrates in New Haven were selected by popular vote to punish criminals "according to the mind of God revealed in this world."[72] The law of God was looked to here also when gaps were found in positive law.

Another source for theories of natural law were the universities of England and America. Many a young colonist was sent to school in England, from whence "the young men brought back more vice than acquired education,"[73] but while they were there these young men were exposed to the doctrines of Locke then commonplace. At home, at Harvard, Yale and Princeton, the same theories were available in the original as well as in books of interpretation. Of the various sources of natural law Jonathan Mayhew could write: "Having been initiated, in youth, in the doctrines of civil liberty as they were taught by such men as Plato, Demosthenes, Cicero and other renowned persons among the ancients; and such as Sidney and Milton, Locke and Hoadley, among the moderns, I liked them; they seemed rational."[74] With the outbreak of opposition to England in America, this ready-made and accepted doctrine of natural law became the justification for opposition to arbitrary British rule.

As early as 1761 James Otis argued that "an Act [of Parliament] against natural equity is void."[75] The occasion was his opposition to the application of a British customs official for a general warrant to search for smuggled goods. Again in 1764 Otis argued against the absolute and arbitrary power of Parliament. In his *Rights of the British Colonies Asserted and Proved* he contended that the supreme power in a state belongs only to God; that, although parliaments declare what is for the common good, it is the higher authority of God that makes it so and not these declarations; and further, that any act of Parliament against God's natural laws "would be contrary to eternal truth, equity and justice, and consequently void."[76] He quoted Locke to prove the natural rights of the colonists.

John Adams argued against the Stamp Act as "against our Rights as Men, and our Privileges as Englishmen."[77] The struggle between England and the colonies was, he argued, "founded in principle so indisputable in the moral law, in the revealed law of God, in the true constitution of Britain, and in the most apparent welfare of the British nation, as well as of the whole body of the people in America, that it rejoices my very soul."[78]

George Mason embodied his theories of natural rights in the Virginia Declaration of Rights of June 12, 1776, when he wrote:

"That all men are by nature equally free and independent, and have certain inherent rights, of which, when they enter into a state of society, they cannot by any compact deprive or divest their posterity; namely, the enjoyment of life and liberty, with the means of acquiring and possessing property, and pursuing and obtaining happiness and safety.

"That all power is vested in, and consequently derived from the people; that all magistrates are their trustees and servants, and at all times amenable to them."[79]

On the eve of the Revolution James Wilson refuted Blackstone's theory "That there is and must be in every state a supreme, irresistible, absolute, uncontrolled authority, in which the *jura summi imperii*, or the rights of sovereignty, reside."[80] Wilson contended that by the nature of things all men are equal and free, that the consent of the governed is necessary for all lawful government, that consent is given to assure the increased happiness of the governed "above what they could enjoy in an independent and unconnected state of nature."[81]

Formal rejection of the theory of sovereignty on which the English law of speech and press was founded, and in its place the substitution of a theory of natural rights and justice, appeared in two of the five irrevocable rights claimed by the First Continental Congress in the 1774 address to the inhabitants of Quebec. The first was the right of the people to share in their government by representatives chosen by themselves; to be governed by laws which the people themselves approve through their elected representatives, and not by edicts of men over whom they have no control. The second, enumerated as the last in the address, was freedom of the press. It was said to consist, "besides the advancement of truth, science, morality, and acts in general, in its diffusion of liberal sentiments on the administration of Government, its ready communication of thoughts between subjects, and its consequential promotion of union among them, whereby oppressive officers are shamed or intimidated, into more honorable and just modes of conducting affairs."[82]

Complete acceptance of natural rights and justice was perfected by the Declaration of Independence in which it is written, "We hold these truths to be self-evident, that all men are created equal, that they are endowed by their Creator with certain unalienable Rights, that among these are Life, Liberty and the pursuit of Happiness. That to secure these rights, Governments are instituted among Men, deriving their powers from the consent of the governed." The adoption of the Constitution of the United States and its first ten amendments set out the rules by which these "unalienable rights" were to be secured.

36

THE FIGHTING FAITH OF THE AMERICAN REVOLUTION: THE EXTENT TO WHICH IT SURVIVES TODAY

A DOCTRINE TRANSPLANTED

A quarter of a century ago Roscoe Pound wrote that in America natural law was kept alive long after it had become moribund and had ceased to be a living theory of law in the old world.[1] In Europe natural law scarcely survived the eighteenth century and the nineteenth was the century of history in legal as well as political thought. On the other hand, in this country the last decade of the eighteenth and a good part of the nineteenth comprised the formative era of American law to which, according to Pound, natural law was admirably suited. This was especially so because it was written constitutions, state and federal, all of which laid emphasis on individual rights, that had to be interpreted as the legal apparatus was set up and rules worked out. In each of these constitutions a characteristic feature was a bill of rights the purpose of which was to make secure and enforce the notion "that all men are created equal, that they are endowed by their Creator with certain unalienable Rights."

Later there was to be a change in the legal thinking of this country as there had been earlier in the legal thinking of the countries of Europe. However, that had to wait until the "young brood of lawyers" weaned on the "honied Mansfieldism of Blackstone" of which Jefferson complained[2] had taken over and for the extension of the influence of Bentham and Austin to these shores. Meanwhile, James Wilson could teach with approbation in the lectures he delivered at the College of Philadelphia in 1795 that all law may be divided into two species: divine and human; that the former is called natural or revealed, depending on whether it is promulgated by reason and the natural moral sense or by the holy scriptures, but that whether natural or revealed, it flows from the same divine source—the law of God. He could also

37

teach that the latter, human law, "must rest its authority, ultimately, upon the authority of that law, which is divine."[3]

One imprint of the general acceptance in this country of the idea of an overriding law of nature which endures to this day is judicial review as it is known in both our state and federal systems. A bulwark which favors minority and property rights, this represents a practical application of natural law concepts which were incorporated into the judicial system of this country under the guidance of men who not only were nurtured on the fighting faith of the American Revolution, but who were also very familiar with Sir Edward Coke's doctrine of judicial supremacy. Indeed, there were state court decisions with overtones that favored judicial review even before the Federal Constitution was adopted.[4] Henry St. George Tucker alluded to such a concept in his American edition of Blackstone's *Commentaries*[5] which was published the same year that Chief Justice John Marshall delivered the opinion of the Supreme Court of the United States in *Marbury* v. *Madison*.[6] Soon, with the start of the nineteenth century, judicial review became an accepted part of the American judicial scene and it has remained so ever since.

The earlier cases in which this imprint made itself felt and in which direct references to natural law are found all involved property interests in one form or another. Perhaps one hint of the reason why can be found in an assertion by Gouverneur Morris at the Federal Convention even before the Constitution became a reality: "Life and liberty were generally said to be of more value than property. An accurate view of the matter would, nevertheless, prove that property was the main object of society."[7]

Perhaps another hint of the reason can be found in the emphasis that Locke placed on the right of property, a natural right that he considered antecedent to the formation of government.[8] Whatever the reason, in 1795 while he was sitting as a Circuit Judge in *Van Horne's Lessee* v. *Dorrance*,[9] the trial of a title to land, Mr. Justice Patterson instructed a Pennsylvania jury "that the right of acquiring and possessing property, and having it protected, is one of the natural, inherent, and inalienable rights of man." Three years later in *Calder v. Bull*,[10] a case that questioned the validity of a resolution of law passed by a Connecticut legislature which set aside a lower court decree disapproving a will, Mr. Justice Samuel Chase wrote: "I cannot subscribe to the *omnipotence* of a *State Legislature*, or that it is *absolute and without controul;* although its authority should not be *expressly* restrained by the *Constitution* or *fundamental law*, of the State."[11] In 1810 in *Fletcher* v. *Peck*[12] a state was prevented from rescinding a land grant "either by general principles which are common to our free institutions, or by the particular provisions of the Constitution of the United States."[13] Mr. Justice Johnson concurred in Mr. Chief Justice Marshall's opinion for the court "on a general principle, on the reason and nature of things: a principle which will impose laws even on the deity."[14]

The same thing was true as late as 1874 in *Loan Association* v. *Topeka*,[15] a case that involved the power of a state legislature to enact a statute which authorized municipalities to issue bonds the proceeds of which would be used to encourage the establishment of manufactures, and other enterprises, as would tend to develop and improve the city. The action was brought by a savings and loan association against the city for interest on bonds issued by it pursuant to the statute as a *donation* to one enterprise. The city resisted payment on the grounds that the act placed no restriction on the amount a city might issue insisting that this failure of the legislature to limit or restrict the power granted violated the Kansas Constitution. The Supreme Court struck down the Kansas statute. "It must be conceded," Mr. Justice Miller wrote for the Court, "that there are such rights in every free government beyond the control of the State. A government which recognized no such rights, which held the lives, the liberty, and the property of its citizens subject at all times to the absolute disposition and unlimited control of even the most democratic depository of power, is after all but a despotism."[16] Observing that our theory of government is opposed to any deposit of unlimited power, he continued: "There are limitations on such power which grow out of the essential nature of all free governments. Implied reservations of individual rights, without which the social compact could not exist, and which are respected by all governments entitled to the name."[17]

During the last quarter of the nineteenth century a change in legal thinking took place in this country as it had about a century earlier in Europe. A Lawrence Lowell, later President of Harvard, described this as "a sudden change of base"[18] with the victors in the struggle that had lasted two and one-half centuries, the proponents of the natural rights of man, "adopting the opinions of the vanquished,"[19] that there can be no limitation or restraint on the authority of the sovereign. This "sudden change of base" Lowell attributed to two causes, the first of which he described as follows: "So long as the reins of government were in the hands of a king or an aristocracy, it was natural that the advocates of popular rights should seek to restrain his power; but after the people had obtained control of the state, it was not to be expected that they would show the same respect for principles which fettered the exercise of their own authority. The ascendency of the popular party had, therefore, an inevitable tendency to upset those doctrines which were designed to limit the exercise of power by others."[20] The second cause was, wrote Lowell, the attention that Bentham[21] and Austin[22] now attracted in this country, the former with his greatest happiness for the greatest numbers as the sole test for legislation, the latter with his novel form of the doctrine that sovereignty is essentially incapable of limitatiin. Austin was described as having "obtained a mastery over the legal thought of the English-speaking people, which has never been equaled in the history of the race."[23]

But even as the pattern of legal thinking progressed through this change, and from this one through others after the turn of the twentieth century—all the way to legal positivism—still the imprint of natural law persisted and traces of it continued to creep into the opinions of the Supreme Court. As late as 1910 the first Mr. Justice Harlan could adopt a line of thought reminiscent of the early history of equity. In an opinion upholding the validity of an act of Congress that empowered the Secretary of War to require that obstructions to navigation be removed, he wrote for the court: "Suffice it to say, that the courts have rarely, if ever, felt themselves so restrained by technical rules that they could not find some remedy, consistent with the law, for acts, whether done by government or by individual persons, that violated natural justice or were hostile to the fundamental principles devised for the protection of the essential rights of property."[24]

Even Mr. Justice Holmes, who dismissed natural law as one way to satisfy man's demand for the superlative (another way for those less fortunate was, he said, to get drunk),[25] felt compelled as a judge to call for "fair play" and "substantial justice."[26]

At the very time legal thinking in this country was gaining momentum away from the faith of the founding fathers, natural law was given impetus in at least one area as the Court was faced with the ambiguities of the due process clause of the Fourteenth Amendment. Thus, in *Holden* v. *Hardy*,[27] as it upheld the right of the State of Utah to impose an 8-hour day in underground mines, and in smelters and ore reduction works, the Court was reluctant to attempt to precisely define

40

the clause. It was content to say "that there are certain immutable principles of justice which inhere in the very idea of free government which no member of the Union may disregard."[28] The same thing was repeated in *Twining* v. *New Jersey*,[29] where a state law that permitted an inference to be drawn against the accused for failure to testify was upheld, and the Fifth Amendment was held not applied to the states through the Fourteenth.

The manner of selection by which some, but not all, of the basic provisions of the Federal Bill of Rights have been absorbed by the Fourteenth Amendment has itself been made to rest on a natural law process. Thus, in *Hebert* v. *Louisiana*[30] the Fourteenth Amendment was said to require "that state action, whether through one agency or another, shall be consistent with the fundamental principles of liberty and justice which lie at the base of all our civil and political institutions and not infrequently are designed as 'law of the land.' "[31]

The Supreme Court upheld the Louisiana court's construction of a penal statute that paralleled the Eighteenth Amendment as not a denial of due process, and it found a double prosecution (one under state and the other under federal law) not against double jeopardy. Even more explicit was the test laid down in *Palko* v. *Connecticut*[32] a case in which a state statute permitting appeals to be taken by the state in criminal cases was unsuccessfully challenged as violative of the Fourteenth Amendment. The test was said to be: "Does it violate the 'fundamental principles of liberty and justice which lie at the base of all our civil and political institutions'?"[33] As explicit and more recent is the test laid down in *Kent* v. *Dulles*,[34] a case that was concerned with two applications for passports that had been denied by the Secretary of State. In this case the right to travel was found to be "a part of the 'liberty' of which the citizen cannot be deprived without due process of law under the Fifth Amendment."[35] Even the Solicitor General conceded that. "If that 'liberty' is to be regulated," concluded the Court, "it must be pursuant to the law-making functions of the Congress."[36] As to the delegation of this function the Court said: "Where activities or enjoyment, *natural* and often necessary to the well-being of an American citizen, such as travel, are involved, we will construe narrowly all delegated powers that curtail or dilute them."[37] The Court went on to hold that under existing law the Secretary of State did not have authority to deny the passports because of the applicants' Communist beliefs and associations or their refusal to file affidavits concerning present or past membership in the Communist Party.[38]

It must not be assumed, however, that all of this was without dissent. At the very start Mr. Justice Iredell disputed the applicability of natural law. Although he went along with the Court in the result arrived at in *Calder* v. *Bull*,[39] he disagreed with some of the reasoning. "It is true," he wrote, "that some speculative jurists have held, that a legislative act against natural justice must, in itself, be void; but I cannot think that under such a government, any Court of Justice would possess a power to declare it so."[40] Much to the same effect was a dissent by Mr. Justice Clifford to Mr. Justice Miller's statement in behalf of the Court in *Loan Association* v. *Topeka*.[41] But perhaps no more forceful a dissent can be found than Mr. Justice Black's statement in *Adamson* v. *California*,[42] a self-incrimination case in which the proposition was rejected that the Fourteenth Amendment incorporates the Fifth and applies it to the states. He wrote of *Twining* v. *New Jersey*,[43] decided thirty-nine years earlier, "I think that decision and the 'natural law' theory of the Constitution upon which it relies degrade the constitutional safeguards of the Bill of Rights and simultaneously appropriate for this Court a broad power which we are not authorized by the Constitution to exercise."[44]

But however long natural law may have survived as a living theory of law in this country after it had been laid aside in Europe, and however much it may have suited the American scene during the formative era of American law—whether as the basis for a novel concept of judicial review, or as a principle with which to interpret the ambiguities of the Fourteenth Amendment—in no area did it have less influence than in the interpretation of the speech and press provisions of the First Amendment. Indeed, within a decade after the Federal Convention it was the English common law of speech and press that had prevailed in the colonies before the Revolution that carried the day. How unpopular the outcome proved to be is well illustrated by the effort that Congress made to remit the fines that were imposed in the Alien and Sedition Trials.[45] Later, even after the First Amendment provision had been absorbed into the Fourteenth through a natural law process of selection, natural law thinking continued to be set to one side in the actual interpretation of what liberty of speech and press amount to. And in more recent eras, as pressures caused by increasingly unsettled international political atmospheres have fluctuated, problems of speech and press have become ever more perplexing. The outcome has been a search that continues to this day for a theory, a concept, or even a formula, again divorced from the thinking that motivated the Declaration of Independence, the Constitution, and the Bill of Rights, that will fit all occasions. That is the subject of the chapters that follow.

CHAPTER V

THE ALIEN AND SEDITION LAWS: ABSENCE OF PREVIOUS RESTRAINT

ADOPTION OF THE LAWS

In 1798, less than ten years after the adoption of the First Amendment, the Alien and Sedition Laws were enacted by the Federalist majority in Congress. The first of these, the Naturalization Act,[1] extended from five to fourteen years the time required for full citizenship; the second and third, the two Alien Acts,[2] related to aliens in this country. The last of these laws, the Sedition Act,[3] provided in part as follows in Section 2: "And be it further enacted, That if any person shall write, print, utter or publish, or shall cause or procure to be written, printed, or uttered or published, or shall knowingly and willingly assist or aid in writing, printing, uttering or publishing any false, scandalous and malicious writing or writings against the government of the United States, or either house of the Congress of the United States, or the President of the United States, with intent to defame the said government, or either house of the said Congress, or the said President, or to bring them, or either of them, into contempt or disrepute; or to excite against them, or either or any of them, the hatred of the good people of the United States . . . shall be punished by a fine not exceeding two thousand dollars and by imprisonment not exceeding two years."

It is true that by the third section of the Sedition Act the truth of the matter charged as a libel could be given in evidence in defense and a jury could determine both law and fact under a court's direction. Nevertheless, this was strange legislation for a government that had so recently insisted that guarantees against the infringement of speech and press be incorporated into its constitution. The safeguards of the third section of the act notwithstanding, the implications of the second section were altogether too evident. To understand what had brought

44

this about, a knowledge of local and international events of the times is necessary.

Although these laws were enacted while the United States was at peace, war with France, a recent ally, was expected momentarily. This was motivated by the following sequence of events: The Jay Treaty, the temporary solution of our difficulties with Great Britain, irritated the French who were then at war with England. In retaliation the French seized and confiscated American shipping bound to and from English ports. Charles Pinckney, John Marshall, and Elbridge Gerry were sent to France to settle this new controversy, only to be met by the Directory with disrespect, humiliation and insult. The efforts of the American mission were received with the suggestion, transmitted through intermediaries, that a loan to France and the payment of a *douceur* were the prerequisites to any negotiations. When all of this was revealed to Congress April 3, 1798, with the disclosure of the famous X, Y, Z letters, a furor arose in this country. A recommendation was made to the President that this country prepare for war and steps to that end were initiated.

Aside from the furor caused by the X, Y, Z affair, the war between England and France had considerable effect on the American political scene. The Federalist party, the party in power, supported England; the Republican party, with Jefferson as its leader, favored the French.[4] Sentiment on both sides was at a fever pitch. Furthermore, the Federalists were angered by insults directed at them by Republican journalists and pamphleteers. They feared abuse and misrepresentation at a time when war seemed inevitable, and they had no love for the foreign press in this country which exploited freedom of the press to the utmost. It was with this in mind that Congress enacted the Alien and Sedition Laws, but not without strong opposition from Jefferson and his party.

REACTION TO THE LAWS; THE KENTUCKY AND VIRGINIA RESOLUTIONS

The Sedition Act made truth a defense, required an actual intent to cause injury, and it made the jury the judge of criminality. Nevertheless, the act was considered by the opposition as an infringement of freedom of speech and of the press as well as a weapon in the hands of the party in power to perpetuate its authority.[5] At first, even Hamilton, an ardent Federalist, wrote as follows of the measure when it was introduced in the Senate: "There are provisions in this bill, which, according to a cursory view, appear to me highly exceptionable, and such as, more than any thing else, may endanger civil war. I have not had time to point out any objections by this post, but I will do it to-morrow. Let us not establish tyranny. Energy is a very different thing from violence. If we make no false step, we shall be essentially united, but if we push things to an extreme, we shall then give to faction body and solidity."[6]

The contention that the aim of the Sedition Act was to silence opposition, as well as to muzzle violent and unrestrained criticism of the government, was not as far fetched as it might seem and it had considerable support. Thus when John Allen of Connecticut opened the debate in the House of Representatives on the proposed legislation he said of it: "I hope this bill will not be rejected. If there ever was a nation which required a law of this kind, it is this. Let gentlemen look at certain papers printed in this city and elsewhere, and ask themselves whether an unwarranted and dangerous combination does not exist to overturn and ruin the Government by publishing the most shameless falsehoods against the Representatives of the people of all denominations, that they are hostile to free Government and genuine liberty, and of course to the welfare of this country; that they ought, therefore, to be displaced, and that the people ought to raise in insurrection against the Government."[7] To prove his point Mr. Allen then proceeded to read long passages from offending newspapers which, to say the least, were quite unfriendly to the administration and the party in power.[8]

The proponents of the measure argued its constitutionality by resorting to the traditional English definition of freedom of the press as enunciated by Mansfield. For instance, Mr. Robert Harper of South Carolina is reported to have argued that he "had often heard in this place, and elsewhere, harangues on the liberty of the press, as if it were to swallow up all other liberties; as if all law and reason, and every right, human and divine, was to fall prostrate before the liberty of the Press; whereas, the true meaning of it is no more than that a man shall be at liberty to print what he pleases, provided he does not offend against the laws, and not that no law shall be passed to regulate this liberty of the press."[9]

In 1799, after the law had been put into effect, Hamilton wrote, with an apparent change of sentiment: "To preserve confidence in the officers of the general government, by preserving their reputations from malicious and unfounded slanders, is essential to enable them to fulfill the ends of their appointment. It is, therefore, both constitutional and politic to place their reputations under the guardianship of the courts of the United States."[10]

Widespread resentment against the Federalist party and its Alien and Sedition Laws burst forth as soon as the contents of these became generally known. Although Jefferson apparently did not object when the legislation was first proposed and he heard of it, later he added kindling to the fire of resentment with the nine Kentucky resolutions that he drafted and which were adopted by the Kentucky legislature November 10, 1798. The third of these declared that, as a general principle and expressly so by the Constitution as amended, all powers neither delegated to the United States nor prohibited to the states were reserved to the latter; that no power over religion, speech or press was delegated to the United States or forbidden to the states by the Constitution. Therefore, because of this and because of the express prohibition of the First Amendment, it stated that the Sedition Act "which does abridge the freedom of the press, is not law, but is altogether void, and of no force."[11]

When Jefferson sent him a copy of these resolutions, Madison took the cue, rewrote them, and had his version presented to the Virginia legislature along with a report that he wrote. The Virginia legislature reacted favorably and adopted Madison's measures December 21, 1798. This version protested the Alien and Sedition laws as unconstitutional and called for the cooperation of all of the states "in maintaining unimpaired the authorities, rights, and liberties, reserved to the states respectively, or to the people."[12] In his report Madison denied the existence of a federal common law that could sanction the Sedition Act, and he denied that the Federal government had the power to legislate to the abridgment of the freedom of the press.

The states that did respond to the call for cooperation opposed the resolution,[13] but the people at large reacted with a bountiful crop of remonstrances, petitions and memorials condemning the laws which they addressed to Congress.

However sincere Jefferson may have been in this matter, he too could become irritated at the press. Thus, in 1803, while he was President, he wrote to Governor McKean of Pennsylvania as follows: "The federalists having failed in destroying the freedom of the press by their gag-law, seem to have attacked it in an opposite form, that is by pushing it's licentiousness & it's lying to such a degree of prostitution as to deprive it of all credit. And the fact is that so abandoned are the tory presses in this particular that even the least informed of the people have learnt that nothing in a newspaper is to be believed. This is a dangerous state of things, and the press ought to be restored to its credibility if possible. The restraints provided by the laws of the states are sufficient for this if applied. And I have therefore long thought that a few prosecutions of the most prominent offenders would have a wholesome effect in restoring the integrity of the presses. Not a general prosecution, for that would look like persecution: but a selected one . . . If the same thing be done in some other of the states it will place the whole band more on their guard."[14] Jefferson enclosed a copy of an "offending" newspaper to illustrate his point.

Meanwhile, Jefferson had found his issue for the election of 1800.

TRIALS OF LYON, HASWELL, COOPER AND CALLENDER

How many prosecutions took place for violations of the Sedition Law is not accurately known. Anderson states that twenty-four or twenty-five persons were arrested, at least fifteen indicted, ten or possibly eleven tried, and ten pronounced guilty.[15] He divides the cases in which indictments were returned into the following classes: leading Republican newspapers, minor Republican newspapers, individuals of national or local importance, persons of no great significance. The trials took place amidst charges of unfairness and of packed juries.

By its terms the Sedition Act expired with the 5th Congress,[16] and as soon as Jefferson became President all persons convicted or awaiting trial for its violation were immediately pardoned or released.[17] For these reasons no trial ever reached the Supreme Court of the United States and the constitutionality of the act was never finally determined. Nevertheless, Associate Justices William Patterson and Samuel Chase presided over four of the reported trials, and these illustrate how the Federalist packed judiciary impregnated with English case law, usages and customs sought to incorporate the English common law of seditious libel into American law. Indeed, it was not until 1812 that the Supreme Court of the United States decided that sedition is not a part of the common criminal law of this country.[18]

Matthew Lyon, a Representative to Congress from Vermont, was the first to be convicted for a violation of the Sedition Act.[19] He was accused of having the intent "to stir up sedition, and to bring the President and government of the United States into contempt." His crime consisted of a letter in which he had written of the President that "every consideration of the public welfare [was] swallowed up in a continued grasp for power, in an unbounded thirst for rediculous pomp, foolish adulation, and selfish avarice."[20] A second count accused Lyon of a seditious intent. The basis for this was a letter that he had received, but which he had published and used for political purposes. In it the difficulties with France were attributed to a "bullying speech" of the President and a "stupid answer" of the Senate.

At Lyon's trial, Justice Patterson instructed the jury that it had nothing whatever to do with the constitutionality or unconstitutionality of the Sedition Act; that if it found that the intent of Lyon was to render odious or contemptible the President and the Government, and to bring them both in disrepute, a verdict of guilty should be returned.[21] Conviction followed and punishment by fine and imprisonment was imposed. But while he was in prison Lyon was overwhelmingly re-elected to Congress. He was, however, prevented from resuming his seat until his fine had been paid and his sentence served.

The second trial before Justice Patterson was that of Anthony Haswell,[22] a Revolutionary War soldier and editor of the *Vermont Gazette*. One part of Haswell's crime consisted of publishing an advertisement for a lottery to raise money with which to pay Lyon's fine. The advertisement was addressed "To the enemies of political persecution in the western district of Vermont." As a preface to the details of the plan it advised: "Your representative (Matthew Lyon) is holden by the oppressive hand of usurped power in a loathsome prison, deprived almost of the right of reason, and suffering all the indignities which can be heaped upon him by a hard-hearted savage, who has, to the disgrace of Federalism, been elevated to a station where he can satiate his barbarity on the misery of his victims. But in spite of Fitch (the marshal) and to their sorrow, time will pass away; the month of February will arrive, and will it bring liberty to the defender of your rights? No. Without exertion it will not. Eleven hundred dollars must be paid for his ransom."[23]

Haswell had also reprinted in his newspaper an excerpt from the *Aurora*, another Republican newspaper: "At the same time the administration publicly notified that Tories, men who had fought against our independence, who had shared in the desolation of our homes, and the abuse of our wives and daughters, were men who were worthy of the confidence of the government."[24]

Justice Patterson instructed the jury that although the common law had been modified by statute to admit truth in evidence, unless the justification came up to the charge it was no defense; that unless the evidence sustained the language descriptive of Lyon's treatment no defense was made out; and that as to the statement about the Tories, if they believed beyond a reasonable doubt that the intent was defamatory and there was publication, they must convict. During the trial evidence was ruled inadmissible because it would not have been a flat justification, even though it would have established that the administration occasionally favored the appointment of Tories to office. Again there was a conviction and punishment by fine and imprisonment.

The first trial over which Justice Samuel Chase presided was that of Thomas Cooper,[25] editor of the *Sunbury and Northumberland Gazette*. In the midst of a political controversy Cooper had published a justification of a request for a political appointment that he had made to President Adams some time earlier. Cooper had written that at the time of the request, President Adams "was hardly in the infancy of political mistake: even those who doubted his capacity thought well of his intention. Nor were we saddled with the expense of a permanent navy, or threatened, under his auspices, with the existence of a standing army. Our credit was not yet reduced so low as to borrow money at eight per cent . . . nor had he yet interfered, as President . . . to influence the decisions of a court of justice . . . an interference without precedent, against law and mercy. This melancholy case of Jonathan Robbins, a native citizen of America, forcibly impressed by the British, and delivered up, with the advice of Mr. Adams, to the mock trial of a British court-martial . . . a case too little known, but to which the people ought to be fully appraised, before the election, and they shall be."[26]

This served as the basis for Cooper's indictment.

During the trial Justice Chase started his long instruction to the jury with the statement: "When men are found rash enough to commit an offense such as the traverser is charged with, it becomes the duty of the government to take care that they should not pass with impunity."[27] He stated in his statement of the law that all governments about which he had read or heard of punished libels against themselves; he added: "If a man attempts to destroy the confidence of the people in their officers, their supreme magistrate, and their legislature, he effectually saps the foundation of the government."[28] Justice Chase then proceeded to refute all of the charges made by Cooper. At one point he exclaimed that he could not suppress his feelings "at this gross attack upon the President."[29] He advanced the conclusion: "This publication is evidently intended to mislead the ignorant, and inflame their minds against the President, and to influence their votes on the next election."[30]

The inevitable verdict of guilty was again followed by fine and imprisonment. Stephen Girard paid the fine but Cooper served the sentence.

The second Sedition Act trial over which Justice Chase presided was that of James Callender.[31] Later his conduct of this trial served as one of the reasons for his impeachment.[32]

Callender was indicted as the author of a book entitled *The Prospect Before Us* which he had written with the encouragement of Thomas Jefferson.[33] The book was a violent attack on Adams' administration which was characterized as "one continued tempest of malignant passions."[34] It spoke of Adams as a "professed aristocrat" who "had proved faithful and serviceable to the British interest;" it ridiculed him by asking: "Reader, dost thou envy that unfortunate old man with his twenty-five thousand dollars a year, with the petty parade of his birth-day, with the importance of his name sticking in every page of the statute book? Alas! he is not an object of envy, but of compassion and of horror."[35] It concluded by advising the people: "Take your choice, then, between Adams, war and beggary, and Jefferson, peace and competency."[36]

Justice Chase read the book while he was presiding at the Circuit Court at Annapolis. As he did so he marked the passages that he considered libellous with the intention of taking it with him to Richmond as the proper subject for prosecution. He remarked "that before he left Richmond, he would teach the people to distinguish between the liberty and licentiousness of the press."[37] On the way to Richmond, when he was told that Callender was said to have been once arrested for vagrancy he answered, "it is a pity you have not hanged the rascal."[38]

At the start of the trial there was considerable bickering about how prospective jurors should be challenged. Any question relating to whether or not a prospective juror had formed and delivered any opinion on the book was excluded. The only proper question was ruled to be, "Have you ever formed and delivered an opinion upon this charge?"[89] Justice Chase felt that otherwise the trial would never take place because everyone had heard of the case and formed an opinion.

During the trial, evidence which could only justify part of the charge was declared inadmissible because of the fear that once heard, illegal evidence might make an undue impression. For that reason, all questions intended to be asked the witnesses by the defense were required to be submitted in writing to the Court in advance. As the trial progressed there were numerous interruptions and witty remarks by Justice Chase until finally both defense counsel sat down and refused to proceed. The trial ended with a long discussion by the Justice on why juries should not decide the constitutionality of laws.

Like the others, Callender was convicted and sentenced to fine and imprisonment.

At the conclusion of the Callender trial Justice Chase proceeded to New Castle, Delaware, where, at the opening of court, he announced that he had heard of a seditious newspaper in that state. He advised the United States District Attorney to search all of the newspaper files for abusive language. Even though there was no other business to transact, the Justice held the grand jury for an additional day for them to return an indictment should anything be found. When the District Attorney reported nothing but an unpleasant reference about the Justice himself, no action was taken.[40]

Only Justices Patterson and Samuel Chase actually presided over prosecutions for violations of the Sedition Act. However, other members of the Supreme Court of the United States that sat between 1798 and 1801 expressed their sentiments about the act in addresses to grand juries. Justice Cushing defended the act in a charge to a Virginia grand jury September 23, 1798, as an amelioration of English law;[41] Justice Iredell delivered an address to a grand jury in Philadelphia April 11, 1799, in which he not only upheld the Alien and Sedition Laws, but also quoted Blackstone's definition of freedom of the press as "the definition . . . nowhere more happily or justly expressed."[42] In addition, Justice Oliver Ellsworth expressed his approval of the act in a letter to Timothy Pickering, Secretary of War.[43]

THE SEDITION ACT AND THE ENGLISH LAW OF SEDITIOUS LIBEL

Fear brought about the Sedition Act of 1798 just as fear had brought about the statute *De Scandalis Magnatum* 524 years earlier in England. In both instances, the motivating force was apprehension over the possible effects of adverse criticism; the purpose of both acts was to silence unfavorable comment on the government and to protect those of authority in the government from verbal and written attack. The later act, the Sedition Act, sought to incorporate the English law of seditious libel into American law by statutory enactment. Fortunately, the only use made of it was to silence the more violent of those who criticised President Adams.

Both at English common law and under the Sedition Act, to blame the government and its officials was forbidden. It was believed that to bring either or both into disrepute tended to the overthrow of the government. Until 1792, the criminal intent charged to the defendant was merely a matter of form at English common law, and it was not a part of the definition of libel; it required no proof of the matter by the prosecutor and it admitted no proof in rebuttal by the defendant. The Sedition Act required an evil intent,[44] but this was rendered a fiction when bad intent was inferred from the tendency of publications as framers of public opinion.

It is true that the Sedition Act made truth admissible as evidence in defense, whereas truth was not allowed as a defense in England until 1843. But this was little protection under the American act because of the manner in which it was administered. To amount to a defense truth not only had to be proved "to the marrow,"[45] but the entire matter had to be proved by a single witness. If it fell short of this, the testimony of a witness was ruled inadmissible.[46] Thus in Callender's trial Justice Chase ruled that "to admit evidence, which went to an argumentative establishment of the truth of a minute part of the charge by one witness would be irregular and subversive of every principle of law . . . "[47] Furthermore, the Federal Judiciary which enforced the Sedition Act believed that the English common law was essential for the suppression of crime. It subscribed to the English definition of freedom of the press stated by Lord Mansfield as follows: "The liberty of the press consists of printing without any previous license, subject to the consequences of law. The licentiousness of the press is *Pandora's* box, the source of every evil."[48] Indeed, even before 1793 prosecutions had already taken place in the Federal courts in which the applicability of this English common law had been upheld.[49]

There can be little doubt that had the Supreme Court of the United States been confronted with the constitutionality of the Sedition Act the law would have been upheld. A majority of the members who sat on the Court while it was in effect and for some time thereafter had expressed their approval even without having the issue presented. Nevertheless, by today's standards, as it was enforced this law violated the Constitution. The publications of Callender, Cooper, Haswell and Lyon were not necessarily false and they expressed opinions that were allowable. These men neither taught nor advised the use of force and violence to bring about the defeat of Adams in an election. Instead, they sought to accomplish this result by the expression of political opinions. Without a doubt, these opinions were unrestrained and even in bad taste. But then, the political arena has never been a proper setting for the thin skinned or the over sensitive. Furthermore, Callender and the others were punished for their criticism of the President and his administration of public affairs. In its enforcement or otherwise, no law that restricts the free and open discussion of such matters can be consistent with the prohibitions of the First Amendment.

THE GHOST OF THE ENGLISH THEORY AS EXPRESSED BY BLACKSTONE

Although as a final act of contrition at least some of the fines imposed for violations of the Sedition Act were ultimately remitted by Act of Congress,[50] the ghost of the British theory as expressed by Blackstone, the theory under which these convictions took place, lingered on. As late as 1907 it was restated in the best common law tradition by Mr. Justice Holmes in *Patterson* v. *Colorado*,[51] the first of the decisions on speech and press that the Justice rendered as an Associate Justice of the Supreme Court of the United States.

This was the review of an information for contempt issued by the Supreme Court of Colorado. The information had been issued against those responsible for the publication of articles and cartoons alleged to reflect on the motives and conduct of the court in cases still pending; an intent to embarrass the impartial administration of justice was charged. Local law, the state constitution, and the Fourteenth Amendment were all raised by motion to quash. When this failed, the truth of the matter published was set up along with the claim of the right to prove the truth under the applicable provisions of the Constitution of the United States.

With the statement, "We leave undecided the question whether there is to be found in the Fourteenth Amendment a prohibition similar to that in the First,"[52] Mr. Justice Holmes asserted that even if it should be assumed that the prohibitions of the First Amendment apply to the states as well as to the United States, the position of Patterson would not be improved. At this early date he defined these prohibitions as follows: "In the first place, the main purpose of such constitutional provisions is to 'prevent all such *previous restraints* upon publications as had been practiced by other governments,' and they do not prevent the subsequent punishment of such as may be deemed contrary to the public welfare. *Commonwealth* v. *Blanding*, 3 Pick. 304, 313, 314;

54

Respublica v. *Oswald*, 1 Dallas, 319, 325. The preliminary freedom extends as well to the false as to the true; the subsequent punishment may extend as well to the true as to the false. This was the law of criminal libel apart from statute in most cases, if not in all. *Commonwealth* v. *Blanding, ubi sup;* 4 Bl. Com. 150."[53] Parenthetically, it should be noted that Mr. Justice Holmes is better known for the "clear and present danger" test he developed years later.[54]

The first toll of the death-bell of the ghost of the theory as expressed by Blackstone was not sounded until 1931. The bell-ringer was Mr. Chief Justice Hughes in his opinion for the Court in *Near* v. *Minnesota*.[55] Although the theory was upheld, the Chief Justice wrote: "The exceptional nature of its limitations places in a strong light the general conception that liberty of the press, historically considered and taken by the Federal Constitution, has meant, principally although not exclusively, immunity from previous restraints or censorship. The *conception of the liberty of the press in this country had broadened with the exigencies of the colonial period and with the efforts to secure freedom from oppressive administration.*"[56]

In 1936 the vigil was finally ended with *Grosjean* v. *American Press Co.*[57] in which Mr. Justice Sutherland wrote for the Court: "It is impossible to concede that by the words 'freedom of the press' the framers of the amendment intended to adopt merely the narrow view then reflected by the law of England that such freedom consisted only in immunity from previous censorship; for this abuse had then permanently disappeared from British practice . . . Undoubtedly, the range of a constitutional provision phrased in terms of the common law sometimes may be fixed by recourse to the applicable rules of that law. But the doctrine which justifies such recourse, like other cannons of construction, must yield to more compelling reasons whenever they exist . . . And, obviously, it is subject to the qualification that the common law rule invoked shall be one not rejected by our ancestors as unsuited to their civil or political conditions."[58]

After enjoying a long and exciting career, the theory had suffered a long, hard, lingering death.

CHAPTER VI

LIBERTY VERSUS LICENSE

BIRTH OF THE THEORY

In our century there has been a marked increase in freedom of speech and press cases to which a number of causes have contributed. Significant have been two World Wars that all but engulfed the entire world; a "police action" and in its wake a "cold war" that threatens to do so at any time; a depression such as the world had never experienced before, together with world-wide political, social and economic upheavals; and last, but of utmost importance, the recognition that the Fourteenth Amendment encompasses the prohibitions of the First which it applies to state action.

First one theory has been advanced and then another to meet the ever increasing and perplexing problems caused by the impact of these forces on speech and press, and also to replace the archaic theory found in Blackstone which had all but broken down by the end of the first decade of the century. Still the problem has not been solved. Some of these theories have recognized the magnitude of the problem, others have not. For instance, in 1920 Attorney General A. Mitchell Palmer offered the opinion that a deadline could easily be drawn across which men would not be permitted to go in the exercise of their right of free speech. He explained exactly how to do it,[1] but subsequent history has proven that this is not so easy to accomplish.

First to be advanced was the use-abuse or the liberty versus license theory, a theory that seeks to draw a sharp line between speech and press that is right, and speech and press that is wrong. On one side is liberty, on the other abuse or licentiousness. The former is protected, the latter is not. But this was not something new. It was a distinction which had developed in England over a century earlier as an aftermath of the Fox Libel Act.[2] Lord Kenyon had used it in his charge to the jury in the *Trial of John Cuthell:* "The liberty of the press is dear to England; the licentiousness of the press is odious to England: the liberty of it can never be so well protected as by beating down the licentiousness."[3] In 1918 Chief Justice White came close to it when he wrote for the Court: "It suffices to say that, however complete is the right of the press to state public things and discuss them, the right, as every other right enjoyed in human society, is subject to the restraints which separate right from wrongdoing."[4]

Equally close was the language used by Mr. Justice Sanford in 1925: "It is a fundamental principle, long established, that the freedom of speech and of the press which is secured by the Constitution, does not confer an absolute right to speak or publish, without responsibility, whatever one may choose, or an unrestricted or unbridled license that gives immunity for every possible use of language and prevents the punishment of those who *abuse this freedom*."[5] He cited Joseph Story in support of the proposition that reasonably limited, "this freedom is an inestimable privilege in a free government; without such limitation, it might become the scourge of the republic."[6]

In the practical application of the theory a number of labels have been used to distinguish use from abuse, liberty from license, right from wrong. "Reasonable tendency" or "bad intent," "direct" or "indirect incitement" have all had their turn. It was the first of these that Chief Justice White used in *Toledo Newspaper Co.* v. *United States*,[7] a contempt of court case in which the offending newspaper allegedly had assailed and challenged the right of a court to grant relief sought in an impending proceeding. "[T]he character of the act done and its direct tendency to prevent and obstruct the discharge of judicial duty"[8] was held to be the test. And although it was not shown that the presiding judge had seen the articles objected to, the "reasonable tendencies" and not the "substantially impossible assumptions on the subject" were said to control—"the reasonable tendency of the acts done to influence or bring about the baleful result."[9]

THE FIRST OF THE ESPIONAGE ACT CASES

Along with American participation in World War I came the Espionage Act cases which were convictions for violations of the Espionage Acts of 1917[10] and 1918.[11] Most of these cases arose from violations of Title I, § 3, of the 1917 act as originally passed and as amended by the 1918 act. Some were finally disposed of during the war, others after the war had ended, but all were upheld with use-abuse or liberty versus license as the main prop.

As originally enacted, Title I, § 3, made it punishable for anyone, when the United States is at war, to willfully "make or convey false reports or false statements with the intent to interfere with the operation or success of the military or naval forces of the United States or to promote the success of its enemies;" to "willfully cause or attempt to cause insubordination, disloyalty, mutiny, or refusal of duty, in the military or naval forces of the United States;" or to "willfully obstruct the recruiting or enlistment service of the United States, to the injury of the service of the United States."[12] The 1918 act left the 1917 act intact except that it added "attempts to obstruct the recruiting or enlistmen service," plus nine other offenses.

The first noteworthy case, *Masses Publishing Co.* v. *Patten,* never went beyond the Court of Appeals.[13] Nevertheless it set the pattern. It started out as a "direct incitement" case but it ended up as one that hinged on "bad tendency." The former was used by the lower court and the latter in the intermediate court. The case arose when the Postmaster of New York City excluded from the mails an issue of *The Masses,* a monthly revolutionary journal. The publication printed cartoons and text attacking the war which were considered objectionable under the provisions of the 1917 act declaring non-mailable any publication violating its criminal section. District Judge Learned Hand was appealed to by the publisher for a preliminary injunction against the postmaster which he granted.

In his opinion Judge Hand laid down rules that followed the "direct or indirect incitement" test. Outside of the boundaries of free speech he placed counsel or advice to others "to violate the law as it stands."[14] "Words," he observed, "are not only the keys of persuasion, but the triggers of action, and those which have no purport but to counsel the violation of law cannot by any latitude of interpretation be a part of that public opinion which is the final source of government in a democratic state." Within the boundaries he placed conduct which "stops short of urging upon others that it is their duty or their interest to resist the law."

In summarizing his philosophy of free speech, Judge Hand declared: "Political agitation, by the passions it arouses or the convictions it engenders, may in fact stimulate men to the violation of law. Detestation of existing policies is easily transformed into forcible resistance of the authority which puts them in execution, and it would be folly to disregard the causal relation between the two. Yet to assimilate agitation, legitimate as such, with direct incitement to violent resistance, is to disregard the tolerance of all methods of political agitation which in normal times is a safeguard of free government. The distinction is not a scholastic subterfuge, but a hard-bought acquisition in the fight for freedom, and the purpose to disregard it must be evident when the power exists."[15]

Judge Hand was reversed not on his determination of what speech is or is not protected, but on a principle of administrative law. By the provisions of the act, whether or not something is mailable must be determined by the Postmaster in the exercise of his judgment and discretion; his decision is conclusive and cannot be reversed by the courts unless it is clearly wrong. Nevertheless, for good measure the Court of Appeals threw out Judge Hand's determination of free speech and substituted "bad tendency." "If," it held, "the natural and reasonable effect of what is said is to encourage resistance to a law, and the words are used in an endeavor to persuade to resistance, it is immaterial that the duty to resist is not mentioned, or the interest of the persons addressed in resistance is not suggested."[16]

The first of the Espionage Act cases to reach the Supreme Court of the United States was *Schenck v. United States*.[17] Schenck, the defendant, had attended to the printing and distributing of leaflets which advocated opposition and resistance to the World War I draft. He had done this in his capacity as general secretary of the Socialist Party. The prohibitions of the First Amendment against infringement of speech and press were set up as a defense. A unanimous Court upheld the conviction with an opinion written by Mr. Justice Holmes in which he launched his classic "clear and present danger" test. "The question in every case," he wrote, "is whether the words used are used in such circumstances and are of such a nature as to create a clear and present danger that they will bring about the substantive evils that Congress has a right to prevent."[18] At this point, however, the now famous test had not yet matured. It was still but an embryo. Although it provided a more liberal tone to what had already been said on the subject of speech and press, it was still coupled with "bad intent" and "bad tendency." Thus wrote the Justice: "If the act (speaking, or circulating a paper,) its tendency and intent with which it is done are the same, we perceive no ground for saying that success alone warrants making the act a crime."[19]

Seven days after his opinion in the *Schenck* case, Mr. Justice Holmes delivered two more unanimous opinions for the Court. Both upheld convictions for violations of the Espionage Act, and in both he reverted to "bad tendency" as the test.

Objected to in the first case, *Frohwerk* v. *United States*, [20] were articles published in a German language newspaper which were critical of the war effort and of the recruiting program. Admittedly the case was decided by the Supreme Court on an unsatisfactory record,[21] but to the objection that there was not sufficient allegation of intent it was answered: "intent to accomplish an object cannot be alleged more clearly than by stating that parties conspired to accomplish it."[22]

The decision in the second case, *Debs* v. *United States*, [23] upheld the conviction of Eugene Debs. It arose from a speech that he delivered before a convention which had as its main theme the growth and ultimate success of Socialism. During the course of the speech Debs expressed approval of the conduct of persons who had been convicted for aiding and abetting the failure to register for the draft. He spoke of war as an instrument with which to support capitalism, and he branded the declaration of war as a crime both against the United States and against the nations of the world. In the trial court the jury was instructed in part: "In passing upon the question of specific intent, I wish to say something additional thereto. Disapproval of war is, of course, not a crime, nor is the advocacy of peace a crime under this law, unless the words or utterances by which the expression or advocacy is conveyed shall have been willfully intended by the person making them to commit the acts forbidden by this law, and, further, not even then unless the natural and reasonably probable tendency and effect of such words and language as he may use will have the effect and consequences forbidden by the law."[24] The issue of freedom of speech was raised as a defense, but Holmes dismissed this as disposed of in *Schenck* v. *United States*.

FOUR MORE ESPIONAGE ACT CASES

There were yet four Espionage Act cases to be decided by the Supreme Court of the United States: *Abrams* v. *United States*,[25] *Schaefer* v. *United States*,[26] *Pierce* v. *United States*,[27] and *Milwaukee Publishing Co.* v. *United States*.[28] But in none of these was Mr. Justice Holmes to speak for or go along with the majority. From now on it was to be Holmes and Brandeis dissenting, preaching the virtues of "clear and present danger," while the majority held the line for "bad intent" and "reasonable tendency."

Historically, these cases are of interest primarily for the contributions that the dissenting opinions made to the development of "clear and present danger" as a test. It was in these that the embryo conceived in *Schenck* v. *United States* was nurtured to maturity. However, that is another story which will be developed later.[29] For the present the discussion is limited to the decision of the first three cases and to the majority opinions which applied the "use-abuse" or "bad tendency" theory.

The facts in all three cases bore some similarity in the sense that they were all concerned with the circulation of printed materials that were critical of the war effort. In the first case, *Abrams* v. *United States*, nine thousand circulars, some printed in Yiddish and some in English, which were distributed by the Russian-born defendants denounced President Wilson as a coward, assailed the government for its intervention in Russia, called upon Russian immigrants to withdraw their sympathy and help from the prosecution of the war with Germany, and urged revolutionary organizations to unite and keep United States forces busy at home. The defendants in the second case, *Schaefer* v. *United States*, published a German language newspaper of limited circulation in which they republished news taken from other newspapers, sometimes with omissions, additions, and changes. In the third case, *Pierce* v. *United States*, pamphlets were distributed that declared abhorrence for conscription, criticised the activities of the Attorney General of the United States, characterized the war with Germany as one to protect loans made to the Allies by American investment bankers, and declared the opposition of the Socialist Party, the sponsor of the pamphlet, to war and conscription.

The indictments in all three cases charged violations of the Espionage Act. Although they varied to fit the facts of each case, there was some resemblance between all of them, especially between those of the *Schaefer* and *Pierce* cases. The *Abrams* case charged conspiracy to bring the form of the Government of the United States into contempt, scorn, contumely and disrepute, an intent to incite, provoke, and encourage resistance to the United States in the war, as well as a conspiracy to urge, incite and advocate curtailment of production essential to the war effort;[30] the *Schaefer* case charged false publication with the intent to promote the success of the enemies of the United States, and the *Pierce* case charged false satements with the intent to interfere with the operation and success of the military and naval forces of the United States; both the *Schaefer* and the *Pierce* cases charged obstruction to the recruiting and enlistment services of the United States, as well as attempts to cause insubordination, disloyalty and refusal to duty in the military and naval services of the United States.

In all of these cases the issue of freedom of speech and press was raised but was dismissed or brushed aside by the majority of the Supreme Court without much ceremony. In *Abrams* this was said to have been sufficiently discussed in the *Schenck* and *Frohwerk* cases. Instead, the case was decided on a question of evidence—whether the evidence placed before the jury was competent and substantial enough to sustain the verdict. An obvious intent to provoke and encourage resistance to the United States in time of war was found to be present and a verdict of guilty upheld.

As the Court upheld the conviction in *Schaefer,* it limited its scrutiny "to the sedate and guiding principles of criminal justice."[31] The effect of the articles could not be shown, but the Court dismissed this as not necessary. Said the Court: "The tendency of the articles and their efficacy were enough for the offense in their 'intent' and 'attempt', for those are the words of the law, and to have required more would have made the law useless."[32]

Pierce, the third case, was very much a repetition of the other two. Again it was a question of the probable effect of the circulation of material and of the defendants' motives—"whether the statements contained in the pamphlet had a natural tendency to produce the forbidden consequences, as alleged"[33]—a jury question as was the question whether the proximate result would be a material interference with recruiting and the success of the war. As for the reflections cast on the Attorney General and the American investment bankers, common knowledge was found sufficient by the majority of the Court to prove their falsity.

Perhaps Mr. Justice Clarke held the key to the decision of all three cases, even more so than did Justices Holmes and Brandeis in their celebrated "clear and present danger" dissents and concurrences.[34] In his separate dissent to the *Schaefer* case he observed: "I cannot see, as my associates seem to see, that the disposition of this case involves a great peril either to the maintenance of law and order and governmental authority on the one hand, or to the freedom of the press on the other. To me it seems simply a case of flagrant mistrial, likely to result in disgrace and great injustice, probably in life imprisonment for two old men, because this court hesitates to exercise the power, which it undoubtedly possesses, to correct, in this calmer time, errors of law which would not have been committed but for the stress and strain of feeling prevailing in the early months of the late deplorable war."[35]

In 1902, as a consequence of the assassination of President McKinley, the State of New York enacted a law making criminal anarchy a statutory crime.[36] Both during and after World War I a number of other states enacted laws of a similar nature. Those enacted during the war were similar in content and purpose to the Federal Espionage Act; the others, those enacted after the war, had as their purpose the outlawry of criminal syndicalism and anarchy.[37] It was inevitable that sooner or later the constitutionality of these acts should be tested by the Supreme Court of the United States. And when, during the 1920's, convictions for the violations of some of the acts did reach the Court "clear and present danger" was expressly excluded as the test.[38] Instead, the legislative determination of the existence of a substantive evil was accepted as conclusive unless arbitrarily and unreasonably arrived at. The purpose and probable effect of printed matter circulated in violation of the acts were factors taken into consiedration[39] "Use-abuse" was still the test with "bad tendency" and "bad intent" still the yardsticks.

An example of a war-time state sedition law is found in *Gilbert* v. *Minnesota.*[40] the review of a conviction for the violation of such a law enacted by Minnesota in 1917.[41] The statute declared it unlawful within the State of Minnesota to discourage or interfere with enlistments in the armed forces of the United States or of Minnesota, to teach or advocate by speech and writing that men should not enlist in these forces or that the citizens of Minnesota should not assist the United States in war against its public enemies. Gilbert was convicted under the statute for a false and malicious representation in a speech of the motives and objects behind the entry of the United States into the war against Germany.

The first objection advanced against the statute was that it encroached on the national war power which the Constitution of the United States conferred expressly on Congress and withheld from the states. Mr. Justice McKenna disposed of this for the majority by affirming that the states as well as the United States are intimately concerned with the outcome of war; that victory or defeat depends on the morale, spirit and determination of all.

The second objection asserted that the state statute was an infringement of the guaranteed right of free speech which was claimed as a natural and inherent right. Mr. Justice McKenna was willing to concede this for the purposes of this case. However, even with this concession he held that it could not be an absolute right, but rather one subject to limitations and restrictions—a right not "intended to give immunity for every possible use of language."[42] Not only was Gilbert's conviction upheld and the statute found constitutional, but as this was done a majority of the Court said of Gilbert's claim of the right of free speech: "It would be a travesty on the constitutional privilege he invokes to assign him its protection."[43]

During the October Term, 1925, the Supreme Court of the United States reviewed a conviction under one of the peacetime acts. The case was *Gitlow* v. *New York*[44] and the act was the 1902 New York act[45] that prohibited advocacy of criminal anarchy by word of mouth or writing. Criminal anarchy was defined in the act as "the doctrine that organized government should be overthrown by force or violence, or by the assassination of the executive head or of any of the executive officials of government, or by any unlawful means." Gitlow, the defendant, was convicted for writing a Socialist pamphlet which declared indispensable a proletarian revolution and a Communist reconstruction of Society. There was, however, no evidence that anything resulted from the publication or the circulation of the pamphlet. The due process clause of the Fourteenth Amendment was raised as a defense.

As the Court took up this defense it held for the first time that the protection given speech and press by the First Amendment is also encompassed within the due process clause of the Fourteenth. However, as in earlier First Amendment cases this protection was interpreted not to mean an absolute right without responsibility, but rather a protection subject to the power of a state to punish its abuse "by utterances inimical to the public welfare, tending to corrupt public morals, incite to crime, or disturb the public peace."[46] It was a protection that did not include "utterances endangering the foundations of organized government and threatening its overthrow by unlawful means."[47] For, declared the Court, "Such utterances, by their very nature, involve danger to the public peace and to the security of the State. They threaten breaches of the peace and ultimate revolution. And the immediate danger is none the less real and substantial, because the effect of a given utterance cannot be accurately foreseen. The

State cannot reasonably be required to measure the danger from every such uttrance in the nice balance of a jeweler's scale."[48]

In upholding the statute the majority decreed that great weight, and every presumption in favor of its constitutionality, must be accorded a legislative determination that to advocate the violent overthrow of the government constitutes such a substantial evil that it must be guarded against by the exercise of the police power. The Court held the statute applicable "to every utterance—not too trivial to be beneath the notice of the law—which is of such a character and used with such intent and purpose as to bring it within the prohibition of the statute."[49] "Clear and present danger" was ruled out when, as in this case, the existence of a substantive evil has already been determined by the state, the body "primarily the judge of regulations required in the interest of public safety and welfare."[50]

During the October Term, 1926, that followed the precedent-making *Gitlow* decision, the Supreme Court reviewed three more convictions for violations of state criminal syndicalism statutes. Although these three cases were argued on different dates, they were all decided on the same day, May 16, 1927. One of these, *Whitney* v. *California*,[51] was a reaffirmance of the *Gitlow* case. The majority again held that freedom of speech does not mean an absolute right, but rather a right limited by the right of the state to punish speech that is contrary to the public welfare—to punish speech which tends to incite crime, disturb the public peace, or which threatens the overthrow of organized government by unlawful means.

The California statute outlawed "criminal syndicalism" and its advocacy. "Criminal syndicalism" was defined as "any doctrine or precept advocating, teaching or aiding and abetting the commission of crime, sabotage . . . or unlawful acts of force and violence or unlawful methods of terrorism as a means of accomplishing a change in industrial ownership or control, or affecting any political change."[52] In upholding the statute, a majority of the Court repeated what it had said in *Gitlow* v. *New York:* when a legislative determination has been made that certain defined acts constitute such a danger to public peace and security that they should be penalized, such a legislative determination must be given great weight and accorded every presumption in favor of constitutionality.

The decision in *Burns* v. *United States*,[53] the second of these three cases, also upheld a conviction for a violation of the California syndicalism law. Although the case is not important for the constitutional questions that it presented (these were held to have been disposed of in *Whitney* v. *California)*, it is important for what the Court said about the amount and character of proof required.

In its instruction to the jury the trial court had referred to evidence that the offending organization, of which the defendant was a member, "amongst other things, advocated what is known as slowing down on the job, slack or scamped work, such as loading of a ship in such a way that it took a list to port or starboard and therefore had to limp back to port, *and things of that kind*."[54] Commenting on objections to the use of this language, the Court said: "By the instructions complained of, the consideration of the jury was limited to 'things of that kind.' The advocating of the malicious commission of such acts to teach and abet sabotage—physical damage and injury to physical property; it also is to teach and abet crime and unlawful methods of terrorism. It was not necessary for the prosecution to show that the elements of criminal syndicalism were advocated or taught with the precision of statement required in indictments for criminal acts involved . . . The purpose and probable effect of the printed matter circulated and of the things said in furtherance of the declared purposes of the organization are to be considered having regard to the capacity and circumstances of the persons sought to be influenced. When there is taken into account the evidence referred to and the parts of the charge preceding and following the part of the charge here assailed— and especially the giving and reiteration of the statutory language defining sabotage—it is quite apparent that the instruction was not erroneous."[55]

In the third case, *Fiske* v. *Kansas*,[56] an opposite result was reached. Although the Kansas act defined criminal syndicalism in much the same terms as the California act, the state offered no evidence of the teachings of the I.W.W. except a copy of the preamble of its constitution. From this the Court concluded that no substantial inferences were presented "that the organization taught, advocated or suggested the duty, necessity, propriety, or expediency of crime, criminal syndicalism, sabotage, or other unlawful acts or methods."[57] There was nothing to be found that advocated "the overthrow of the existing industrial or political conditions by force, violence or unlawful means."[58]

SHORTCOMINGS OF "USE-ABUSE"

The shortcomings of the "use-abuse" theory with its criteria of "reasonable," "natural" or "bad tendency" have been variously described. The theory has been pictured as so broad and so vague that no one can predict with any reasonable degree of certainty what it means. At best, it has been said, one can only guess. The theory has been compared to a dragnet ready to enmesh all who dare speak out. Its use, it has been argued, destroys free expression, and the fear of the threat of censorship reduces this freedom to "mere intellectual abstraction."[59] In its omnipresence only those who wish to live dangerously dare discuss matters of public concern; the others are reduced to the discussion of academic, non-controversial or colorless issues.

It has also been said that this theory reduces the element of intent to a fiction—that a bad or evil intent may be inferred where none in fact exists, especially if in time of stress juries are free to find supposed intent to bring about a prohibited result. In the *Abrams* opinion the Court had said: "Men must be held to have intended, and to be accountable for, the effects which their acts were likely to produce."[60] Citing the *Abrams, Schaefer, Pierce* and *Gilbert* cases, no less an authority than Mr. Justice Frankfurter has voiced the opinion that "[i]n some instances we have too readily permitted juries to infer deception from error, or intention from argumentative or critical statements."[61] Perhaps equally applicable is the statement that another judge made several centuries earlier: ". . . car commen erudition est à l'entent d'un home ne serr trie, car le Diable n'ad conusance de l'entent de homme."[62]

Support for "reasonable tendency" as the appropriate test has been sought and found on the familiar ground of history. The provisions of the Constitution have been depicted as not mathematical formulas "having their essence in their form,"[63] but as "organic institutions transplanted from English soil."[64] Their significance, it has been said, "is to be gathered not simply by taking the words and a dictionary, but by considering their origin and the line of their growth."[65] To reject the age old formula in contempt cases and to substitute for it "clear and present danger" has been described as ". . . not only to turn one's back on history but also to indulge in an idle play on words, unworthy of constitutional adjudication."[66] Indeed, the right of a state to model its judiciary on "the qualities and standards attained by the English administration of justice" has been defended as has the means "deemed appropriate to that end by English courts."[67]

But the familiar ground of history has served equally well to oppose "reasonable tendency." To turn one's back on history, it has also been said, is exactly what was intended when the prohibition against infringement of speech and press became a part of the American creed.[68] It has been further said that "to assume that English common law in this field became ours is to deny the generally accepted historical belief that 'one of the objects of the Revolution was to get rid of the English common law on liberty of speech and of the press.' "[69] And this latter interpretation of the effect of history appears to have prevailed. These were the words with which the Supreme Court prefaced its express rejection of "reasonable" or "inherent tendency."[70]

Chapter VII

CLEAR AND PRESENT DANGER: GENESIS, GESTATION AND ECLIPSE

A MINORITY DOCTRINE

Even while "use-abuse" held sway, another theory that was to replace it later was in the process of formulation. Moreover, this was taking place in the very cases that "use-abuse" prevailed with its criteria of "reasonableness," "natural," "remote," or "bad tendency."[1] The genesis of this new theory that later became known as "clear and present danger" originated in Mr. Justice Holmes' opinion for a unanimous Court in *Schenck* v. *United States*.[2] It was, however, in the minority and concurring opinions written by Justices Holmes and Brandeis during the 1920's in the Espionage Act and the State Criminal Syndicalism Act cases that "clear and present danger" took shape and was made ready for a later date. There was, however, to be a lapse of all of a decade after "use-abuse" had itself passed from the scene before this later date would come, but once it did it saw the resurgence and the extension of Mr. Justice Holmes' creation to an extent that perhaps not even its originator envisioned.[3]

GENESIS

Justice Holmes' treatment of speech and press in the *Schenck* case marked a radical departure from his earlier statement on the subject in *Patterson* v. *Colorado*.[4] Nevertheless, he held to his earlier statement as if to defend it in a self-conscious way. He now expressed the thought that it might be that the prohibitions of the First Amendment were not confined to previous restraint, but that to prevent previous restraint may have been its main purpose. Once that had been disposed of he set himself adrift from *Patterson* v. *Colorado*, returned to the case under consideration, and pointed out that "the character of every act depends on the circumstances in which it is done;"[5] that in many places and in ordinary times Schenck would have been within his constitutional rights in printing and distributing anti-draft leaflets. Then, in the following words, the Judge gave his first exposition of "clear and present danger": "The question in every case is whether the words used are used in such circumstances and are of such a nature as to create a clear and present danger that will bring about the substantive evils that Congress has a right to prevent. It is a question of proximity and degree. When a nation is at war many things that might be said in time of peace are such a hindrance to its effort that their utterance will not be endured so long as men fight and that no court could regard them as protected by any constitutional right."[6]

Here Mr. Justice Holmes was spokesman for a unanimous Court. Consequently, in this, his first statement of his historic test, he was able to supply but a bare skeleton of what was to come later when he spoke in dissent, unhampered by the limitations imposed upon him by his bretheren whenever he acted as spokesman for the majority. He wrote to Pollock of these limitations and of his opinions which he considered mutilitated as a result: "The boys generally cut one of the genitals out of mine, in the form of some expression that they think too free."[7] On occasion, Holmes must have been irritated by the removal of these "genitals" and perhaps he was in such a frame of mind when he wrote again to Pollock, "I am very hard at work again as we are sitting, but in good shape and enjoying it, preparing small dismonds for people of limited intellectual means."[8]

Seven days after his opinion in the *Schenck* case, Justice Holmes delivered unanimous opinions in the *Frohwerk* and the *Debs* cases[9] in which two more convictions for violations of the Espionage Act were upheld. In neither of these did Holmes avail himself of the opportunity to elaborate on his "clear and present danger" test. Zechariah Chafee once suggested that perhaps Holmes was waiting for a more opportune moment and a decision that he considered clearly wrong.[10] Chafee pointed out that as it happened Holmes could launch his novel theory with the backing of a unanimous Court, something that he could not have done otherwise. Consequently, Chafee was of the opinion that freedom of speech profited more as a result than if Holmes had voted for a reversal. This is interesting in the light of comments which Holmes made on the *Debs* case in two of his letters to Pollock.

In his letter of April 5, 1919, Holmes wrote to Pollock: "I am beginning to get stupid letters of protest against a decision that Debs, a noted agitator, was rightly convicted of obstructing the recruiting service so far as the law was concerned. I wonder that the Govern-

70

ment should press the case to a hearing before us, as the inevitable result was that fools, knaves, and ignorant persons were bound to say he was convicted because he was a dangerous agitator and that obstructing the draft was a pretence. How it was with the Jury of course I don't know, but of course that talk is silly as to us. There was a lot of jaw about free speech, which I dealt with somewhat summarily in an earlier case—*Schenck* v. *U. S.* . . . also *Frohwerk* v. *U. S.* . . . As it happens I should go farther probably than the majority in favor of it, and I daresay it was partly on that account that the C. J. assigned the case to me."[11]

In his letter of April 27, 1919, Holmes wrote further: "Of course there were people who pitched into the Court for sending Debs to prison under the espionage act, but there was no doubt that the jury was warranted in finding him guilty or that the act was Constitutional. Now I hope the President will pardon him and some other poor devils with whom I have more sympathy. Those whose cases have come before us have seemed to me poor fools whom I should have been inclined to pass over if I could. The greatest bores in the world are the come-outers who are cocksure of a dozen nostrums. The dogmatism of a little education is hopeless."[12]

If what Holmes was waiting for was a more opportune moment he apparently found it in *Abrams* v. *United States*.[13] Here he expressed his views by way of dissent, unhampered by any fear that one of the "vital organs" would be cut from his opinion. By his own admission, it was in this dissent that he intended to set out the full limits of "clear and present danger" as he meant it.[14]

After a recitation of the circumstances of the distribution of the two pamphlets that formed the basis of the indictment and a description of the inflammatory nature of their contents,[15] the Justice started his discussion of the law with an elaboration of the meaning of "intent." He recognized that as vaguely used in ordinary legal discussion, "intent" means knowledge of the facts at the time an act is committed from which common experience indicates that certain consequences will follow, whether or not foreseen by the actor. But he drew a distinction where words are used exactly, and the statute had to be taken to use its words in a strict and accurate sense. He wrote: "a deed is not done with intent to produce a consequence unless that consequence is the aim of the deed."[16] In other words, actual intent is necessary. He reaffirmed that the *Schenck, Frohwerk* and *Debs* cases were correctly decided, and then he continued:

71

"I do not doubt for a moment that by the same reasoning that would justify punishing persuasion to murder, the United States constitutionally may punish speech that produces or is intended to produce a clear and imminent danger that it will bring about forthwith certain substantive evils that the United States constitutionally may seek to prevent. The power undoubtedly is greater in time of war than in time of peace because war opens dangers that do not exist at other times.

"But as against dangers peculiar to war, as against others, the principle of the right to free speech is always the same. It is only the present danger of immediate evil or an intent to bring it about that warrants Congress in setting a limit to the expression of opinion where private rights are not concerned. Congress certainly cannot forbid all effort to change the mind of the country."[17]

Actual intent Holmes considered essential where a further act of the actor is required to complete the substantive crime, or where success depends on the acts of others. Indeed, the actor's aim might be brought about, but without the evil sought to be checked. And in this case an intent to prevent interference in Russia might have been satisfied without provoking resistance to the war effort of the United States against Germany. Abrams, Holmes felt, was guilty of expressing opinions and exhortations privileged by the Constitution. He defended this privilege as follows:

"Persecution for the expression of opinions seems to me perfectly logical. If you have no doubt of your premises or your power and want a certain result with all your heart you naturally express your wishes in law and sweep away all opposition. To allow opposition by speech seems to indicate that you think the speech impotent, as when a man says that he has squared the circle, or that you do not care wholeheartedly for the result, or that you doubt either your power or your premises. But when men have realized that time has upset many fighting faiths, they may come to believe even more than they believe the very foundations of their own conduct that the ultimate good desired is better reached by free trade in ideas—that the best test of truth is the power of the thought to get itself accepted in the competition of the market, and that truth is the only ground upon which their wishes safely can be carried out. That at any rate is the theory of our Constitution. It is an experiment, as all life is an experiment. Every year if not every day we have to wager our salvation upon some prophecy based upon imperfect knowledge. While that

72

experiment is part of our system I think that we should be eternally vigilant against attempts to check the expression of opinions that we loathe and believe to be fraught with death, unless they so imminently threaten immediate interference with the lawful and pressing purposes of the law that an immediate check is required to save the country. I wholly disagree with the argument of the Government that the First Amendment left the common law as to seditious libel in force. History seems to me against the notion. I had conceived that the United States through many years had shown its repentance for the Sedition Act of 1798, by repaying fines that it imposed. Only the emergency that makes it immediately dangerous to leave the correction of evil counsels to time warrants making any exception to the sweeping command, 'Congress shall make no law . . . abridging the freedom of speech.' Of course I am speaking only of expressions of opinion and exhortations, which were all that were uttered here, but I regret that I cannot put into more impressive words my belief that in their conviction upon this indictment the defendants were deprived of their rights under the Constitution of the United States."[18]

The *Abrams* dissent was the first of six opinions by Justices Holmes and Brandeis that carried forward the genesis of "clear and present danger."[19] With the exception of one that was a concurring opinion,[20] all were likewise dissents. Three, including *Abrams*, were in Espionage Act cases [21] and three were cases that involved state criminal anarchy and syndicalism statutes.[22] In all but one[23] the two Justices stood together, sometimes with one and sometimes with the other as spokesman.

Justice Brandeis was the spokesman in the two Espionage Act case dissents, both leaflet cases, that followed the *Abrams* dissent. In the first of these, *Schaefer* v. *United States*,[24] he characterized "clear and present danger" as a rule of reason which, if correctly applied, would preserve freedom of speech "both from suppression by tyrannous, well meaning majorities and from abuse by irresponsible minorities."[25] Then he went on to make interesting observations on the function of judge and jury in the application of the rule. Whether particular words were within permissible curtailment was, according to his view, a question of degree as a consequence of which the discretion of the jury should be wide in the exercise of its judgment. But, he continued, "If the words were of such a nature and were used under such circumstances that men, judging in calmness, could not reasonably say that they created a clear and present danger that they would bring

73

about the evil that Congress sought and had a right to prevent, then it is the duty of the trial judge to withdraw the case from the consideration of the jury; if he fails to do so, it is the duty of the appellate court to correct the error."[26]

In the other Espionage Act case, *Pierce* v. *United States*.[27] Justice Brandeis reasoned as to part of the indictment that a verdict should have been directed for the defendants not only for lack of proof of an attempt willfully to "cause insubordination, disloyalty, mutiny, or refusal of duty, in the military or naval forces" within the terms of the act,[28] but also because the leaflet itself and the circumstances under which it was distributed were not such "as to create a clear and present danger of causing either insubordination, disloyalty, mutiny or refusal of duty in the military or naval forces."[29] At best, the leaflet objected to, which was distributed to civilians rather than to military or naval forces, was said to contain lurid and perhaps exaggerated pictures of the horrors of war.

THE STATE CRIMINAL ANARCHY AND SYNDICALISM CASES

The three criminal anarchy and syndicalism act cases served two purposes: first, to complete the genesis of "clear and present danger"; second, to demonstrate that even between Holmes and Brandeis there could be differences in so vital an area as speech and press. Two cases, *Gitlow* v. *New York* [30] and *Whitney* v. *California*,[31] served for the former; one case, *Gilbert* v. *Minnesota*,[32] served for the latter. In all three the Supreme Court upheld the constitutionality of the state acts and it affirmed conviction for their violations.

With his usual penchant for brevity, in his *Gitlow* dissent Justice Holmes held out for "clear and present danger" as it had been announced by the full Court in the *Schenck* case. He considered that a "clear and present danger" was not created by utterances as a consequence of which the defendants were convicted for violating the New York anarchy statute.[33] To the assertion that these utterances were incitements and not mere theory he answered: "Every idea is an incitement. It offers itself for belief and if believed it is acted on unless some other belief outweighs it or some failure of energy stifles the movement at its birth. The only difference between the expression of an opinion and an incitement in the narrower sense is the speaker's enthusiasm for the result. Eloquence may set fire to reason. But whatever may be thought of the redundant discourse before us it had no chance of starting a present conflagration. If in the long run the beliefs expressed in a proletarian dictatorship are destined to be accepted by the dominant forces of the community, the only meaning of free speech is that they should be given their chance to have their way."[34]

Justice Brandeis completed the Holmes-Brandeis presentation of "clear and present danger" in the concurring opinion he wrote in the *Whitney* case. He agreed with the majority that the rights of speech and assembly are not absolute although they are fundamental, but he differed with this majority on the test to be applied to determine when a restriction should be applied to protect the state from destruction, or from political, economic or moral injury. He argued for "clear and present danger" even in the presence of a legislative pronouncement that a danger exists which calls for protective measures. To him, even though constitutional on its face, a statute must be open to challenge to determine whether the facts to which it is applied meet the test of "clear and present danger." He argued that such a statute and such a legislative pronouncement constitute but rebuttable presumptions. One wonders that Holmes would go so far as to agree with this, especially in view of the extent of his belief of the right of the legislature to experiment, but agree he did.[35]

As Justice Brandeis further elaborated on "clear and present danger" he expounded on the beliefs that he claimed motivated the adoption of the prohibitions against abridgment of speech and press. He described these as beliefs that "the final end of the State was to make men free to develop their faculties; and that in its government the deliberative forces should prevail over the arbitrary."[36] He further characterized these as beliefs "that freedom to think as you will and to speak as you will are means indispensable to the discovery and spread of political truth; that without free speech and assembly discussion would be futile; that with them, discussion affords ordinarily adequate protection against the dissemination of noxious doctrine."[37] Law and order, he added, could not be assured by fear and repression, but rather by free discussion of supposed grievances and proposed remedies. As he saw it, more than fear of serious injury alone is necessary to justify suppression of free speech and assembly. There must exist a contemplated evil which is so eminent that there is no opportunity for full and free discussion; there must be present a danger of such a character that the remedy of education by more speech cannot be relied on to avert the evil.

75

HOLMES AND BRANDEIS IN DISAGREEMENT

In *Gilbert* v. *Minnesota*[38] Justice Holmes concurred in the result arrived at by the majority although he disagreed with the reasoning, but Justice Brandeis dissented. Although Holmes did not specify what the ground was, he wrote to Pollock of his friend's dissent: "he had one ground worthy of serious consideration and others that I thought all wrong."[39] Thus accentuated, this was "The Gulf Between" to borrow a phrase used elsewhere.[40]

By way of dissent in the *Gilbert* case, Justice Brandeis objected to the Minnesota statute[41] because it imposed a restriction on speech and press under all circumstances, rather than to avert a "clear and present danger" in a particular emergency; he objected because its prohibitions bore no relation to the needs of government and applied even though recruiting was neither in process nor contemplated. He held the right to discuss Federal government functions freely to be a privilege and an immunity of every citizen of the United States which was protected from state interference even before the adoption of the Fourteenth Amendment.

To Brandeis the maintenance of the armed forces, the preservation of government, both state and federal, and the conduct of war were responsibilities in which Congress had superior rights. In relation to these responsibilities and these superior rights he maintained that no state could act except at the direction of Congress. Consequently, he considered the Minnesota statute objectionable at the time of its enactment before the Federal Espionage Act became law because it was then the policy of Congress to permit free discussion of governmental functions; he considered it objectionable after the enactment of this act not only because it went beyond the prohibitions of the Federal act, but also because it invaded a field in which Congress had exclusive power, and in this particular instance a field in which Congress had spoken.

The result arrived at by the majority supported the validity of a state statute which was the exposition of the wishes of the dominant group and a device to further the survival of the fittest—something to be respected according to the philosophy that Holmes subscribed to. Furthermore, this result fitted into his scheme of things which favored the right of the legislature to experiment, a right that he did not particularly wish to see interfered with even though he himself did not agree with the wisdom of the experiment.[42] Later, for these same reasons, he was to dissent from decisions which held unconstitutional state laws which prohibited the teaching of any modern language but English in primary schools.[43]

The reasons that compelled Holmes to agree with the result arrived at by the majority also compelled him to disagree with Justice Brandeis' dissent, one which would have struck down the Minnesota statute. Brandeis did not subscribe to his friend's idea that the majority should be allowed to experiment with legislation to the extent that it was to the detriment of the rights of minorities. Instead, he required of legislation that it have a desirable end and that it be for the public good. For that reason, these two Justices who were so often together in dissent could not agree in the decision of this case. They could not agree then any more than they could on another occasion already referred to when Holmes would have upheld, and Brandeis would have rejected, the right of states to prohibit the teaching of modern languages other than English in primary schools.

It has been suggested that Justice Holmes' "clear and present danger" test was the natural outgrowth of his theories of law and sovereignty—theories that rejected natural law and its concepts of good and evil, truth as an absolute, the free will of man and his God-given dignity.[44] When this reasoning is pursued the "clear and present danger" test as it was conceived by Holmes becomes a reflection of his "bad man" theory of law, a theory that defines knowledge of the law as the ability to predict how much the "bad man" can get away with before he will be made to suffer disagreeable consequences.[45] Just as this "bad man" theory depends on limits beyond which one cannot go without being subjected to the public force and punished, the "clear and present danger" test sets limits beyond which freedom of speech and press, the rights guaranteed by the First Amendment, cannot be relied on for the protection of self-expression. Good and evil, truth and falsehood, play little part. The prime consideration is a limit or a point short of which there is protection, and beyond which there is none. In every case, this limit or point depends on the time, the manner, and the place in which the "bad man" chooses to exercise his right of self-expression.

According to this reasoning, the "clear and present danger" test can in essence be considered a practical application of what Holmes considered a legal right to be—nothing but a permission to exercise one's powers of self-expression so long as it is supported by the public force. Beyond this permission there is the point of "no return." Morality plays no part for morality Holmes dismissed as nothing but mob prefcrence, "a body of imperfect social generalizations expressed in terms of emotions."[46] Whether what is said or written is morally good or morally bad depends on whether the mob likes or dislikes it—it depends on what the mob is accustomed to. Therefore, how can morality be set as the test? To do so would but lead to confusion, for rights in the moral sense and rights in the sense of the law and the Constitution may or may not be coextensive.

However one may feel about all of this, and although Mr. Justice Holmes rejected natural law as nothing more than one way of satisfying man's persistent quest for the superlative,[47] the fact still remains that he probably came as close as anyone, and more so than many, in making an absolute of freedom of speech and press. He would have extended this freedom to that which is generally considered bad as well as to that which is generally considered good, so long as there is not created a "clear and present danger" that a substantive evil would result which Congress has a right to prevent. Perhaps here again his "can't helps"[48] which he attributed to associations played a part. But whatever the cause, he still would have gone further than the majority of his day in favor of free speech and free press, and he suspected that it was partly on this account that the Chief Justice assigned *Schenck* v. *United States* to him.[49]

GESTATION AND ECLIPSE

Notwithstanding its apparent immediate acceptance by a unanimous Court, throughout the two decades that followed its initial presentation "clear and present danger" was relegated very much to the rear ranks in so far as a majority of the Court was concerned. After *Schenck* v. *United States* two decades were to pass before the test could again achieve majority status. Indeed, it was only during the first of the two decades that followed its conception that it had any status at all. During this time it was very much in the nature of an unborn child. It was there and it made its presence felt as it gathered life, but only in the dissenting or concurring opinions of two men. After that, it suffered ten years of eclipse during which little if anything was heard of it. It is true that during the years 1919 and 1920, at the start of the twenty years of gestation or eclipse, the Schenck case was cited with approval by majorities of the Supreme Court in at least six cases.[50] However, this was more a matter of citing authority for upholding court convictions than for reliance on the principle for which the case became known. Indeed, the principle was not even so much as mentioned. In the *Gilbert* case, the last of the six and one in which Holmes concurred, the Court cited the *Abrams* and *Schaefer* cases in which Holmes had dissented as well as the *Schenck, Frohwerk* and *Debs* cases in which he had written the majority opinions. Later, between 1920 and 1930, "clear and present danger" was mentioned in only one majority opinion,[51] and then only to be distinguished and found not applicable to the facts of the case. But then, this was anything but fatal for these were the years of gestation during which Holmes and Brandeis did more than merely keep the test alive. Speaking in dissent or in concurrence on six occasions, they were able to shape and nurture this brain-child, unhampered by the limitations that would inevitably have been present had they spoken for the majority.

The decade from 1930 to 1940 was one of obscurity, and even of eclipse, for the test. Again it came to the surface in only one majority opinion,[52] once more only to be distinguished and rejected as not applicable. But even worse, it saw the light of day in only one minority opinion.[53] Although this one was written by no less a person than Mr. Justice Cardozo, the test had to await yet another day for its resurrection.

CHAPTER VIII

DECADE OF FLUX

DIVISION OF AUTHORITY

1930 marked the start of a new decade during which the law of speech and press was in a state of flux as the way was paved for a later rejection of the theory that prevailed during the 1920's.

During the latter half of the decade of the 1920's there had been a marked division of authority over the meaning of freedom of speech and press. One school of authority, ostensibly predominant, followed the "use-abuse" or "dangerous tendency" theory; another school fought valiantly for the adoption of the new theory of "clear and present danger." During the 1930's neither was the former expressly rejected nor the latter adopted. Instead, a course midway between the two was followed. The Court remained aloof from both, although the presence of one or the other could be felt on occasion in the background. There were two reasons for this: (1) the fears of the 1920's were, to a great extent, dormant; (2) Charles Evans Hughes was Chief Justice of the United States.

Five years before he became Chief Justice, Hughes expressed alarm over the growth of intolerance in this country. He saw in the growing demand for uniformity a grave danger to the progress that had been made in the struggle for liberty. Freedom meant more to him than disposing dynasties, successfully ridding ourselves of autocracy and privilege, and the winning of suffrage.[1] Three years later, in 1928, he wrote as follows of the conflicts over the meaning of the liberty of speech and press: "The division in the Court illustrates the vast importance of its function, as, after all, the protection both of the rights of the individuals and those of society rests not so often on formulas, as to which there may be agreement, but on a correct appreciation of social conditions and a true appraisal of the actual effect of conduct."[2]

Under the strong guidance of a man who shared these views it was inevitable that the prevailing attitude should give way in one direction or another. The direction that this attitude took is well illustrated by three cases that were decided while he presided over the Court, and which set the pattern of the law of speech and press for his era. The first two were decided soon after he took office, the third midway through his term. In all three he wrote for the Court.

The first case, *Stromberg* v. *California*,[3] involved review of a conviction for a violation of the California "red flag" law that condemned the display of a "red flag, banner or badge or any flag, badge, banner, or device of any color or form whatever in any public place or in any meeting place or public assembly or from or on any house, building or window as a sign, symbol, or emblem of opposition to organized government or as an invitation or stimulus to anarchistic action or as an aid to propaganda that is of a seditious character."[4] The defendant, a member of the Young Communist League, was a supervisor in a summer camp for children. She daily displayed a red flag, a reproduction of the flag of Soviet Russia, which the children were taught to salute in a ritual in which they pledged allegiance "to the worker's red flag, and to the cause for which it stands; one aim throughout our lives, freedom for the working class." The state appellate court doubted the constitutionality of the first clause of the statute as all too-embracing. Nevertheless, it upheld the conviction under the other two. On appeal to the Supreme Court of the United States, the case was reversed.

The Court recognized that freedom of speech is not absolute; that a state may punish "those who indulge in utterances which incite to violence and crime and threaten the overthrow of organized government by unlawful means."[5] It also expressed the conviction that "The maintenance of the opportunity for free political discussion to the end that government may be responsive to the will of the people and that changes may be obtained by lawful means, an opportunity essential to the security of the Republic, is a fundamental principle of our constitutional system."[6] The Court found no reason to object to the second and third clauses as construed, but it did object to the first. This one it found so vague and indefinite on its face and as authoritatively construed that it permitted the punishment of the fair use of free political discussion. The verdict was general and it did not appear on which of the three clauses it rested. Therefore, the case was reversed.

In the second case, *Near* v. *Minnesota*,[7] the Supreme Court revitalized the age-old doctrine of "previous restraint" to strike down a Minnesota statute that declared a nuisance the publication of "(a) an obscene, lewd or lascivious newspaper, magazine or periodical, or (b) a malicious, scandalous and defamatory newspaper, magazine or periodical."[8] The truth of the matter published was available as a defense to alleged violations of "(b)", but only if publication was "with good motives and for justifiable ends."

Writing for the majority, the Chief Justice made some interesting, though brief, observations on the limits of sovereignty. He admitted "the authority of the state to enact laws to promote the health, safety, morals and general welfare of its people." But there were limits to this sovereign power which, he wrote, "must always be determined with appropriate regard to the peculiar subject of its exercise."[9] In so far as liberty of speech and press were concerned, he turned to history. A part of the Minnesota statute he found reminiscent of the law of speech and press as it had formerly existed in England before it was changed by the Fox Libel Act when malice could be inferred from the mere publication of defamatory matter. In fact, as the Court pointed out, in this case judgment proceeded from the mere proof of publication. The Chief Justice admitted that there are limits to prohibitions against previous restraint, but only in exceptional cases: in times of war, the actual obstruction of the recruiting service or the publication of the sailing dates of troop transports, incitement to acts of violence and to the overthrow of orderly government by force. However, he did not recognize these limits as extending to criticism of public officials.

Near v. *Minnesota,* was relied on by the Court to invalidate still another state statute, a license tax imposed on newspaper owners. The occasion was *Grosjean* v. *American Press Co.*[10] in which Justice Sutherland, writing for the Court, also turned to historic concepts and to the circumstances that had motivated the adoption of the First Amendment. This time it was the story of the English licensing taxes that provided the background for the Court to strike down a Louisiana statute that imposed a two percent tax on the gross receips of newspapers and periodicals with circulations over 20,000 a week. The purpose of the statute was to strike back at the press that opposed Huey Long. Indeed, it was described in a circular distributed to the legislature by Long and the Governor during its consideration as "a tax on lying, two cents per lie."[11] Taking notice of the suspicious manner in which the tax was imposed, the Court recognized that its plain purpose was to penalize the publishers and curtail the circulation of a "selected group of newspapers."[12]

In *De Jonge* v. *Oregon*,[13] the Chief Justice extended still further the lead already established in *Stromberg* v. *California*. Again he recognized the right of a state to protect itself from abuse of speech and press—in this instance, incitements to the overthrow of government by force and violence. But the state can protect itself, he said, "only by dealing with the abuse. The rights themselves must not be curtailed."[14] In so far as the enforcement of the criminal syndicalism statute was concerned, it was the purpose for which a public meeting was called and not its auspices that mattered to him. Those who conducted a lawful meeting could not, he reasoned, be branded as criminals regardless of the objectives of the sponsors. If those who conducted a meeting had committed crimes elsewhere by conspiring against the public peace and welfare, they should have been prosecuted for these crimes under the appropriate laws. They should not be prosecuted for them by making participation in a peaceful meeting the basis for a criminal charge.

The prevailing attitude had indeed given way. It was no longer "dangerous tendency" or the search for a formula that served as a guide. Instead, in each case the Court sought "a correct appraisal of social conditions and a true appraisal of the actual effect of conduct."[15] In this manner it was believed that both the rights of the individual and those of society would be protected.

However glimly individual members of the Court may have viewed the social legislation of the era, the Court itself was aided to no small extent by this legislation once it took hold. It is true that the period was marked by unemployment and depression, but the discontent and uncertainty of the previous decade was largely taken care of by corrective legislation of one type or another. There was hope. In the matter of speech and press, the colossus of world Communist conspiracy had not reached the proportions that it would at the end of World War II. But even so, the Hughes Court had set its course in the solution of problems of speech and press, problems which ultimately it alone could solve. Right or wrong, the course was consistent and from it the Court never wavered. There were times, it must be admitted, when the majority was slim, but somehow it was always there to follow the straight line laid down by the Chief Justice. No case typifies better the temper of this course than *Herndon* v. *Lowry*,[16] decided midway through the Hughes era. The decision was close, five to four. Mr. Justice Roberts wrote for the Court. He was joined by the Chief Justice, Justices Brandeis, Stone and Cardozo.

Angelo Herndon, a member and an organizer of the Communist Party of Atlanta, had been convicted and sentenced to from eighteen to twenty years imprisonment for attempting to incite insurrection in violation of a Georgia statute. When he was apprehended he had in his possession a pamphlet urging the "Self-Determination of the Black Belt" and other literature advocating a revolutionary struggle for power. There was, however, no evidence that he had distributed any of this material, although he stated that it was intended for distribution at his meetings. The minutes indicated no intent to overthrow organized government.

When the *Herndon* case reached the Supreme Court of the United States one side urged "dangerous tendency" as the test to be applied, the other "clear and present danger." The two clashed head on, but in setting aside the conviction the majority accepted neither although it leaned toward the latter. For guidance it turned to what Chief Justice Hughes had written in 1928[17] and to what he had written in his opinion in *De Jonge* v. *Oregon*.[18] The Court refused to draw any inference from the possession of the literature and it pointed out that membership in the Communist Party had not been declared unlawful by the leslature of Georgia. The question was, it said, "Did he thus incite to insurrection by reason of the fact that they agreed to abide by the tenets of the party, some of them lawful, others, as may be assumed, unlawful, in absence of proof that he brought the unlawful aims to their notice, that he approved them, or that the fantastic program they envisaged was conceived of by anyone as more than an ultimate ideal?"[19] Although the majority conceived of circumstances in which the answer could be "yes," the answer which they gave under the circumstantial evidence of the case was "no."

The standard of guilt formulated by the Supreme Court of Georgia was rejected. Under it "a defendant need not advocate to force . . . Indeed, he need not be active in the formation of a combination or group if he agitate for a change in the frame of government, however peaceful his own intent . . . Proof that the accused in fact believed that his efforts would cause a violent assault upon the state would not be necessary to conviction. It would be sufficient if the jury thought he reasonably might foretell that those he persuaded to join the party might, at some time in the indefinite future, resort to forcible resistance of government. The question thus proposed to a jury involves pure speculation as to future trends of thought and action . . . The law, as thus construed, licenses the jury to create its own standard in each case."[20] As construed and applied, the statute was described "as a dragnet which may enmesh anyone who agitates for a change of government if a jury can be persuaded that he ought to have foreseen his words would have some effect in the future conduct of others."[21]

Lovell v. *City of Griffin*,[22] *Schneider* v. *State* (*Town of Irvington*),[23] *Cantwell* v. *Connecticut*,[24] *and Cox* v. *New Hampshire*,[25] were all "Jehovah Witness" cases. Here again Chief Justice Hughes took the initiative and led the way. He wrote the opinions in the first and last of these: in the first he liberated freedom of the press from its narrow confines of newspapers and periodicals, and extended it to pamphlets and leaflets; in the last he set the limits to which this extended liberty could be found to exist.

The decision in the first case, *Lovell* v. *City of Griffin*,[26] set aside a conviction for the violation of a municipal ordinance which prohibited absolutely the distribution of pamphlets without first having obtained written permission from a city manager. The ordinance was not limited to literature considered obscene or offensive to public morals, or to literature advocating unlawful conduct. Instead, it was broad and sweeping. It applied to literature of any kind. As the Court rejected the ordinance as unconstitutional, it appraised this as legislation of the type that would reimpose licensing and censorship in its "baldest form." In the second and third cases,[27] broad and sweeping legislation of a similar nature was also struck down.

The legislation questioned in the last case, *Cox* v. *New Hampshire*,[28] was of a different nature. In effect, it provided for a board to license theatrical or dramatic representations, parades or processions in public streets, and open meetings. The Court found this administered in a fair and non-discriminatory manner. Furthermore, it recognized the social need for such legislation—the need for the safeguard of good order and for the safety and convenience of the public in the use of public streets. The legislation was upheld.

From the extension of the guarantees of speech and press to pamphlets and leaflets in *Lovell* v. *Griffin*,[29] it was a short step for the Hughes Court to extend these guarantees to peaceful picketing. This was done in *Thornhill* v. *Alabama*.[30] With Mr Justice Murphy the spokesman of the Court, peaceful picketers were guaranteed "the liberty to discuss publicly and thruthfully all matters of public concern without previous restraint or fear of subsequent punishment."[31]

85

This case also marked the end of one decade, the start of another, and the resurgence of "clear and present danger."

"Prior restraint" and the prominent position that the doctrine occupied after it was revitalized in *Near* v. *Minnesota*,[32] was the major feature of the decade from 1930 to 1940. It was an ancient and celebrated doctrine that predated both the Constitution and the First Amendment; its earliest trace could be dated as early as 1695 when the English House of Commons refused to extend the Licensing Act of 1662.[33] After that the doctrine gradually assumed the status of common law which Blackstone summarized as follows in his often quoted statement of the eighteenth century concept of freedom of the press: "The liberty of the press is indeed essential to the nature of a free state; but this consists in laying no previous restraints upon publication, and not in freedom from censure for criminal matter when published. Every freeman has an undoubted right to lay what sentiments he pleases before the public: to forbid this is to destroy the freedom of the press, but if he publishes what is improper, mischievous, or illegal, he must take the consequences of his own temerity."[34]

In the hands of Hughes even this concept could be made to work so that freedom of speech and of the press became more of a reality than ever before. But there were also dangers that could accompany raising this theory to the level of a constitutional doctrine. To discover the nature of these dangers one has only again to turn back the pages of history to the period immediately prior to the American Revolution—to Mansfield's definition of liberty of the press in the *Dean of St. Asaph's Case:* "To be free, is to live under a government by law. The *liberty of the press* consists in printing without any previous license, subject to the consequences of law. The licentiousness of the press is *Pandora's* box, the source of every evil."[35]

But however one may feel about *Near* v. *Minnesota* and "previous restraint"—and the case has been criticised as a resurgence of an eighteenth century doctrine that has outlived its usefulness[36]—the Court was provided with a "trump card" that has served it well, especially for the case to which nothing else has seemed applicable.[32] It has been turned to time and again.

CHAPTER IX

RESURGENCE OF "CLEAR AND PRESENT DANGER"

A TEST BECOMES A FORMULA, 1940-1950

The decade from 1940 to 1950 witnessed the resurgence of "clear and present danger"; it saw the test finally come into its own as a majority view and saw it extended to dimensions that perhaps not even Holmes and Brandeis envisioned. Time after time, and in a variety of situations, it was turned to by the Court during this period when civil liberties achieved a status that was frequently referred to as a "preferred position."[1] "Clear and present danger" now became a formula with which to keep men out of jail rather than to put them in as it had theretofore been.

PICKETING

The earliest, and certainly one of the most important, new areas to which the test was extended during the decade of the 1940's was that of labor picketing. The range that the Supreme Court covered in this particular area during this period is well exemplified by the first and the last picketing cases that it decided from 1940 to 1949. In the first one, *Thornhill* v. *Alabama* which was decided at the very start of the decade,[2] "clear and present danger" served to uphold the right to picket and to bring it within the shelter of the First Amendment; in the last one, *Giboney* v. *Empire Storage and Ice Co.*[3] "clear and present danger" served not to overturn but to uphold an injunction against picketing that was peaceful.

At issue in the *Thornhill* case was an Alabama statute entitled "Loitering or picketing forbidden" which was struck down as invalid on its face. The Court recognized that the rights of both employers and employees to compete for a share of the products of industry "are subject to modification or qualification in the interests of the society in which they exist."[4] However, the statute made it a misdemeanor for any person or persons to go near to or loiter about a lawful place

87

of business "for the purpose, or with the intent of influencing, or inducing other persons not to trade with, buy from, sell to, have business dealings with, or be employed by such persons, firm, corporation, or association, or who picket[ed] the works or place of business of such persons, firms, corporations, or associations of persons, for the purpose of hindering, delaying or interfering with or injuring any lawful business or enterprise of another."[5]

As the court interpreted the Alabama statute, it embraced every practicable and effective means, be it picketing or something else, whereby the public might be enlightened of the nature and the cause of a labor dispute; it would have impaired the right to freely and effectively discuss industrial relations, matters of public concern. Indeed, as construed and applied by the state court the Alabama statute even prohibited a single person from walking back and forth slowly, peacefully, and without speaking to anyone, in front of an employer's premises carrying a sign stating the facts of a labor dispute. Were this upheld, said the Court, it "could be used to support abridgment of freedom of speech and of the press concerning almost every matter of importance to society."[6] That the Court refused to agree to. Indeed, it found that "Abridgment of the liberty of such discussion can be justified only where the clear danger of substantive evils arises under circumstances affording no opportunity to test the merits of ideas by competition for acceptance in the market of public opinion."[7] The Court considered the danger to an individual concern neither so serious nor so imminent as to justify so sweeping a proscription to freedom of discussion as this statute imposed.

No more convincing was the argument that the purpose of the statute was to protect the community from the violence and the breaches of the peace that, it was said, must accompany picketing. The Court did not doubt that there is the power and the duty to take steps adequate to preserve the peace and to protect life and property. "But," it concluded, "no clear and present danger of destruction of life or property, or invasion of the right of privacy, or breach of the peace can be thought to be inherent in the activities of every person who approaches the premises of an employer and publicizes the facts of a labor dispute involving the latter."[8]

On the same day that the Court decided the *Thornhill* case it also ruled on *Carlson* v. *California*,[9] another picketing case. This time it did not specifically mention "clear and present danger," nevertheless it did make specific reference to the reasons set forth in its earlier opinion as it struck down a municipal ordinance which made it unlawful for any person to carry or display a sign, banner or badge in the vicinity of any business establishment with the purpose of inducing others to refrain from working or buying there, or for any one to "loiter" or "picket" for that purpose in the vicinity of any place of business. The "sweeping and inexact terms of the ordinance"[10] were deemed not to differ from the statute in the *Thornhill* case, and to disclose a threat to freedom of speech in the same way.

Justice Douglas probably best summarized the law of speech and press as it was applied to picketing as a consequence of the *Thornhill* and *Carlson* cases. In his concurring opinion in *Bakery & Pastry & Helpers* v. *Wohl* he wrote:

"Picketing by an organized group is more than free speech, since it involves patrol of a particular locality and since the very presence of a picket line may induce action of one kind or another, quite irrespective of the nature of the ideas which are being disseminated. Hence those aspects of picketing make it the subject of restrictive regulation.

"But since 'dissemination of information concerning the facts of a labor dispute' is constitutionally protected, a State is not free to define 'labor dispute' so narrowly as to accomplish indirectly what it may not accomplish directly."[11]

State regulation of picketing or court action against it was upheld, as indeed it was in *Hotel & Restaurant Employees Local* v. *Wisconsin Employment Relations Board*,[12] so long as its purpose was to prohibit violence rather than to interfere with picketing of a peaceful nature. It was not upheld when, as in *Cafeteria Employees Union* v. *Angelos*,[13] picketing was enjoined merely because of isolated abuses that fell short of violence.

In a sense the Court's decision represented a return to *Senn* v. *Tile Layers Protective Union*[14] which upheld a Wisconsin statute[15] that made peaceful picketing lawful. Sometimes the law as it was now enunciated was applied with reference to "clear and present danger," and sometimes it was not. Thus, less than a year after the *Thornhill* case the Court again decided two picketing cases on the same day. Both were from action of the same court, the Supreme Court of Illinois, and in both the problem was the validity of labor injunctions. In one it was a question of picketing blended with violence, in the other a question of picketing continued by a union after it had been unsuccessful in an attempt to unionize the shop picketed. In the first,

Milk Wagon Drivers Union v. *Meadowmoor*,[16] the Court was careful to reaffirm the *Thornhill* and *Carson* decisions, but then it went on to uphold the injunction. Instead of invoking "clear and present danger," the Court proceeded on the theory that "utterance in a context of violence can lose its significance as an appeal to reason and become part of an instrument of force." And that, the Court ruled, the Constitution was not meant to shelter. However, in the second case, *American Federation of Labor* v. *Swing*,[18] the Court found "an instance of 'peaceful persuasion' disentangled from violence and free from 'picketing *en masse* or otherwise conducted' so as to occasion 'imminent and aggravated danger'."[19] The injunction was struck down as a ban inconsistent with freedom of speech.

The point is again illustrated by yet two other cases decided on the same day by the Supreme Court a scant two years after the *Thornhill* case. In *Carpenters & Joiners Union* v. *Ritter's Cafe*,[20] the union picketed a restaurant at which no labor controversy existed because its owners had contracted with a builder for the construction of a building a mile-and-a-half distant as well as entirely disassociated from the restaurant, and the builder used non-union carpenters and painters in the course of the construction. The picketing was enjoined as a violation of the state anti-trust law. In the other case *Bakery & Pastry Drivers & Helpers* v. *Wohl*,[21] the union picketed not only the bakeries from which self-employed non-union peddlers obtained bakery products, but also the business establishments to which these products were sold. It seems that these peddlers worked a seven-day week whereas union peddlers could only work a six-day week. To even the score, the union sought to force the independent peddlers to work a six-day week and hire a union member at the union rate for the seventh day. The trial court found that no labor dispute existed. For that reason, it ruled that the self-employed non-union peddlers could not be subjected to picketing and an injunction was issued.

In the first case the Supreme Court was concerned with the constitutionality of Texas policy to localize industrial conflict which it upheld, and not with its wisdom. While it is true that picketing is constitutionally protected as a means of communicating the fact of a labor dispute, this did not imply to the Court that a state is devoid of power to confine the sphere of this communication to that which is directly related to a dispute. In the second case, the *Wohl* case, the Court discarded the idea that a "labor dispute" as defined by state law was essential for the exercise of the right to publicize grievances in a labor matter. And in this case it could perceive no "substantial evil of such magnitude as to mark a limit to the right of free speech which the petitioners sought to exercise."[22]

Giboney v. *Empire Storage and Ice Co.*,[23] mentioned earlier, the last picketing case to be decided during the decade of the 1940's, involved a question of state policy as did the *Ritter* case, but unlike the *Ritter* case this one was decided in terms of "clear and present danger." The controversy was again between union and non-union peddlers, this time in the ice business, and the picketing was directed against a company that refused to agree not to sell to non-union peddlers. The picketing was found to have as its sole purpose to induce a violation of a valid criminal law, and the Constitution was said not to immunize speech or writing that is an integral part of conduct which is in violation of state law. Unless restrained there was "clear danger, imminent and immediate,"[24] the Court ruled, that this union activity would render a dead letter the Missouri policy expressed in its anti-trade-restraint law.[25]

JEHOVAH'S WITNESSES—STATE STATUTES, MUNICIPAL ORDINANCES, AND SALUTE TO THE FLAG

Less than a month after the *Thornhill* decision, "clear and present danger" was extended still further and applied to Jehovah's Witnesses cases in *Cantwell* v. *Connecticut*.[26] This was a case in which the Supreme Court used both "prior restraint" and "clear and present danger." "Prior restraint" served to strike down a state statute which forbade any person from soliciting money, services or other valuables, for any alleged religious, charitable, or philanthropic cause unless the person had obtained the approval of a designated official who was charged with determining that a particular cause was a religious one, or that its object was one of bona fide charity or philanthropy.[27] All of the appellants had been convicted for violating this law. "Clear and present danger" came into play in the case of one of them who had been convicted for a breach of the peace, a result of the method that the group used to sell and distribute its literature and to solicit contributions. Members of the group accosted passers-by in the streets and urged them to listen to a phonograph that they carried. When permission was granted, they played records that not only described the literature but also attacked organized religion and in particular the Roman Catholic Church. The attack on the religious faith of two who consented to listen, both Roman Catholics, caused them to become incensed and to threaten the defendants, whereupon the latter simply went on their way.

As the Court struck down the conviction for a breach of the peace that resulted, it reasoned: "When clear and present danger of riot, disorder, interference with traffic upon the public streets, or other immediate threat to public safety, peace or order, appears, the power of the State to prevent or punish is obvious."[28] But equally obvious was the fact that "a state may not unduly suppress free communication of views, religious or other, under the guise of conserving desirable conditions."[29] It is true that in this particular instance it was not unnatural that the phonograph records should arouse animosity. Nevertheless, said the Court, "in the absence of a statute narrowly drawn to define and punish specific conduct as constituting a clear and present danger to a substantial interest of the state,"[30] the conduct of the appellants did not raise a menace to the public that in itself was clear and present.

The advance that was made by "clear and present danger" in the *Cantwell* case the Court refused to extend further in *Douglas* v. *City of Jeanette*,[31] a class suit that originated in a federal district court to restrain the enforcement of a city ordinance against a Jehovah's Witness group. As it affirmed the judgment below which denied the relief sought for want of equity, the Supreme Court considered that Federal Courts should, in the exercise of their discretionary power under the Constitution to review federal questions in criminal causes that arise under state law, refuse to interfere in state court proceedings "save in those exceptional cases which call for the interposition of a court of equity to prevent irreparable injury which is clear and imminent."[32] The Court felt that in this particular instance adequate protection was available in the state courts.

"Clear and present danger" was scarcely the sole novel principle applied to Jehovah's Witness cases during this period. There was also "preferred position." The two went hand in hand once speech, press and religion were raised to the latter status. With these freedoms thus enshrined, it was not enough that an ordinance was nondiscriminatory and it mattered not that a town was company owned. Constitutionally, an ordinance was repugnant if it served as a guise to impose a license tax as a condition to the activities of a religious sect.[33] The same was true if that was the excuse used to punish the distribution of religious literature.[34]

Because of this "preferred position," an ordinance could not make a commercial enterprise out of evangelism merely because religious literature was sold rather than donated.[35] Moreover, evangelists were not thereby converted into hucksters and peddlers any more than were preachers of the more orthodox faiths who depended on their calling for a living. For, in the eyes of the Court, religious freedom is not restricted to those "with a long purse."[36]

Even if a town is company-owned its residents are free citizens of state and country, and they must make decisions that effect the community as well as the nation. For that reason they must be as well informed as the citizens of municipally owned towns. Therefore, in *Marsh* v. *Alabama*[37] freedom of speech, press, and religion were found to be "preferred" for all regardless of the nature of the community.

In another case, *Saia* v. *New York*,[38] an ordinance which sought to regulate sound amplification devices could not stand if its effect was to impose a previous restraint. The ordinance required prior permission of the chief of police but it failed to prescribe adequate standards. It had all of the vices already struck down in earlier decisions, and to have upheld it would have meant a retreat from the "preferred" treatment accorded speech, press and religion in these earlier decisions.[39]

SALUTE TO THE FLAG AND "CLEAR AND PRESENT DANGER"

In the course of human events, especially in times of stress, it sometimes happens that out of sincere concern for national security measures emerge which are intended to secure and preserve national life, but which on occasion collide with the religious scruples of some and the personal convictions of others. Inevitably, constitutional guarantees are invoked and conflicts precipitated which, in this country, can only be resolved by the Supreme Court of the United States. That was the case with the compulsory flag-salute measures which were adopted in several states immediately prior to, or at the start of, World War II. Once again "clear and present danger" ultimately played its part.

The first time that the flag-salute problem came before the Supreme Court there was no mention of "clear and present danger," and the regulation was upheld as a valid one. This was in *Minersville School District* v. *Gobitis*,[40] decided in 1940, in which a parent brought suit to enjoin the enforcement of a local compulsory flag-salute regulation against his children. All of the members of the family were Jehovah's Witnesses and the children were expelled from public school when, for religious reasons, they refused to conform to the regulation. As a consequence, the parent had to send his children to a private school to comply with state compulsory school attendance laws, and it was from the necessity of this expense that he sought relief.

Although the Court recognized that the Constitution places beyond the reach of law "the affirmative pursuit of one's convictions about the ultimate mystery of the universe and man's relation to it,"[41] it also considered that there is the matter of political responsibilities and from these, it said, one is not discharged by "the mere possession of religious convictions which contradict the relevant concerns of a political society."[42] The regulation was upheld as an appropriate means with which to foster and evoke a sentiment of national unity among public school children. The aim was said to be neither to promote nor to restrict beliefs, but rather to encourage an attachment for the institutions of the country. Furthermore, the Court did not believe that it should act as a school board for the entire country, or pass on legislative determinations of the wisdom of such programs. There was but one dissent, that of Associate Justice, later Chief Justice Stone.[43] Mr. Justice Stone was not to stand alone for very long.

A scant three years after the *Gobitis* decision the flag-salute question came up again in *West Virginia Board of Education* v. *Barnette*.[44] Meanwhile, three of the Justices who had been with the majority in the earlier decision, Justices Black, Douglas and Murphy, had announced that they believed that the earlier case had been wrongly decided. They had done this in a joint statement that they had appended to their dissent in the first *Jones* v. *Opelika* decision.[45] In addition, Chief Justice Hughes and Justice McReynolds had retired. All that was now needed for an opposite result was the vote of one of the two new Justices, Jackson and Rutledge. As it happened, both of these voted to overrule and one of them, Mr. Justice Jackson, wrote the opinion of the Court.

The root of the second flag-salute controversy was a West Virginia statute the stated purpose of which was to teach, foster and perpetuate the "ideals, principles and spirit of Americanism, and increas[e] the knowledge of the organization and machinery of the government."[46] Pursuant to this statute, the Board of Education prescribed that all public school teachers and pupils participate in the salute and the pledge of allegiance to the flag. Nonconformity meant expuslion from school for insubordination; readmission was denied until there was compliance, and parents or guardians were subject to prosecution if their children refused to conform. The case reached the Supreme Court by way of an injunction that was granted by a federal district court. The enforcement of the law was restrained as to the appellees, all Jehovah's Witnesses, who had either suffered or had been threatened with the penalties that the law imposed.

This time the Court was quick to point out that the problem presented was not that of a state stepping in to determine where the rights of one individual ended and those of another began. There was not the matter of a freedom asserted by one colliding with the right claimed by the other. Instead, it was the question of a conflict between the rights of individuals and the authority of the state. The crux of the issue was the right of self-determination in matters of individual opinion and personal attitude versus a power asserted by the state to condition a public education on the performance of a prescribed sign or profession, while at the same time coercing attendance with a threat of punishment to parent and child.

The regulation left no doubt that it required an affirmation of a belief and an attitude of mind. It did, however, leave unclear whether there was contemplated an unwilling conversion and a foregoance of contrary convictions, or whether it would have been satisfied with barren gestures and words uttered with disbelief. In this connection, the Court took pains to affirm that it was "now a commonplace" that suppression or censorship of self-expression could be tolerated by the Constitution only where the expression presented a "clear and present danger" of action such as the state is empowered to prevent and punish.[47] To the Court it seemed that there ought to be grounds more immediate and urgent than silence before an involuntary affirmation should be commanded. And here the power to so command was set forth without even an allegation that to remain passive during a salute to the flag would so much as create a "clear and present danger" as would justify an effort to muffle expression. The Court now held that before compulsory flag salute could be upheld it would have to say that the Bill of Rights, the safeguard of an individual's right to speak his mind, left it open to public authorities to force one to utter that which was not in his mind.[48]

In the *Gobitis* case the Court had reasoned that it was committed to legislatures, as well as to courts, to guard the liberties that are cherished—that constitutionally it is appropriate to "fight out the wise use of legislative authority in the forum of public opinion and before legislative assemblies rather than to transfer such a contest to the judicial arena,"[49] because "effective means of inducing political changes are left free."[50] But now the Court did not consider that true in every situation. As an example, it cited the difference between the regulation of a public utility and the restrictions of speech, press, religion, or assembly. The former may be regulated and restrictions imposed to the extent that a legislature has a "rational basis," but the latter may not be curbed on such slender ground. Indeed, the Court now held that these are susceptible of infringement only so far as it will "prevent grave and immediate danger to interests which the State may lawfully protect."[51]

In the *Gobitis* case the Court had also reasoned that "National unity is the basis of national security,"[52] but now that could no longer be the excuse to permit compulsion such as was contemplated here as a means to achieve that national unity. *Minersville School District* v. *Gobitis* was overruled and the judgment enjoining the enforcement of the West Virginia regulation affirmed.[53]

OUT-OF-COURT PUBLICATIONS CONCERNING PENDING CASES

Out-of-court publications concerning pending cases was a third area to which "clear and present danger" was extended. During the 1940's this was done in *Bridges* v. *California*,[54] *Pennekamp* v. *Florida*,[55] and *Craig* v. *Harney*,[56] all state contempt of court cases. Prior to these decisions, the only experience that the Supreme Court had with the power of state courts to punish out-of-court publications by contempt was in *Patterson* v. *Colorado*,[57] but even this case was not squarely in point. It was decided sixteen years before the prohibitions of the First Amendment were applied to the states through the Fourteenth. In it, even though in his opinion for the Court Mr. Justice Holmes had managed to make pronouncements on speech and press, the question whether or not a prohibition similar to that in the First Amendment was to be found in the Fourteenth had been specifically left undecided. The Supreme Court did, however, have experience with the question of contempt in the federal courts.

The Federal Courts and the Act of March 2, 1831

The problem of contempt in the federal courts has a history that reaches all the way back to the Judiciary Act of 1789 which empowered the courts of the United States "to punish by fine or imprisonment, at the discretion of said courts, all contempts of authority in any cause or hearing before the same."[58] This broad, undefined

96

power was immediately taken to grant judicial authority to punish summarily and, to borrow a phrase used by Chancellor Kent as he argued for the common law doctrine of contempt, "with the celerity of lightning."[59] Abuses arose which culminated in an impeachment proceeding brought against Federal District Judge James H. Peck after he had imprisoned and suspended from practice one Lawless, an attorney who had had the audacity to publish a criticism of one of the Judge's opinions.[60] During the impeachment proceeding, James Buchanan, who was in charge of the prosecution, told the Senate: "I will venture to predict, that whatever may be the decision of the Senate upon this impeachment, Judge Peck has been the last man in the United States to exercise this power, and Mr. Lawless has been its last victim."[61]

Judge Peck was acquitted, but within ten days Buchanan reported a bill to the House of Representatives[62] which led to the law of March 2, 1831,[63] that still empowered courts to punish contempts of their authority, but only "*Provided,* That such power to punish contempts shall not be construed to extend to any cases except the misbehavior of any person in their presence, or so near thereto as to obstruct the administration of justice."[64]

The immediate effect of the 1831 act was more than an expression of federal policy. It set an example for the states so that by 1860 twenty-three of the thirty-three then in the Union had followed suit with similar statutory limitations. Between 1831 and the Civil War in only two states were publications held summarily punishable for contempt.[65] The Civil War, however, appears to have served as a point of demarcation after which the power gradually reasserted itself in an increasing number of jurisdictions. After the turn of the century it reappeared even in the federal courts by way of the construction given to the "so near" clause of the federal statute. The reversal of policy became complete in 1918 when the Supreme Court decided *Toledo Newspaper Co. v. United States,*[65] a case that upheld a summary conviction of contempt for the publication of articles and cartoons during a pending injunction proceeding in which a district judge was intimated to be biased in favor of one of the parties involved. The Court not only interpreted the 1831 act as conferring "no power not already granted" and as imposing "no limitations not already existing," but it gave the phrase "so near to" a causal meaning that embraced actions with a "reasonable tendency" to obstruct the administration of justice.[67]

So the law stood until 1941 and *Nye* v. *United States*[68] when the *Toledo Newspaper Co.* case interpretation was rejected as an historic "inaccuracy" and a geographical connotation adopted in the place of "reasonable tendency." Nye's behavior, it seems, consisted of undue influence exerted more than 100 miles from the court to induce an administrator to terminate a suit for wrongful death. In turn, the geographical connotation of the *Nye* case led to the application of "clear and present danger" eight months later in *Bridges* v. *California*,[59] a contempt by publication case that came to the Supreme Court from a state court.

The State Court Cases and "Clear and Present Danger"

Bridges v. *California* was the review of two state court convictions for contempt by publication. One was that of an editor and a publisher of a newspaper for publishing editorials and comments about cases that were pending in the sense that verdicts of guilty had been rendered and the defendants were awaiting sentence. Among other things, these defendants had been characterized as "gorillas" who should not be granted probation. The other was the conviction of Harry Bridges the West Coast labor leader, for the publication of a telegram that he sent to the Secretary of Labor in which he criticized the decision of a state judge in a labor case, and in which he indicated that a strike would follow the enforcement of the decree.

Writing for the Court, Justice Black noted the history of contempt in the federal courts and the events that were contemporaneous with the adoption of the First Amendment. He rejected as historically unsound the contention that such publications belong to a special category marked off by history, deeply embedded in English common law, which was carried over into American law. He concluded: " 'one of the objects of the Revolution was to get rid of the English common law on liberty of speech and of the press.' "[70]

The Supreme Court did admit that courts have the power to protect themselves from disturbances and disorder in the courtroom, but it subscribed to neither "inherent" nor "reasonable tendency" as the proper measure of this power. Instead, it turned to "clear and present danger," and the way for this was made easy because the state court judgments in question were not "encased in the armor wrought by prior legislative deliberation."[71] Rather, they were judgments couched in the generalities of the common law and thus did not present state policy which had to be weighed. Under the circumstances, the Court concluded that it fell to itself to determine as an original question whether the publications created such a likelihood of a substantive evil as to deprive them of constitutional protection. To resolve the problem it looked to Holmes speaking for a unanimous Court in the *Schenck* case, and to Holmes and Brandeis concurring or dissenting in the *Schaefer,* the *Abrams* and the *Whitney* cases. From these it deduced "a working principle that the substantive evil must be extremely serious and the degree of imminence extremely high before utterances can be punished."[72] The Court did not, however, consider that these cases marked "the furthermost conditional boundaries of protected expression." Instead, it concluded that they did no more than "recognize a minimum compulsion of the Bill of Rights." The unequivocal language of the prohibitions of the First Amendment the Court took "as a command of the broadest scope that explicit language, read in the context of a liberty-loving society, will allow."[73]

In the light of what it said on "clear and present danger," the Court decided that there was no justification for the restrictions on free expression that both cases entailed. The possible influence of the editorials was dismissed as negligible. Also, under no construction, it said, could the Bridges' telegram be considered a threat to follow an illegal course. It was addressed to an individual whose duties comprised the prevention of strikes and who was entitled to all available information concerning an impending or threatened strike. Moreover, at no time during the proceeding below was it claimed that a strike would run afoul of the decree or of California law.[74]

The second case, *Pennekamp* v. *Florida*,[75] not only reaffirmed the Bridges case, but it provided a little further elaboration. In this one, judges had been criticized in editorials and caricatured in cartoons while cases were up for new trial or reindictment as using "every possible technicality of the law to protect the defendant, to block, thwart, hinder, embarass and nullify prosecution."[76] The petitioners, the publisher and the associate editor of a newspaper, contended that their only intent was to criticize and condemn practice and procedure as it then existed by statute in Florida. They invoked the freedom of the press. The indictment on which the two had been convicted had alleged that the publications reflected on and impugned the integrity of the courts, wilfully withheld and suppressed the truth, and tended to obstruct fair and impartial administration of justice in pending cases.

When this reached the Supreme Court, Mr. Justice Reed pointed out for the Court that in the *Bridges* case "reasonably well-marked limits" had been fixed "around the power of courts to punish newspapers and others for comments upon or criticism of pending litigation."[77] The orderly operation of the courts had, he continued, been placed "as the primary and dominant requirement in the administration of justice" and this had been held "consonant with a recognition that freedom of the press must be allowed in the broadest scope compatible with the supremacy of order." Moreover, "clear and present danger" had been adopted as the "theoretical determinant of the limit for open discussion."[78] Afflicted with the "vice of uncertainty" as this rule was admitted to be, it was none the less expected that out of its repeated application by the courts, and with decent self-restraint on the part of the press, there would emerge standards of permissible comment which would adequately safeguard the courts and yet allow fair play to the good influences of open discussion. This, the Justice was careful to point out, did not diminish the power of courts to ward off and punish by contempt any disturbance or disorder in the courtroom.

After weighing the impact of the words printed (all criticism of judicial action already taken) against the protected right of public comment, the Court concluded that there was neither the clearness nor the immediacy necessary. The danger to fair, impartial judicial administration was not such that it closed the door to permissible public comment.

The importance of the last case, *Craig* v. *Harney*,[79] in which a publisher, an editorial writer, and a news reporter had been adjudged guilty of constructive criminal contempt by a state court, is that it laid aside any doubt whether the doctrine of the *Bridges* and *Pennekamp* cases applied to litigation between private litigants. All the fire and brimstone in the case stemmed from a forcible detainer case in which a lease was held to have been forfeited for non-payment of rent. While the case was pending, news items and an editorial deplored the judge's handling of the case. For instance, his ruling instructing the jury to bring in a verdict for the plaintiff at which the jury balked several times but finally complied with under protest was described as "arbitrary action" and a "travesty of justice"; the fact was deplored that he was a layman rather than a lawyer; he was said to have brought down "the wrath of public opinion on his head" by his conduct, and groups were reported to have labeled his ruling a "gross miscarriage of justice" and as giving a service man a "raw deal."[80]

The state appellate court admitted that "clear and present danger" was controlling, and that it was in the light of this test that the case had ultimately to be decided. Nevertheless, it tried to distinguish this one from the *Bridges* case on the theory that there were published threats of further criticism unless the case was disposed of according to the wishes of the publisher, and that the alleged contempt arose during litigation that was between private individuals—litigation in the outcome of which the public, as such, had no interest. The gist of the argument apparently was that there is a greater range of permissible comment in pending cases that generate public concern as in the *Bridges* case than there is in those that do not. Although the Supreme Court admitted that the nature of a case might be relevant to determine whether the "clear and present danger" test is satisfied, it held that the rule of the *Bridges* and *Pennekamp* cases was "fashioned to serve the needs of all litigation, not merely select types of pending cases."[81]

PUBLIC ASSEMBLIES AND "CLEAR AND PRESENT DANGER"

The two cases in which "clear and present danger" was applied to public assemblies are perhaps as good an example as any of the range that the test was made to travel during the decade of the 1940's. In one, *Thomas* v. *Collins*,[82] it was used to protect the right of an individual to address a peaceful, friendly audience; in the other, *Terminello* v. *Chicago*,[83] it was used to enforce the right of an individual to make a provocative, challenging speech in an atmosphere of turbulence, disorder, and animosity. Both were five to four decisions.

The first one, *Thomas* v. *Collins*, centered around a Texas statute[84] that was but one of a number of similar state efforts to curb the growing power of labor unions. Adopted in 1943, this one required labor organizers to register and procure an organizer's card before they could solicit union membership. The controversy arose when the appellant, a union official, was committed for contempt for violating an order restraining him from soliciting membership without first having complied with the statute. His contempt was alleged to have taken place when, after having been served with the order, he went ahead and delivered a previously scheduled address to a peaceful and orderly labor meeting. His prepared address closed with a general invitation to nonunion members present to join to which he added

101

an oral solicitation to one Pat O'Sullivan, a nonunion man in the audience whom he had never previously seen.

The appellant contested the validity of the statute as a previous restraint as well as a denial of the equal protection of the laws, and he relied on "clear and present danger." On its part, the State urged that the statute was no more than a registration law designed to assure previous identification and that it conferred ministerial rather than discretionary power. Its adoption was termed a recognition that a labor organizer does more than merely talk. There was not, the State said, any question of speech and press, but instead one of the regulation of a "business practice." Consistent with this, it argued that the appropriate standard should be the one applied to state regulatory statutes under the commerce clause. When the case reached the Supreme Court of the United States the decision was five to four with the majority of the Court adopting the former view, that of the appellant, and the minority the latter, that of the State.

The majority rejected the idea that the First Amendment is not applicable to business or economic activity. It restated the "preferred position" to which the freedoms of the First Amendment had been elevated, and it upheld the view that the only restrictions of speech and press that are justified are those that create a "clear and present danger" to a public interest. It said: "Only the gravest abuses, endangering paramount interest, give occasion for permissible limitation."[85]

The Court did not doubt that labor unions are subject to state regulation to the extent required by the public interest. But whatever this interest might be, such regulation may not invade the domain reserved for free speech and assembly. And within this domain the Court had already placed "[f]ree discussion concerning the conditions in industry and the causes of labor disputes . . . indispensable to the effective and intelligent use of the processes of government to shape the destiny of modern industrial society."[86] The State Supreme Court was found to have given insufficient weight to these considerations; it had failed to take into account the "blanketing effect" of the application of the prohibitions and of the bearing of "clear and present danger" on the matter.

But even apart from the "business practice" theory, the Texas statute was found objectionable as imposing an invalid restriction. There had been dictum in *Cantwell v. Connecticut*,[87] on which the State apparently relied, to the effect that a statute that went no further than to require previous identification would be sustained. Nevertheless, in the present case the Court rejected as incompatible with the First Amendment the requirement that one must register before a speech could be made in which support for a lawful movement was enlisted. In the absence of a grave and immediate danger to an interest which the state has a right to protect, lawful public assemblies cannot be called instruments of harm that require previous identification of speakers. And this, the majority reasoned, is as true of workmen and unions as it is of businessmen, farmers, educators, and members of political parties.

Although Justice Jackson went along with the majority and provided the fifth vote, he wrote a concurring opinion in which he indicated that he felt some qualms about the lot of the employer and the rules that were applied to him. Here the Court was striking down an attempt by a state to bring within its licensing system speech that was otherwise beyond its reach by associating it with "solicitation." On the other hand, at the Federal level employer speech which would otherwise have been free had been brought within the Labor Board's power to suppress it by associating it with "coercion" or "domination." Therefore the Justice felt that the Supreme Court was "applying to Thomas a rule the benefit of which in all its breadth and vigor [the] Court deni[ed] to employers in National Labor Relations Board cases."[88] He proposed that the same rule be applied to all.

The other public assembly case, *Terminello* v. *Chicago*,[89] was decided at the end of the decade. As a result of this one the Supreme Court was praised by some for having extended "clear and present danger" again to the advancement of the cause of free speech, but damned by others who maintained that the Court was able to reach the decision that it did because it failed to apply "clear and present danger" to the facts of the case. Indeed, so impassioned was Mr. Justice Jackson who belonged to the latter group that he warned by way of dissent "that, if the Court does not temper its doctrinaire logic with a little wisdom, it will convert the constitutional Bill of Rights into a suicide pact."[90]

The petitioner, a Catholic priest who was under suspension by his bishop, had been found guilty of disordely conduct in violation of a city ordinance forbidding breaches of the peace. The case arose from a public address that he delivered in a context of violence and disorder to a public meeting held in Chicago. He spoke to a capacity audience in an 800-seat auditorium outside of which a picket line of several hundred formed, and a crowd of about one thousand gathered to protest. Disturbances took place in spite of the efforts of seventy police. The meeting was held in an atmosphere of people being escorted through picket lines, clothing being torn, stench bombs and other missiles thrown at the building, epithets hurled at those who attended the meeting, windows broken, and attempts made, one by a flying wedge of forty boys, to rush the auditorium.

Added to this was the conduct of the petitioner. During his address not only did he condemn the conduct of the crowd outside, but he denounced with considerable vigor various political and racial groups as inimical to the welfare of the nation, and he spoke derisively of officials who favored a harsh post-war policy toward Germany, not to mention an unkind remark that he directed at the widow of the late President of the United States.

When the case reached the Supreme Court the argument centered on whether or not this address was composed of such derisive, fighting words, that placed it outside the scope of constitutional guarantees. A majority of the Court found it unnecessary to reach this question. Instead, it reached to the instructions to the jury in the trial court in which it was said that "breach of the peace" consisted of any "misbehavior which violates the public peace and decorum," and held that the "misbehavior may constitute a breach of the peace if it stirs the public to anger, invites dispute, brings about a condition of unrest, or creates a disturbance, or if it molests the inhabitants in the enjoyment of peace and quiet by arousing alarm."[91]

But, said Justice Douglas for the Court, under our system of government the function of free speech is to invite dispute; further, it may even serve its high purpose best "when it induces a condition of unrest, creates dissatisfaction with conditions as they are, even stirs people to anger." Provocative and challenging as speech often is, "[i]t may strike at prejudice and preconceptions and have profound unsettling effects as it presses for acceptance of an idea."[92] And that is why, although it is not absolute, speech is protected from censorship or punishment except when there is a likelihood that it will produce a "clear and present danger" of a serious substantive evil far above public inconvenience, annoyance, or even unrest.

Even though the petitioner had not objected to the trial judge's instructions, he had objected to the ordinance as a violation of his right of free speech. To the majority of the Court that was sufficient under the precedent of *Stromberg* v. *California*[93] in which exception to instructions had not been taken, yet a judgment of conviction based on a general verdict under a state statute had been set aside because one part of the statute was unconstitutional. As construed and applied to Terminello, the ordinance here was found to be a denial of the right of free speech guaranteed by the Constitution. And this was true even though, throughout the proceedings, the state appellate courts had assumed that only conduct amounting to "fighting words" were punishable under the ordinance.[94] Here too the verdict was general and for all that anyone knew the petitioner was convicted under the parts of the statute that were unconstitutional. "We cannot," wrote Justice Douglas, "avoid that issue by saying that all Illinois did was to measure petitioner's conduct, not the ordinance, against the Constitution."[95]

THE DECADE OF THE 1940's : A RECAPITULATION

When Justice Holmes first suggested his "clear and present danger" test in 1919 in *Schenck* v. *United States* he spoke for a unanimous court; twenty-one years later when Justice Murphy revived the test in *Thornhill* v. *Alabama* one justice, Justice McReynolds, refused to go along with the majority. Thus, Justice Murphy was not quite as successful in the numerical superiority that supported his revival as Holmes had been in his initial presentation. Nevertheless, it is largely due to the revival in the *Thornhill* case that the then all but forgotten test gained lasting recognition. Mr. Justice Murphy started a cycle that held full sway for all of a decade during which "clear and present danger," aided by "preferred position," dominated civil liberties litigation.

It is true that at the start of this cycle, for about the first three years, "clear and present danger" served as not much more than a supplement to the age old concept of "prior restraint." But even this marked a change from the preceding decade when "prior restraint" stood alone as the alternative to "dangerous tendency." However, before "clear and present danger" could achieve the commanding position that it was destined to occupy only a little later, two things had to take place: first, Justices Black, Douglas and Murphy had to repudiate the *Gobitis* decision in which they had voted with the majority as erroneously decided; second, the liberal Black-Douglas-Murphy block that was taking shape had to gain reinforcement. The former took place in 1942 when these three justices made their gratuitous statement as they joined Chief Justice Stone in his *Jones* v. *Opelika* dissent, the latter took place in 1943 when Justice Rutledge replaced Justice Byrnes who resigned. That there would be a change became quite evident the very day Mr. Justice Rutledge took his seat, February 15, 1943, when a rehearing was granted in *Jones* v. *Opelika*. The decision was overruled on May 3rd. A little more than a month later the same fate befell the original flag-salute case as it too was overruled. And so it continued until the deaths of Justices Murphy and Rutledge within a few months of each other in 1949.

It has been written that if "clear and present danger" ever was "the law" it was during the time that Justices Black, Douglas, Murphy and Rutledge were together on the Supreme Court.[96] While this is true, it should not be assumed that majorities in its favor were always readily available. At best, it never had more than these four as consistent supporters, and throughout the decade there were only two decisions in which it was used that were unanimous.[93] More often, it was a question of finding a fifth vote from among the other members of the Court, none of whom were particularly enthusiastic about the test. And there were occasions when this meant a fifth who would only join in the result arrived at rather than the language of the four as in *Thomas* v. *Collins*.[98] There were also decisions during this decade in which "prior restraint" served to sustain First Amendment claims without "clear and present danger." This has been referred to as vote "purchasing" to achieve a desired result.[99]

The "clear and present danger" test that prevailed during the decade of the 1940's was, it is true, a resuscitation of the Holmes-Brandeis creation of several decades earlier. There was, however, some difference between the two. In the original version, the test was directed only at the constitutionality of the application of statutes rather than at the constitutionality of the statutes themselves. In the later version the test was applied to both. Moreover, the earlier version was directed at content rather than at the form of speech and press. When the question was state action aimed at form—time, place, manner of expression—the guide was the reasonable basis rule, a rule that was discarded soon after the revival of the test in 1940. Finally, Justices Holmes and Brandeis used "clear and present danger" only in cases that involved national security; the revived version was applied to a variety of situations.

CHAPTER X

THE START OF A NEW DECADE: "CLEAR AND PRESENT DANGER" CIRCUMSCRIBED AND ABRIDGED

Even while it reigned supreme during the decade of resurgence and extension, "clear and present danger" was not without opposition and criticism. Hardly had the decade started than the voice of Mr. Justice Frankfurter made itself heard in dissent. In the *Bridges* case he held out for "reasonable tendency," a test that he considered historic, and he objected to its displacement with a phrase that had gained currency a scant twenty-years earlier. He deemed the Constitution "not a formulary," and he thought the duty it imposes on the Court not ended "with the recitation of phrases that are the short-hand of a complicated historic process." He objected to "idle play on words," and "clear and present danger" he termed but "an expression of tendency and not of accomplishment;" he dismissed the literary difference between it and "reasonable tendency" as "not of constitutional dimension."[1]

Throughout the decade the Justice continued his attack on what he believed to be a misconception of the origin and purpose of "clear and present danger." He was convinced that when Mr. Justice Holmes coined the phrase he "was not enunciating a formal rule that there can be no restriction upon speech, and, still less, no compulsion where conscience balks, unless imminent danger would thereby be wrought 'to our institutions of government.' "[2] As he saw it, the phrase originated in a case in which speech alone served as a means to bring about sedition in wartime. Therefore, when the Court sought to settle the flag salute question with "clear and present danger" it not only assumed "a legislative responsibility that does not belong to it," however unwittingly it may have done so, but it took ". . . a felicitous phrase out of the context of the particular situation where it arose and for which it was adapted."[3] And again, when it was a question of contempt of court based on two editorials and a cartoon he was certain that " 'clear and present danger' was never used by Mr. Justice Holmes to express a technical legal doctrine or to convey a formula for adjudicating cases." Instead, "[i]t was a literary phrase not to be distorted by being taken from its context."[4] Later, when "clear and present danger" served to exonerate another publisher and another editorial writer of constructive criminal contempt, Mr. Justice Frankfurter concluded that "clear and present danger" had become "merely a phrase for covering up a novel, iron constitutional doctrine." "Only the pungent pen of Mr. Justice Holmes could," he continued "adequately comment on such a perversion of the purpose of his phrase."[5]

At the end of the decade of resurgence and extension, Mr. Justice Frankfurter broadened his attack and brought "preferred position" within its scope. His objection to this was much the same as it was to "clear and present danger." He summarized "preferred position" as "a complicated process of constitutional adjudication by a deceptive formula . . . Such a formula makes for mechanical jurisprudence."[6]

With the start of another decade in 1950 and the change in the personnel of the Court, at the very outset there was strong premonition that the Justice would have his way—that "clear and present danger" would soon be subjected at least to circumscription and abridgment and not only to dissent and criticism. The occasion was *American Communications Ass'n* v. *Douds*,[7] a consolidation of two cases in which the Court upheld the constitutionality of the non-Communist affidavit requirement of the Labor-Management Relations Act, 1947.[8] The unions, the appellants in one and the petitioners in the other, took positions on "clear and present danger" which the Court did not consider consistent. In one the union contended that the legislation under scrutiny could not, under any circumstances, meet the "clear and present danger" test as applied by the Court. Belief, it said, could never constitute such a "clear and present danger." Moreover, it continued, it was difficult, if not impossible, "to conceive how the expression of belief, or the joining of a political party, without more, could ever constitute such a danger."[9] In the other, the union argued that absent a showing that political strikes are a "clear and present danger" to the security of the nation or that they threaten widespread, and even substantial, industrial unrest, under the "clear and present danger" rule no basis existed to sustain the restrictions placed on protected freedoms by the contested portions of the act.[10]

Writing for the Court, Mr. Chief Justice Vinson attributed this "confusion" to the attempt to apply "clear and present danger" as a mechanical test in every First Amendment case without regard "to the context of its application." He characterized the provisions of the Constitution as "organic living institutions transplanted from English soil," rather than "mechanical formulas having their essence in their form," and he theorized that "[i]t is the considerations that gave birth to the phrase, 'clear and present danger,' not the phrase itself, that are vital in our decision of questions involving liberties protected by the First Amendment."[11] Finally, he neatly came to the conclusion that the question with which the Court was faced was different from that which Justices Holmes and Brandeis "found convenient to consider in terms of clear and present danger."[12] The roots upon which "clear and present danger" had stood for better than a decade were loosened to no small degree with the statement that "even harmful conduct cannot justify restrictions upon speech unless substantial interests of society are at stake. But in suggesting that the substantive evil must be serious and substantial, it was never the intention of this Court to lay down an absolutist test measured in terms of danger to the Nation. When the effect of a statute or ordinance upon the exercise of First Amendment freedoms is relatively small and the public interest to be protected is substantial, it is obvious that a rigid test requiring a showing of imminent danger to the security of the Nation is an absurdity."[13]

INDICATIONS OF A TREND

Within a year after the *Douds* case Chief Justice Vinson wrote for the Court in three more First and Fourteenth Amendment cases, all decided on the same day and all indicative of a trend. In the first, *Niemotko* v. *Maryland*,[14] applications for permits to use the city park for Bible talks were submitted to the city council of Havre de Grace, Maryland, only to be refused for no apparent reason other than dislike for the applicants and their views. The appellants were arrested when they held their meetings without permits. In the second case, *Kunz,* v. *New York*,[15] a permit already granted was revoked on evidence that the appellant had ridiculed and denounced other religious beliefs. Again there was conviction when the appellant persisted and spoke without a permit. In the third, *Feiner* v. *New York*,[16] the petitioner was arrested when he refused a police order to step off his box while he delivered an inflammatory speech to a mixed crowd of negroes and whites that had become restless. He was convicted for violating

§ 722 of the Penal Code of New York which, in effect, forbids incitement of a breach of the peace.

In the first case, *Niemotko* v. *Maryland,* neither ordinance nor statute existed to regulate the use of the park—only a "practice" whereby the Park Commissioner and the city council were vested with complete authority to grant or deny permits unguided by adequate standards, narrowly drawn limitations circumscribing absolute power, or a substantial community interest to be served. The conviction was reversed as a denial of the equal protection of the laws.

The second case, *Kunz,* was a repetition of the first. There was an ordinance but it made no mention of reasons for which an application for a permit could be refused. Instead, it granted discretionary power to control in advance the right to speak on religious matters. For that reason, it was declared invalid as a prior restraint that was repugnant to the First Amendment. The conviction was upset. A few years earlier this case would probably have been disposed of in terms of "clear and present danger." As it happened, there was no mention of the test, a fact that seemed peculiar to Mr. Justice Jackson, the sole dissenter.[17]

The last of the three cases, *Feiner* v. *New York,* differed from the first and second in two respects: the conviction was upheld and there was mention of "clear and present danger." Aware as it was that the ordinary murmurings and objections of a hostile audience should not be allowed to silence a speaker, and mindful of the danger that is created when overzealous police officials are vested with complete discretion to break up otherwise lawful public meetings, the Court found that here the petitioner was neither arrested nor convicted for making a speech or for its contents, but rather for the reaction that the speech engendered. As it affirmed the conviction the Court repeated the following language from *Cantwell* v. *Connecticut:* "When clear and present danger of riot, disorder, interference with traffic upon the public streets, or other immediate threat to public safety, peace, or order, appears, the powers of the State to prevent or punish is obvious."[18] It should be noted, however, that the *Cantwell* case was one of the earliest to use "clear and present danger" to keep a man out of jail,[19] whereas in the instant case, and another to follow,[20] the opposite was true. It should also be noted that "clear and present danger" was still acceptable for this type case, although it had "slipped" immeasurably in cases involving national security.

110

THE DENNIS CASE AND THE COURT BECOME QUADRIVIOUS

Eight years after he spoke for the United States Court of Appeals for the Second Circuit in *United States* v. *Dennis*,[21] and seven years after the Supreme Court of the United States had made its pronouncement in this same case, [22] Learned Hand offered the following appraisal of "clear and present danger." "I doubt that the doctrine will persist, and I cannot help thinking that for once Homer nodded."[23]

Perhaps Judge Hand was in this same frame of mind earlier as he meditated over the *Dennis* case and whether or not the defendants, all officials at one time or another of the Communist Party, could be punished under § 3 of the Smith Act for extensive, concerted action in teaching the doctrines of Marxism-Leninism. But, however that may have been, his ensuing construction of "clear and present danger" amounted to a substantial alteration, if not altogether a retailoring, of the test as it had existed before.

Judge Hand prefaced his analysis of the situation with the statement: "The Supreme Court has certainly evinced tenderness toward political utterances since the First World War,"[24] and then he launched into a painstaking review of all of the cases from *Schenck* through *Douds*. But it was from the last one, which in some ways he considered the most important, that he took his cue. As he read the *Douds* case he took it to mean, "that no longer can there be any doubt, if indeed there was before, that the phrase, 'clear and present danger,' is not a slogan or a shibboleth to be applied as though it carried its own meaning; but that it involves in every case a comparison between interests which are to be appraised qualitatively."[25]

And so, although the phrase may have become a shorthand statement for utterances which the First Amendment does not protect, yet for him it could not amount to a *vade mecum*. Instead, Judge Hand chose to consider it as "a way to describe a penumbra of occasions, even the outskirts of which are indefinable, but within which, as is so often the case, the courts must find their way as they can." As he put it, in every case the courts must consider "whether the gravity of the 'evil', discounted by its improbability, justifies such invasion of free speech as is necessary to avoid the danger." He gave the following reason for substituting "improbability" for "remoteness": "Given the same probability, it would be wholly irrational to condone future evils which we should prevent if they were immediate; that could be reconciled only by an indifference to those who come after us. It is only because a substantial intervening period between the utterance and its realization may check its effect and change its importance, that its immediacy is important."[26]

Thus, the question was not whether there existed a confederation that amounted to a "present" danger in all circumstances and at all times, but rather how "imminent," i.e., "how probable," it was of execution at the time the indictment was found. As he reviewed the evidence and took note of international events, he could not conceive of "how one could ask for a more probable danger, unless one must wait till the actual eve of hostilities."[27] He found evident a conspiracy that created a danger of sufficient gravity and enough probability to justify its suppression. He held that there was a danger "clear and present."

Although Judge Hand was skeptical of "clear and present danger," the effect of his opinion was to extend still further the purview of this phrase which he protested was "not a slogan or a shibboleth to be applied as though it carried its own meaning."[29] He did this by applying the test to a situation that was very similar to an earlier one in which the Supreme Court had refused to follow the same course. Twenty-five years earlier in *Gitlow* v. *New York*,[29] the Court had rejected "clear and present danger" as the yardstick for speech that had been declared by legislative determination to be dangerous and inimical to the state. In that case the Court had ruled out the test because of the legislative determination and had limited its function to an examinaion of "the natural tendency and probable effect"[30] of the language used regardless of the immediacy of any danger. Justices Holmes and Brandeis had objected; they had insisted on a showing of "clear and present danger" regardless of the prior legislative determination.

But even as Judge Hand extended the test, he drew away from its traditional meaning as he refashioned it so that it more nearly resembled the doctrine of the *Gitlow* case which had been dormant for a quarter of a century than it did the Holmes-Brandeis concept. The element of imminence which the latter had considered indispensable Hand discarded in favor of the "gravity of the evil discounted by its improbality."[31] The element of time was thus materially altered in the direction of "bad tendency" as the *Gitlow* doctrine had come to be known from the language used, and away from the Holmes-Brandeis insistence that the correction of evils should be left to free public discussion whenever feasible. The alteration did not go all the way but its effect was to provide a sliding scale which could make liberty of speech and press depend on such things as the international political climate.

When the case reached the Supreme Court six of the eight justices who participated joined in the judgment of the Court that upheld the conviction, but a majority was nowhere to be found that would agree on an opinion that could be considered the opinion of the Court. Chief Justice Vinson announced an opinion in which Justices Reed, Burton and Minton joined; Justices Frankfurter and Jackson each wrote concurring opinions; Justices Black and Douglas each wrote dissenting opinions.

On the subject of "clear and present danger" the Chief Justice continued from where he had left off in the *Douds* case. As he expounded further on his understanding of the meaning of the test he took as his starting point the proposition that speech is not absolute, something that probably not too many would argue with. But then the effectiveness of his argument was considerably diminished when he invoked an absolute to prove there are no absolutes: "Nothing is more certain in modern society than the principle that there are no absolutes, that a name, a phrase, a standard has meaning only when associated with the consideration which gave birth to the nomenclature."[32]

To the Chief Justice this case not only presented squarely the application of "clear and present danger," but it also made imperative a decision as to its significance. It could not mean that the Government had to wait until a *putsch* was about to be executed before it could act; even though an attempt to overthrow the government by force was doomed to failure from the outset, there still would be an evil sufficient to be prevented by Congress. Therefore, he rejected success or probability of success as the criterion. Moreover, he found no guidance in the situations with which Justices Holmes and Brandeis were concerned in the *Gitlow* case, and with which the Court was in the *Fiske* and *De Jonge* cases. Just as the Court had distinguished the facts before it in the *Gitlow* case from those of the *Schenck* case, the Chief Justice distinguished the facts now before the Court from those of the predecessor cases. He dismissed the *Gitlow*, *Fiske* and *De Jonge* cases as presenting comparatively isolated events that bore little relation to any substantial threats to the safety of the community, and which he thought not comparable to the situation with which he considered the Court confronted here—"the development of an apparatus designed and dedicated to overthrow the Government, in the context of world crisis after world crisis." Instead, the Chief Justice found his answer in Judge Hand's statement of the rule, a statement which he called "as succinct and inclusive" as any other the Court might devise. He adopted this rephrasing of "clear and present danger" with the following words: "It takes into consideration those factors which we deem relevant, and relates their significance. More we cannot expect from words."[33]

Justice Frankfurter concurred in the affirmance of the judgment. He re-emphasized his dissatisfaction with "clear and present danger" and he made clear that a rephrasing of the test in terms of "probability" did not make it any more palatable. With his customary facility of expression he reviewed the relevant decisions of the Court and he restated the objections that he had voiced before. He rebelled again at "the attempt to use the direction of thought lying behind the criterion of 'clear and present danger' wholly out of the context in which it originated, and to make of it an absolute dogma and definitive measuring rod for the power of Congress to deal with assaults against security through devices other than overt physical attempts."[34] Indeed, it seemed better to him "that the phrase be abandoned than that it be sounded once more to hide from the believers in an absolute right of free speech the plain fact that the interest in speech, profoundly important as it is, is no more conclusive in judicial review than other attributes of democracy or than a determination of the people's representatives that a measure is necessary to assure the safety of government itself."[35]

Justice Jackson still believed in "clear and present danger," but not for this case. He would have saved it for another day as the "rule of reason" to be applied in the type case for which it was devised— for the hot-headed speech on the street corner, the circulation of a few incendiary pamphlets, the parading of zealots behind a red flag, or the refusal of a handful of children to salute the flag. To him the test had meaning and it favored vital freedoms, even if sometimes applied too generously, "where a conviction is sought to be based on a speech or writing which does not directly or explicitly advocate a crime but to which such tendency is sought to be attributed by construction or by implication from external circumstances."[36] But he saw no reason to apply the test in a case such as this one with its well-organized conspiracy.

In his brief dissent Justice Black reaffirmed his confidence in "clear and present danger." He restated the belief that he had expressed earlier when he spoke for the majority in the *Bridges* case. Now, as then, he believed "that the 'clear and present danger' test did not 'mark the furthermost constitutional boundaries of protected expression' but did 'no more than recognize a minimum compulsion of the Bill of Rights.' "[37] With public opinion as it then was he knew that few would protest the conviction of the eleven Communists, but he expressed hope that in calmer times, "when present pressures, passions and fears subside, this or some later Court will restore the First Amendment liberties to the high preferred place where they belong in a free society."[38]

Mr. Justice Douglas recognized that freedom of speech is not absolute and that there are times when it may lose its constitutional immunity. Speech that is innocuous one year "may at another time fan such destructive flames that it must be halted in the interests of the safety of the Republic . . . When conditions are so critical that there will be no time to avoid the evil that the speech threatens, it is time to call a halt."[39] That was his understanding of "clear and present danger"—the likelihood of an immediate injury to society if speech were allowed. However, it was also his understanding that free speech is the rule and not the exception. Therefore, "to support a finding of clear and present danger it must be shown either that immediate serious violence was to be expected or was advocated, or that the past conduct furnished reason to believe that such advocacy was then contemplated."[40]

Justice Douglas would have had no doubts had this been a case in which those who claimed the protection of the First Amendment taught the technique of sabotage, the assassination of the President, the filching of documents from public files, the planting of bombs, the art of street warfare, and the like. But as he saw the present record, it indicated that the petitioners had themselves taught and had organized others to teach Marxist-Leninist doctrines found in books which were not themselves outlawed. He found it impossible to say that the Communists were so potent in this country or were so strategically deployed that they should be suppressed for their speech.

Thus, of the eight Justices who participated in the *Dennis* case seven[41] subscribed to "clear and present danger" in principle. Of the seven only six[42] thought that even in principle it should have been applied to this particular case, and of the six no more than four[43] were with the majority—all that could reach a common understanding

115

as to what the principle now impiled. Moreover, the Vinson-Hand version that these four did agree on bore marked dissimilarity from the traditional version as it substituted "gravity of the 'evil,' discounted by its improbability"[44] for immediacy. But as it happened, the Smith Act successfully met its first test of constitutionality only because these four could resolve their differences with two others[45] who either thought the test not applicable[46] to this type case or did not approve of it at all.[47] Perhaps this was inevitable because of the temper of the times. Even the government admitted on oral argument that had a majority of the Court thought fit to apply the test in its traditional form the Smith Act would have had to fall.[48] As it was, there were only two of the Justices who participated who could be considered disciples of the traditional Holmes-Brandeis exposition, the two who agreed in dissent[49] —all that was left of the bloc that had consistently put over "clear and present danger" during the preceding decade.[50]

Perhaps as good a way as any to describe the consequences of the quadrivious path that the test traveled in *Dennis* v. *United States* is to repeat the proclamation that the French used to announce the death of their kings: Le roi est mort, vive le roi!

THE ROLE OF THE JURY — THE DENNIS CASE

In addition to the meaning of "clear and present danger," the *Dennis* case presented another equally interesting issue—whether the determination of the existence of a "clear and present danger" was a question of fact to be determined by the jury, or, instead, was a question of law to be reserved for the Court. Although the importance of this issue was more momentary than momentous it was, nevertheless, reminiscent of the controversy that had raged earlier in the formative era of the English law of speech and press.

In England, controversy over the role of the jury followed close the assumption that seditious or defamatory writing was not solely a matter for Star Chamber proceedings, but also fell within the jurisdiction of the common law courts even before the Star Chamber was abolished by the Long Parliament in 1641. Once this assumption had been made the position of the jury in libel cases was limited solely to a determination of the question of intentional publication, the court reserving for itself as a question of law whether or not the writing was seditious or defamatory in character.[51] That was not only the rule which prevailed in England well through the eighteenth century, but

116

it was also the rule that was followed in the American colonies until the time of the American Revolution. Thus, when Andrew Hamilton pressed for a general verdict in his defense of Peter Zenger before a New York jury in 1735 he was admonished by the Court: "No, Mr. Hamilton; the jury may find that Mr. Zenger printed and published these papers, and leave it to the Court to judge whether they are libelous. You know this is very common; it is in the nature of a Special Verdict, where the jury leave the matter of laws to the court."[52]

Thomas Erskine protested against this rule as he argued a motion for a new trial in the *Dean of St. Asaph's* case in which a verdict of "guilty" had been entered although the jury had returned a verdict of "guilty of publishing only." He contended that on a plea of not guilty to an indictment or information a jury is entitled to enter a general verdict of guilty or not guilty and should not be limited to a special verdict on the facts.[53] Erskine's contention had no immediate success since Lord Mansfield ruled against it and held that the criminality or innocence of an act is a question of law for the judge. It did, however, have ultimate success since it led to the enactment of the Fox Libel Act which was largely based on Erskine's argument. This act which became law in 1792 authorized a general verdict upon the whole matter put in issue in libel cases.[54] After that, an English jury could no longer be directed by the presiding judge to find a defendant guilty merely upon proof of publication.

In the United States the Alien and Sedition Laws provoked speech and press problems soon after the adoption of the Constitution and the Bill of Rights. These were problems that arose during the trials that took place under the acts, but they were not problems that concerned the role of the jury although there was some question over the type of evidence that was permitted to be presented to the jury.[55] Evidence that could prove only a part of the matter charged was rejected as inadmissible and the proof of an entire matter had to be by a single witness. After the Alien and Sedition Acts had lapsed by their own limitation and Jefferson had freed those convicted under them when he became President, more than a century was to pass before the liberty of speech and press again became an active issue at the national level in this country. Once it did in the World War I Espionage Act cases[56] the role of the jury came up in two cases, *Schaefer* v. *United States*[57] and *Pierce* v. *United States*,[58] both decided in 1920, but thirty more years were to pass before it became a major issue in *Dennis* v. *United States.*[59]

In the *Schaefer* case a majority of the Supreme Court held that the evidence being sufficient, the determination of the falsity of statements that appeared in the defendants' German language newspaper was the function of the jury and not that of the court—that the trial court had acted correctly when it allowed the jurors to draw from their general knowledge of war and war conditions in making the determination. The case is, however, more interesting for what Mr. Justice Brandeis had to say in his dissenting opinion about the role of the jury in its relation to the "clear and present danger" test. To Brandeis the question of the presence of a "clear and present danger" was one of proximity and degree. Therefore, the "field" in which the jury could exercise its judgment was, in his opinion, necessarily wide. It was, however, not unlimited and the trial was still, in his words, "by judge *and* jury," and not one in which the judge could abdicate his function. Treating the existence of a "clear and present danger" as a question of fact, he came to the following conclusion: "If the words were of such a nature and were used under such circumstances that men, judging in calmness, could not reasonably say that they created a clear and present danger that they would bring about the evil which Congress sought and had a right to prevent, then it is the duty of the trial judge to withdraw the case from the consideration of the jury; and if he fails to do so, it is the duty of the appellate court to correct the error."[60]

In the *Pierce* case a general demurrer to an indictment based on the Espionage Act had been overruled by the trial judge. When, subsequent to that, the defendants pleaded not guilty, it was shown in the trial court that they had distributed the pamphlet that formed the basis of the indictment with full knowledge of its contents. The Supreme Court rejected the contention that the trial judge had erred in not sustaining the demurrer: "What interpretation ought to be placed upon the pamphlet, what would be the probable effect of distributing it in the mode adopted, and what were defendants' motives in doing this, were questions for the jury, not the court to decide."[61] Citing the *Schenck, Frohwerk* and *Debs* cases, the Court concluded that whether in fact the printed words would have produced as a proximate result a material interference with the war effort "was a question for the jury to decide in view of all the circumstances of the time and considering the place and manner of distribution."

Thus, before *Dennis* v. *United States* experience with the role of the jury as an issue in speech and press cases was very limited in this country. Nevertheless, existing authority appeared to favor a course that treated such questions as "probable effect" and "clear and present danger" as issues of fact for the jury. The *Dennis* case, however, altered this course as it rejected the contention that it was an error for the trial judge to reserve entirely for himself as a matter of law the question of "clear and present danger." During the trial of the case Judge Medina had instructed the jury that "clear and present danger" was a question of law about which it was not to concern itself: "If you are satisfied that the evidence establishes beyond a reasonable doubt that the defendants, or any of them, are guilty of a violation of the statute, as I have interpreted it to you, I find as a matter of law that there is sufficient danger of a substantial evil that the Congress has a right to prevent to justify the application of the statute under the First Amendment of the Constitution.

"This is a matter of law about which you have no concern. It is a finding on a matter of law which I deem essential to support my ruling that the case should be submitted to you to pass upon the guilt or innocence of the defendants."[62]

In the Court of Appeals Judge Hand approved of this instruction, mindful of *Pierce* v. *United States* in which the Supreme Court had said that "the probable effect of distributing [the challenged pamphlet] in the mode adopted" was a question which should have been left to the jury.[63] Once *Dennis* reached the Supreme Court very much the same reasoning was adopted and Judge Medina's instruction was again upheld.

Writing for a plurality of four of a majority of six, Chief Justice Vinson held that the doctrine of "clear and present danger" was a judicial rule to be applied as a matter of law by the courts. "When facts are found," he wrote, "that establish the violation of a statute, the protection against conviction afforded by the First Amendment is a matter of law."[63] And according to his plurality opinion, the jury had found such facts under proper instructions given by the trial judge. The Chief Justice went to some pains to reject as misplaced petitioners' reliance on Mr. Justice Brandeis' statement in his *Whitney* concurrence that had Miss Whitney chosen to make "clear and present danger" an issue she "might have required that the issue be determined by the *Court or the jury*."[65] Wrote the Chief Justice: "No realistic construction of this disjunctive language could arrive

119

at the conclusion that he [Mr. Justice Brandeis] intended that the question was only determinable by a jury."[66] While this was true as far as it went, it failed to take into consideration Mr. Justice Brandeis' full understanding of the role of judge and jury as he had expressed it in his *Schaefer* dissent.[67] When the *Whitney* statement is read in the light of the latter, "this disjunctive language" could be taken to mean that had Miss Whitney followed the course suggested she could have required that the issue be determined by a jury unless, judging in calmness, a jury could arrive at but one conclusion, i.e., that the circumstances could not reasonably be said to create a "clear and present danger" that they would bring about the evil which Congress sought and had a right to prevent.

Chief Justice Vinson dismissed the statement in the *Pierce* case as "incidental"[68] and of no more persuasive effect than that in the *Whitney* concurrence. To Mr. Justice Douglas, however, the *Pierce* case stated the law as it had been until *Dennis* and as it should continue to be.[69] He believed that the Court erred when it suddenly chose to ignore its earlier decision, the only one on the subject, and suddenly decided to treat the question as one of law. He might have added that should this ruling be viewed in the light of history, one might wonder whether this was not a step in the direction of the English law as it was before the Fox Libel Act when the function of the jury was to determine the fact of publication and no more.

Since *Dennis* v. *United States*, although the jury has been the subject of occasional comment in speech and press cases, the role of the jury has not again been an issue to the extent that the outcome of a case has depended on it. Some of these occasional comments have been in majority opinions[70] and others in dissenting opinions.[71] Those in majority opinions have either dealt with sufficiency of evidence[72] or have been not much more than incidental remarks;[73] those in dissenting opinions have been of a stronger nature as the expression of the personal philosophies of individual Justices.[74] The sum-total of all these, however, has not again brought the role of the jury to the fore in speech and press cases and made it the vital issue that it was in England for so long a period before the Fox Libel Act of 1792.

At this point one may even wonder what the lasting effect of the *Dennis* case will be on the role of the jury in speech and press cases. Since the case was decided in 1951 "clear and present danger" has been returned to the obscurity that it occupied during the decade that preceded its resurrection in *Thornhill* v. *Alabama.* So long as it remains so, and there is no indication that the test is likely to have an immediate new lease on life,[75] this particular phase of the case can perhaps be considered an isolated incident in the history of the liberty of speech and press in this country—a phase that could not muster a majority expression of the Court one way or another since only six Justices committed themselves on the question, and two of these were in dissent to the plurality opinion.[76]

CHAPTER XI

THE SEARCH FOR A NEW STANDARD DURING THE 1950's

THE SEQUEL TO DENNIS V. UNITED STATES

Ever since the *Dennis* case was decided there has been uncertainty as to the status of the "clear and present danger" test. It may even be that Judge Hand's prediction has already come to pass and the doctrine no longer persists. Whether or not that is so, since the *Dennis* case the history of freedom of speech and press seems to indicate a search for a new standard. During the decade of the 1950's "previous restraint" was used on a few occasions, but not to the extent that it can be said to have been the doctrine of the era. There was also resort to a "balancing of interests." The distinguishing feature of the era was, however, that although the Court entertained very much the same gamut of cases that it had during the preceding decade, in none was the decision made to hinge on "clear and present danger." In fact, the test was expressly rejected by the Court as not worthy of consideration in two cases, one a libelous utterance and the other an obscenity case.[2]

In addition to the apparent abandonment of "clear and present danger," this recent decade witnessed another development: an attempt that started out as dictum to impose the liberties of speech and press as a limitation on the power of legislative inquiry, state as well as federal.

ABANDONMENT OF "CLEAR AND PRESENT DANGER"

Picketing

Perhaps nowhere was there better evidence during the 1950's of a shift in emphasis away from "clear and present danger" than in picketing cases. In this area, the first to feel the impact of the resurgence and extension of the test, there were three Supreme Court decisions during the decade after *Dennis*. One came at the very start of this interval, a second one year later, and a third six years later. All were peaceful picketing cases, but in none was there mention of the test so popular in this type case during the prior decade.

The first case, *International Brotherhood of Electrical Workers* v. *N.L.R.B.*, is probably of greater importance to the field of labor law than it is to the history of speech and press. Its effect was to sustain the constitutionality of the application of the anti-secondary boycott provision of the Labor Management Relations Act, 1947,[4] to peaceful picketing. The opinion of the Court did little to elucidate on the rights guaranteed by the First Amendment. The second, *Local Union No. 10 United Association of Journeymen Plumbers and Steamfitters* v. *Graham*,[5] added little more to the case literature on speech and press than did the first. It upheld a state court injunction against peaceful picketing carried on in conflict with the Virginia Right to Work Statute.[6] The immediate result of the picketing indicated potential effectiveness as a practical means of pressuring a general contractor to eliminate nonunion men from the project, whether employed by him or by subcontractors. The last case, *International Brotherhood of Teamsters* v. *Vogt*,[7] is perhaps more important for the *dicta* that is found in the opinion by Justice Frankfurter than it is for the decision itself.

The *Vogt* decision upheld the right of a state to enjoin picketing which coerces an employer to pressure his employees to join a union in violation of a declared state policy. Of itself this was not particularly significant. It reaffirmed prior decisions of the Court according to which, in enforcing some public policy, a state may constitutionally enjoin even peaceful picketing if it is aimed at preventing the effectuation of that policy. Significant, however, was the reappraisal by Mr. Justice Frankfurter of the picketing cases of the earlier decade. According to this, soon after the *Swing* and *Meadowmoor Dairies* cases the "Court came to realize that the broad pronouncements, but not the specific holding, of *Thornhill* had to yield 'to the impact of facts unforeseen,' or at least not sufficiently appreciated."[8] A review of the picketing cases up to and including *Giboney* v. *Empire Storage and Ice Co.* was taken to indicate that "The implied reassessments of the broad language of the *Thornhill* case was finally generalized in a series of cases sustaining injunctions against peaceful picketing, even when arising in the course of a labor controversy, when such picketing was counter to a valid state policy in a domain open to state regulation."[9]

It is impossible to determine whether Justice Frankfurter had "clear and present danger" in mind when he wrote of "broad pronouncements" that had to "yield" and of "implied reassessments" of the broad language of the *Thornhill* case, but it is quite probable that Mr. Justice Douglas did when he wrote in dissent: "The Court has now come full circle."[10]

Municipal Ordinances — Jehovah's Witnesses and Solicitation

During the decade of the 1940's municipal ordinances, like picketing, were fertile ground for "clear and present danger" accompanied with or supplemented by "preferred position." After the *Dennis* case, by 1960 the Supreme Court had reviewed five municipal ordinance cases three of which it reversed, but in none did "clear and present danger" serve as the measure and in only one was "preferred position" mentioned. Two of the cases dealt with the meeting of Jehovah's Witnesses in public parks, a type case in which both principles had played so prominent a part in the previous decade, two with "soliciting," and one with the distribution of handbills.

In the first of the Jehovah's Witness cases, *Fowler* v. *Rhode Island*,[11] the ordinance was struck down because it treated the services of this religious sect different from those of others, a discrimination violative of the First and Fourteenth Amendments. The ordinance prohibited political or religious addresses in public parks and as construed it permitted those of religious faiths other than Jehovah's Witnesses to hold meetings in these parks with impunity. The ordinance in the second Jehovah's Witness case, *Poulos* v. *New Hampshire*,[12] required that religious meetings in public parks be licensed. As construed, the purpose of this one was found merely to call for the adjustment of unrestrained religious exercise to the reasonable comfort and convenience of the entire city. It was upheld in spite of an unlawful refusal of a license because a reasonable method was available to correct the errors that had been committed in this particular instance. The Court distinguished *Cantwell* v. *Connecticut* and *Thomas* v. *Collins*. It said: "It is a *non sequitur* to say that First Amendment rights may not be regulated because they hold a preferred position in the hiarchy of the constitutional guarantees of the incidents of freedom."[13]

The ordinance in the two soliciting cases met the same fate as those in the Jehovah's Witness cases: one was upheld and the other was struck down. The constitutionality of the one that was upheld, *Breard* v. *Alexandria*,[14] was made to depend on a balancing of the householder's desire for privacy and a publisher's right to distribute in the

124

manner calculated to bring the best results. The ordinance forbade solicitation at private residences without prior consent of owners or occupants. The householder won, but to arrive at this decision the Court had to note a dissimilarity between the instant case and *Martin* v. *Struthers* which was concerned with free distribution—invitations to religious services—in which an opposite result was reached. Both cases were made to stand on their own facts, but the Court was careful to note that the liberties of speech and press were not ruled out by the mere fact that a commercial element and a profit motive were present as in the *Breard* case.

The second soliciting case, *Staub* v. *City* of *Baxley*,[15] was reminiscent of *Thomas* v. *Collins*. Again there was an attempt to regulate the solicitation of union membership. This time the Court chose to approach the problem of limitation from the point of view of form rather than of substance as it had earlier. "Prior restraint" sufficed to strike down the ordinance and there was no mention of "clear and present danger," the substantive approach that had been used in the case of the prior decade. The ordinance was said to bestow uncontrolled discretion and to make the enjoyment of speech contingent on the will of a mayor and council. By its terms it was an offense to "solicit" membership in any "organization, union or society" which required of its members the payment of dues or fees without first having obtained a "permit" from the Mayor and Council. The "permit" could be granted or refused depending on the character of the applicant, the nature of the organization, and its effect on the general welfare.

The last municipal ordinance case, *Talley* v. *California*,[16] held void a Los Angeles ordinance which forbade the distribution of handbills that did not carry the name and address of the person who prepared, distributed, or sponsored them. For authority the Court reached back to the pre-"clear and present danger" era and cited *Lovell* v. *Griffin*.

Libel and Obscenity

Within a year after the *Dennis* case, "clear and present danger" was urged as the proper standard when speech and press issues were raised in libelous utterance issues. The case was *Beauharnais* v. *Illinois*.[17] Five years later the same standard was urged in *Roth* v. *United States* and *Alberts* v. *California*, two obscenity cases that were decided together.[18] There was no need for the Court to consider the issues behind the phrase in any of these cases because it placed both libel and obscenity without the area of constitutionally protected speech. Had it not taken this course and had it followed Mr. Justice Douglas' contention in his dissent in the *Roth* case that this was not the answer—instead, that "Freedom of expression can be suppressed if, and to the extent that, it is so closely brigaded with illegal action as to be an inseparable part of it,"[19] it is entirely probable that the Court could then have been driven to the issues of "clear and present danger," or at least to its gravity of the evil refinement of *Dennis.* But as it reached its decisions, both by narrow margins, it found that in the light of history the First Amendment, unconditionally phrased though it is, "was not intended to protect every utterance."[20]

In the *Beauharnais* case, the Illinois Statute was upheld both as enacted and as construed by the State court as not a catchall enactment left at large, but rather as a law aimed at a specifically defined evil, i.e., words "liable to cause violence and disorder."[21] It was a pure and simple criminal libel law designed to punish libel of an individual. This was a common law crime that predated the Revolution which, the majority held, had not been abolished anywhere although the common law element of truth or good motives as no defense had been changed in most states shortly after the adoption of the Constitution either by judicial decision, statute or state constitution. Accordingly, the Illinois statute made truth and publication "with good motives and for justifiable ends" a defense, but both had to be present. Nevertheless, this statute is reminiscent of the old English statute *De Scandalis Magnatum* in the sense that it too represents drastic action taken during turbulent times to preserve the public peace. It was enacted in 1917 when Illinois was struggling to cope with problems created by a wave of new inhabitants sharply divided on national and religious as well as racial grounds, a history of which the majority opinion carefully reviewed to date. The object of the statute was to prevent friction among racial and religious groups, and in this particular case the petitioner had distributed anti-negro pamphlets of an inflammatory nature.

In so far as the *Roth* and the *Alberts* cases were concerned, the former involved the federal statute which makes punishable the mailing of material which is "obscene, lewd, lascivious, or filthy . . . or other publication of an indecent character,"[22] the latter involved the California statute which makes it a misdemeanor to keep for sale, or to advertise, material that is "obscene or indecent."[23] In the *Roth* case the trial judge had instructed the jury that "the words 'obscene, lewd and lascivious' as used in the law, signify that form of immorality which has relation to sexual impurity and has a tendency to excite lustful *thoughts.*" In the *Alberts* case the test applied by the judge was whether the material had "a substantial tendency to deprave or corrupt its readers by inciting lascivious *thoughts* or arising lustful desires."[24]

The Supreme Court found that the trial courts had sufficiently followed adequate standards and had used proper definitions of obscenity so that constitutional safeguards were met. Although it thought objectionable the early standard whereby material was judged merely by the effect of an isolated excerpt upon particularly susceptible persons, a standard which was developed in England and was formerly used by some American courts, it thought adequate the substituted standard which was followed here, i.e., "whether to the average person, applying contemporary community standards, the dominant theme of the material taken as a whole appeals to prurient interest."[25] Thus, by treating obscenity as anti-social in itself it saved the government from having to show the potentially dangerous character of material it seeks to ban as obscene. But as it did this the Court drew a rather interesting distinction between sex and obscenity. As distinguished from obscene material which it defined as "material which deals with sex in a manner appealing to prurient interest," sex itself was defined as "a great and mysterious motive force in human life . . . indisputably . . . a subject of absorbing interest to mankind through the ages; it is one of the vital problems of human interest and public concern."[26] And as to these "vital problems" it quoted from *Thornhill* v. *Alabama* to the effect that freedom of speech and press embrace at least the right to discuss publicly and truthfully all matters of public concern "without previous restraint or fear of subsequent punishment."[27]

An interesting feature of both the *Roth* and *Alberts* cases, particularly of *Roth*, is the manner in which the Court was willing to trust the jury with more responsibility over facts than it was earlier in *Dennis.* Now the jury was permitted to determine for itself whether certain books, pictures, and circulars offended "the common conscience of the community by present-day standards."[28] Indeed, the jurors were told that they alone were the judges of what the common conscience of the community was. In *Dennis* the Court upheld the trial judge when he reserved for himself the effect of the acts complained of on the conscience of the community, i.e., whether or not they created a "clear and present danger" that they would bring about an evil that

127

Congress has a right to prevent. No doubt the difference was due to the fact that in *Dennis* there were crucial questions of national security whereas in *Roth* and *Alberts* there were only questions of dirty books, pamphlets and circulars.

On the same day that the Supreme Court upheld the federal and California obscenity statutes it also upheld a New York law permitting "limited injunctive remedy" against the sale and distribution of written or printed matter considered obscene. In default of the surrender of such publications, an order for their seizure was authorized. The law also entitled persons enjoined "to a trial of the issues within one day after joinder of issues" and to a decision "within two days of the conclusion of the trial."[29] In this particular case, *Kingsley Books, Inc.* v. *Brown*,[30] an injunction was granted *pendente lite*, subsequent to which the booklets involved were enjoined as "dirt for dirt's sake" by a judge sitting in equity. The statute was attacked from the standpoint of prior restraint rather than from that of obscenity.

Just as he had done during the prior decade, Mr. Justice Frankfurter again mounted an offensive against making a rule of decision of a phrase. Earlier he had objected to "clear and present danger" as a "felicitous phrase" taken out of context and distorted as a consequence, now he rejected "prior restraint" as neither "a self-wielding sword," nor as something that could serve "as a talismanic test."[31] Instead, as spokesman for the majority he advocated an application of the thought behind the phrase, i.e., quoting from Professor Freund, "a pragmatic assessment of its operation in the particular circumstances." The Justice found the injunction secured pursuant to the New York law no more a "prior restraint" on freedom of the press than the punishment imposed in the *Alberts* case which the Court had upheld. There the defendant had been fined, sentenced to imprisonment for sixty days, and placed on probation for two years on condition that he not violate the obscenity statute. From this rationale it would seem that a little prior restraint is not *per se* unconstitutional so long as it is "closely confined so as to preclude what may fairly be deemed licensing or censorship."[32] But then, *Kingsley Books, Inc.* v. *Brown* was another five to four decision.

Subversion and the Court Without "Clear and Present Danger"

Six years after the *Dennis* case the Supreme Court came to grips with the Smith Act a second time in *Yates* v. *United States*,[33] The circumstances that surrounded the second encounter were, however,

128

quite different from those of the first. In 1951 when *Dennis* was decided and the conviction of the eleven top Communists in this country upheld, the Korean "police action" raged and it threatened to launch World War III at any moment. By 1957 when the *Yates* case was decided, not only had the "police action" been concluded, but within less than two years the Premier of the Soviet Union would tour this country from coast to coast at the invitation of the President of the United States and he would be entertained at the White House. The "gravity of the 'evil' [the Communist threat]," it would seem, was much more "discounted by its improbability" than it had been six years earlier. Perhaps even in 1957 the "calmer times" about which Justice Black had written in his *Dennis* dissent prevailed. But whether or not that was so, in the *Yates* decision there was no question of "clear and present danger." That had not been heard of for some time, with or without Judge Hand's refinement.

Prior to the *Yates* decision, the closest that the Court came to the historic test of the prior decade took place in *Harisiades* v. *Shaughnessy* decided in 1952,[34] a case in which the ultimate question was whether a legally resident alien may be deported because of membership in the Communist Party that had terminated before the Alien Registration Act, 1940,[35] became law. The First Amendment was one of the barriers invoked against the constitutionality of an act that could be so interpreted. It was contended that even in joining an organization that taught and advocated the overthrow of the Government by force and violence, the alien had merely exercised his First Amendment rights of free speech, press and assembly. There had been a finding below, which was not questioned before the Supreme Court, that during the particular alien's membership the Communist Party did so teach and advocate the overthrow of the Government by force and violence.

With Mr. Justice Jackson writing for the majority, the Court dismissed the First Amendment contention as one that seemed based on a misconception—one that assumed that this Amendment left Congress no room to distinguish between advocacy by the lawful elective process and advocacy of change by force and violence. Instead, the Court reasoned, the Constitution left no excuse for the violent approach when it provided for the attack by ballot. As the Court recognized its duty to distinguish between the two types of advocacy it noted what it termed the two opposite extremes of avoiding the difficulty of this duty: the Communist method of avoiding the inquiry by suppressing everything distasteful on the one hand, and permitting incitement to violent overthrow unless it seems likely of immediate success on the other. However, the Court thought that the test applicable to the Communist Party had been too recently stated to make further discussion profitable at this time.

By the time *Yates* v. *United States* reached the Supreme Court, four of the eight Justices who had participated in *Dennis* were no longer on the Court,[36] of the four of the majority who had formed the plurality in *Dennis* that favored the amended version of "clear and present danger,"[37] one was left;[38] moreover, of the six who had expressed belief in "clear and present danger" in one form or another in *Dennis*,[39] only three were left,[40] and of these three two had been in dissent in the earlier case.[41] If disenchantment was felt over the ramifications of the *Dennis* case, the opportunity for a change was present as well as the climate.

The fourteen petitioners in the *Yates* case were from the lower echelon of the Communist Party hierarchy. In a single count indictment returned in 1951 they had been charged with "conspiracy [1] to advocate and teach the duty and necessity of overthrowing the Government of the United States by force and violence, and [2] to organize, as the Communist Party of the United States, a society of persons who so advocate and teach, all with the intent of causing the overthrow of the Government by force and violence as speedily as circumstances would permit." They were charged with twenty-three overt acts in the conspiracy that was alleged to have originated in 1940 and to have continued until the date of the indictment. Among these acts was membership in the Communist Party knowing of its unlawful purposes, and leadership in carrying out its policies and activities; causing units of the Party to be organized in California and elsewhere; writing articles on the proscribed advocacy and teachings of the Party that were published in the *Daily Worker* and other Party organs; conducting schools to indoctrinate members in the Party's advocacy and teachings; and recruiting new members, particularly among employees in key industries.

As the Court proceeded to consider the problems presented, it approached them from the point of view of three main issues. First, there was the question of the meaning of the term "organize" in the Smith Act,[42] and the effect of the statute of limitations on it. The petitioners contended that the Communist Party was organized by 1945 at the latest and therefore that this part of the indictment was barred by the three-year statute of limitations. The Government argued that the term "organize" connotes a continuing process which goes on throughout the life of an organization and includes recruiting new members, forming new units, regrouping and expanding, etc., as the trial court had charged. The Supreme Court, however, could find no evidence to support this latter thesis. It applied the familiar rule that criminal statutes are to be strictly construed, the term "organize" was given its narrow meaning, and the organizational part of the indictment was thrown out as barred by the statute of limitations.

Second, there was the question of the trial court's instructions to the jury. The petitioners objected to those that had been given because the trial judge had refused to instruct that to convict there had to be advocacy of a kind calculated to "incite" persons to the forcible overthrow of the government—that mere advocacy of forcible overthrow as an abstract doctrine was protected by the First Amendment. The trial judge, however, had rejected any necessity that might have existed at one time for any such distinction as having been removed by the *Dennis* decision. In the trial court the Government had also requested that the jury be instructed in terms of incitement, but before the Supreme Court it urged that the constitutional dividing line was between advocacy as such, irrespective of incitement, and mere discussion or exposition of violent overthrow as an abstract theory.

The Supreme Court disagreed with the Government and held that the distinction that the trial court had rejected is one that has consistently been recognized by the Supreme Court, and one which the legislative history of the Smith Act shows Congress was both aware of and did not intend to disregard. The district court was said to have misconceived the *Dennis* holding. Writing for the majority, Justice Harlan proceeded to summarize this holding in one sentence. In the process he purged it of Chief Justice Vinson's adoption of Judge Hand's rephrasing of Holmes' historic test or, for that matter, of any reference to "clear and present danger" at all. "The essence of the *Dennis* holding," Justice Harlan declared, "was that indoctrination of a group in preparation for future violent action, as well as exhortation for immediate action, by advocacy found to be directed to 'action for the accomplishment' of forcible overthrow, to violence as 'a rule or principle of action,' and employing 'language of incitement,' . . . is not constitutionally protected when the group is of sufficient size and cohesiveness, is sufficiently oriented towards action, and other circumstances are such as reasonably to justify apprehension that action will occur."[43]

The Court construed this as quite different from the view that mere doctrinal justification of forcible overthrow is punishable *per se* under the Smith Act if it is engaged in without the intent to accomplish overthrow. The latter is not a question of being urged to do something, now or in the future, but rather of being urged to believe in something. The Court thought this too remote from concrete action to be within the realm of that which was condemned by *Dennis*, i.e., the advocacy of violence as a rule or principle couched in language of incitement.

The view taken by the Court of Appeals was different from that of the district court, but it was found equally misconceived. Seemingly, the Court of Appeals had recognized that there must be some association of the proscribed advocacy with action, an area in which the instructions to the jury fell short. Nevertheless, it had thought that the requirement that there be proof of an overt act provided an adequate substitute. The Supreme Court again disagreed and judged that the overt act would not necessarily evidence the character of the advocacy, nor would an agreement to advocate forcible overthrow which does not call for advocacy of action of itself be an unlawful conspiracy. In *Dennis*, "[i]t was action, not advocacy, that was to be postponed until 'circumstances' would 'permit.' "[44]

Third, although the determinations already reached would have required a reversal, the Court proceeded to examine the evidence in the exercise of its power to "direct the entry of such appropriate judgment . . . as [might] be just under the circumstances"[45] The effect of setting aside the "organizing" part of the indictment was found to dilute a substantial part of the evidence that the Government had relied on in that aspect of the case. Then, the Government and the trial court had proceeded on the theory that the advocacy of an abstract doctrine was sufficient to offend the Smith Act. Moreover, as indicated by the record in the case and by its briefs, the Government was considered to have proceeded on the theory that a case could be made by showing an active identity between the petitioners and the Party. However, the Court had already rejected as insufficient the advocacy of an abstract doctrine of forcible overthrow, now it found the record deficient in so far as Party advocacy or teaching in the sense of a call to forcible action at some future time was concerned. At best it could find only a half dozen scattered incidents, most of which were not connected with the petitioners or had happened many years prior to the indictment.

The Court ordered acquittals for five of the petitioners and new trials for the nine others.

In the *Dennis* case certiorari had been limited to §§ 2 and 3 of the Smith Act, and there it had been settled that the "advocacy" and "conspiracy" sections of the act did not violate the First and Fifth Amendments. In the *Yates* case there was no limitation on the grant of certiorari and the indictments in the two cases were virtually similar. The latter case provided an opportunity for the Court as it was now constituted to explore the scope and the extent of its *Dennis* holding of an earlier date. As the Court did this nothing was said about "clear and present danger." The outcome was the substitution of acts for the texts that had been relied on in the earlier case. In effect, this was a partial vindication of the positions taken by Justices Black and Douglas in the *Dennis* case although in the later case, as they dissented in part and concurred in part, they still would have held the Smith Act completely unconstitutional. For the time being at least, the upshot of the *Yates* case was that guilt cannot be inferred solely from active membership in the Communist Party— that one cannot be convicted on the basis of "what Marx or Engels or someone else wrote or advocated as much as a hundred or more years ago,"[46] without a further showing of unlawful advocacy on the part of the person himself. This, however, had been decided by a seven-man Court, and of these seven only three gave unqualified support to the opinion of the Court:[47] one concurred in the result, two concurred in part and dissented in part,[48] and one dissented from the decision and the opinion in their entirety.[49]

THE LEGISLATIVE PROCESS AND THE FIRST AMENDMENT

A Kinship Proclaimed

The kinship that was judicially proclaimed to exist between the right of free speech and the process of legislative inquiry presented the most interesting development of the post-*Dennis* decade. The unique feature was that it was proclaimed to exist at the state level as well as at the more familiar Congressional level. This was said not only of the guarantees of the First Amendment as a limitation on the power of Congress to investigate, but also as a limitation on state legislatures by way of the Fourteenth Amendment. There was novelty to the idea, but in reality it was only the latest chapter in the long history of legislative inquiry as a part of the legislative process which, in this country, had its start as early as 1792 when a select committee of the House of Representatives conducted an inquiry into the reasons for the defeat of General St. Clair by the Indians.

The kinship between the First Amendment and the federal power to investigate arose in 1957 in *Watkins* v. *United States*.⁵⁰ The petitioner in that case had been summoned to testify before the House Un-American Activities Committee. He had testified freely as to his own activities and associations, but he had refused to testify as to others he had known to have been members of the Communist Party on the basis that the questions concerning these others were outside the scope of the Committee's activities and not relevant to its work. As a result, he was convicted for violating a statute that dated back as early as 1847 which made it a misdemeanor for a witness before a Congressional committee to refuse to answer questions "pertinent to the question under inquiry."⁵¹

When the case reached the Supreme Court of the United States, was reversed and remanded, the decision was based on the due process clause of the Fifth Amendment. However, by way of dicta, the rights guaranteed by the First were brought in. Speaking for the Court, the Chief Justice summarized the history of Congressional investigations and he took cognizance of the post-World War II type aimed principally, but not exclusively, at subversion in government. As he approached the problem he recognized that there are limitations as well as breadth to the power of Congress to investigate. Thus, no investigation can be an end in itself and there is no authority for Congress to act as a law enforcement or a trial agency. Moreover, Congress cannot investigate for the self-aggrandisement of the investigators any more than it can require a witness to give evidence against himself or subject him to unreasonable search and seizure. There is, he recognized, a duty on the part of all to cooperate in the efforts of Congress to obtain facts needed for intelligent legislation, but that presupposes that the constitutional rights of witnesses will be respected by the Congress as they are by the courts. Although an investigation is not law in itself, it is a part of lawmaking which is justified solely as an adjunct to the legislative process. Then, continued the Chief Justice, "the First Amendment may be invoked against infringement of the protected freedoms by law or by lawmaking."

The Chief Justice did not underestimate the "arduous and delicate

134

task" that is presented by the balancing of the congressional need for particular information as against the individual and personal interest in privacy. However, the Court had already recognized the restraints that the Bill of Rights places on congressional investigations in *United States* v. *Rumely*.[52] That case, wrote the Chief Justice, established "that, when First Amendment rights are threatened, the delegation of power to the committee must be clearly revealed in its character."[53] Then, reaching back to *Kilbourn* v. *Thompson*,[54] a case that grew out of Kilbourn's refusal to answer questions relating to the failure of Jay Cook and Co., he found that although not all inquiries of private matters are barred, nevertheless, "such an investigation into individual affairs is invalid if unrelated to any legislative purpose." Against this background the Chief Justice went on to say: "The critical element is the existence of, and the weight to be ascribed to, the interest of the Congress in demanding disclosures from an unwilling witness. We cannot simply assume, however, that every congressional investigation is justified by a public need that overbalances any private rights affected. To do so would be to abdicate the responsibility placed by the Constitution upon the judiciary to insure that the Congress does not unjustifiably encroach upon an individual's right to privacy nor abridge his liberty of speech, press, religion or assembly."[55] The Court held that the resolution which authorized the Un-American Activities Committee[56] did not meet constitutional standards, especially when read in the light of the history of the Committee to date.

The kinship between free speech and the state legislative power to investigate came up in *Sweezy* v. *New Hampshire*,[57] decided on the same day as the *Watkins* case. This was another instance in which the Court could muster a majority to arrive at a decision but not to join in an opinion. The Chief Justice announced an opinion in which he was joined by Justices Black, Douglas and Brennan; Mr. Justice Frankfurter, joined by Mr. Justice Harlan, announced an opinion in which he concurred in the result; Justices Clark and Burton dissented.

The background for the case was the 1951 New Hampshire Subversive Activities Act which defined criminal conduct in the nature of sedition. It declared "subversive organizations" unlawful, ordered them dissolved, and made "subversive persons" ineligible for employment by the state government.[58] In 1953 the legislature adopted a "Joint Resolution Relating to the Investigation of Subversive Activities"[59] which constituted the Attorney General of the State a one-man committee to enforce the 1951 act. The petitioner testified freely before this one-man committee as to his own past conduct and associations; moreover, he denied that he had ever been a member of the Communist Party or that he had participated in any program to overthrow the government by force or violence; he refused, however, to answer questions concerning the Progressive Party of New Hampshire and concerning persons he had known in that organization, or to answer questions about a lecture he had delivered at the University of New Hampshire. His reasons for this refusal were found in a statement he had read at the outset of the hearing in which he declared that he would not answer questions not pertinent to the inquiry or which transgressed the limitations of the First Amendment as applied through the Fourteenth. According to the procedure set forth in the resolution, the petitioner was then summoned to appear before the State Superior Court and when he persisted again in his refusal to answer the questions he was adjudged in contempt. The Supreme Court of New Hampshire affirmed.[60]

The state court had decided that the need for the legislature to be informed on a subject as elemental as self-preservation of the government outweighed the deprivation of constitutional rights that resulted. The Supreme Court of the United States could have based its decision in this same area and held that circumstances could not justify such an assumption. Instead, the Chief Justice chose, as he had in the *Watkins* case, to delve by way of dicta into the realm of encroachment upon the constitutional liberties of individuals by legislative investigators—this time with the state level added to the federal. Once more he did not doubt that there is a right of legislative inquiry, but he laid emphasis on the fact that the right is subject to limitation. He stressed the importance "that the exercise of the power of compulsory process be carefully circumscribed when the investigative process tends to impinge upon such highly sensitive areas as freedom of speech or press, freedom of political association, and freedom of communication of ideas, particularly in the academic community."[61]

Since the responsibility for the proper conduct of investigations rests upon the legislature itself, when it chooses to authorize inquiries in its behalf by committees of its own creation it must also provide for adequate supervision. Broad, ill-defined jurisdiction can, continued the Chief Justice, nullify this safeguard, and it is because of this that an authorizing resolution can be of particular significance since it can reveal the amount of discretion conferred. To the Chief

Justice and those who joined with him,[62] there was nothing that connected the questioning of Sweezy with fundamental state interest. The record failed to reveal what the reasonable or reliable information was that led the Attorney General to question the petitioner. Moreover, the mandate vested in the Attorney General was so sweeping and uncertain that it was his decision rather than that of the legislature that picked the subject of the investigation, the witness, and the questions. In effect, the legislature had insulated itself from the witnesses whose rights might be affected by the investigation rather than to make known the data it wanted. There was no assurance that the questions the petitioner refused to answer fell within the type of information the legislature sought. The use of the contempt power was found to have violated the requirements of due process.

Justice Frankfurter approached the problem from a different angle. To him the question was not whether the state legislature had acted correctly as it made the Attorney General a one-man committee— that was a state matter to be determined by state law—instead, the case had to be considered as though the entire legislature had posed the questions. As between academic freedom and the right of a citizen to political privacy on one side, versus the right of the state to self-protection on the other, striking a balance implied the exercise of judgment, "[an] inescapable judicial task in giving substantive content, legally enforced, to the Due Process Clause,"[63] ultimately committed to the Supreme Court. And in this particular instance the rights of the individual had to prevail because on the record the subordinating interest of the state was not compelling.

The Kinship Reduced to a "Threat"

Before the *Watkins* and *Sweezy* cases were decided a witness before a congressional committee who chose not to answer questions had two alternatives: he could simply refuse to answer and take his chances on a conviction for contempt, or he could invoke the Fifth Amendment and suffer social ostracism or even loss of employment. When these cases were decided the effect seemed to be to add a third alternative, or at least another defense, that could be used before state as well as federal legislative committees. He could invoke the First Amendment itself, or the First as applied to the states through the Fourteenth. However, the dicta on which this third alternative or added defense was largely based failed to stand the test of time. Within two years its effectiveness was largely reduced to that of a "threat" in the sense that it never achieved the status of a flat holding. Since the initial statement of the dicta at the federal and state levels, this has been distinguished whenever it has been invoked as setting forth a principle of law. Thus far that has happened on four occasions.[64] All were five to four decisions. For this reason the "threat" could well become a reality should the ever-changing membership of the Court shift in a direction that would tip the present delicate balance in the opposite direction. An oddity of all of these cases, starting with *Watkins* and *Sweezy,* is that they were decided in pairs at two year intervals, 1957, 1959 and 1961.

When the second pair of cases came up in 1959, again one presented the question of federal and the other of state legislative power but this time the results were different. Mr. Justice Clark who had dissented in the two earlier cases had now mustered a majority to support his views. He wrote the opinion of the Court in the case involving state power; Mr. Justice Harlan who had apparently been with the majority in the *Watkins* case, but who had only concurred in the result in the *Sweezy* case, wrote the opinion of the Court in the one involving federal power.

The question of state power again involved New Hampshire's one-man legislative investigating committee. The case was *Uphaus* v. *Wyman.*[65] This time the one-man committee which was, *inter alia,* authorized to determine whether there were subversive persons or organizations in the state was interested in a summer camp that was maintained by a voluntary corporation organized under the laws of the state. Although the camp's Executive Director testified freely as to his own activities, he refused to produce the guest lists and other documents for the camp for two summers. As a consequence he was adjudged in civil contempt. He contended that the state was precluded from delving into the investigation of subversives because Congress had completely occupied the field by the Smith Act as construed by *Pennsylvania* v. *Nelson.*[66] He also contested for vagueness the validity of the resolution that set up the committee. In addition he questioned the relevancy of the documents sought, and he invoked his rights to free speech and association.

As to the first contention, the Court did not consider the sweep of its decision in the *Nelson* case to be as broad as the petitioner would have had it. The right of a state to protect itself against sedition was not impaired by it, the Court now said, only the enforceability of a state act which proscribes the same conduct as the federal act does.

The *Nelson* case, it continued, did not deprive a state of the right to protect itself against sedition, but condemned "a race between federal and state prosecutors to the courthouse door."[67]

The case had already been sent back once to the state court to have it considered in the light of *Sweezy* v. *New Hampshire,* but all that the New Hampshire court did was to reaffirm its earlier decision. On the second time around, the Supreme Court of the United States found that its own earlier decision presented no problem. The academic and political freedoms discussed in *Sweezy* two years earlier were said not to exist to the same degree in the present case because the summer camp was neither a university nor a political party. The Court now considered a state matter the authority of the committee to act as it did and this had been upheld by the highest court of the jurisdiction. That left the question whether the public interest in finding out the identity of the individuals that the committee sought overbalanced the individual, private interests which the appellant asserted. This was answered in the affirmative.

It now seemed only logical to the Supreme Court that the Attorney General of the state should seek first to find out what persons were present in the state as he sought to determine whether there were subversives present. His use of the subpoena the Court now found not burdensome. Moreover, although the evidence of a link between the camp and subversive activities may not have been conclusive, the record indicated sufficient relevancy to support the Attorney General's action and offered sufficient justification for the investigation. The camp was a public one and state law required that a register open to sheriffs and public officers be maintained. The fact that compliance with the subpoena could then mean that the register might be exposed to further scrutiny was an inescapable incident. The Court found governmental interest in self-preservation "sufficiently compelling to subordinate the interest in associational privacy."[68]

Barenblatt v. *United States*[69] presented the question of federal power in the second pair of cases. The case grew out of the House Un-American Activities Committee investigation of Communist infiltration into the field of education. Barenblatt, a former graduate student, teaching fellow and college instructor, refused to answer questions as to Communist Party membership but he disclaimed reliance on the Fifth Amendment. Instead, he relied on a previously prepared memorandum based on the First, Ninth and Tenth Amendments in which he contested the right of the Committee to inquire into his

139

political and religious beliefs, or any of his "other personal or private affairs" or associated activities.

Like the Uphaus case, this one was also before the Supreme Court on the second time around after it had been sent back once to the Court of Appeals for further consideration in the light of *Watkins* v. *United States*. As the Court now disposed of the case on its merits it prefaced its opinion with a sort of exordium in which it repeated substantially all that it had said two years earlier about the congressional power of inquiry, and then it went on to refute all of the petitioner's objections which it summarized as three in number.

First, citing the *Watkins* decision, the petitioner objected that the compelling of testimony by the Subcommittee "was neither legislatively authorized nor constitutionally permissible because of the vagueness"[70] of House Rule XI. The Court, however, did not agree that *Watkins* stood for that proposition. While there was criticism of Rule XI in that decision, there was not, the Court now said, the "broad and inflexible holding" the petitioner now sought to attribute to it. Moreover, the Court now looked upon Rule XI as only a part of the total *mise en scène*. And even granting the vagueness of Rule XI, it now held that it could not read this rule "in isolation from its long history in the House of Representatives," which it reviewed. In the light of this history it found the "legislative gloss"[71] on this rule so compelling that it rendered unassailable the legislative authority of the committee to conduct the inquiry under scrutiny.

Second, the petitioner objected that he was not adequately appraised of the pertinency of the Subcommittee's questions to the subject of the inquiry. In the *Watkins* case there was specific objection to questions on the ground of pertinency which the Court could not find in the record of the present case—at best, only contemplated objection to questions yet unasked which was buried in the context of a general challenge to the Subcommittee's power. Not only did the petitioner's memorandum of constitutional objections indicate to the Court an awareness on his part of the Subcommittee's authority and purpose, but the subject-matter of the inquiry had been announced at the start of the investigation, and he had heard the testimony of the witness who had preceded him and who had identified him as a former member of an alleged Communist student organization. Moreover, unlike the petitioner in the earlier case, this petitioner had refused to answer questions as to his own Communistic affiliations.

Third, the petitioner objected that the questions he refused to answer

140

"infringed rights protected by the First Amendment." The Court started off its discussion of this aspect of the case by repeating what it had said in the *Watkins* case: "It is manifest that despite the adverse effects which follow upon compelled disclosure of private matters, not all such inquiries are barred . . . The critical element is the existence of, and the weight to be ascribed to, the interest of the Congress in demanding disclosures from an unwilling witness."[72]

The Court also reached to *Dennis* v. *United States* to rest on the right of self-preservation, "the ultimate value of any society,"[73] the right of Congress to legislate in the field of Communist activity in this country and to conduct investigations pursuant thereto. Here, as there, the Court refused to view the Communist Party as an ordinary political party and it distinguished *Sweezy* v. *New Hampshire* as it rejected the idea that Congress should be denied its power to investigate solely because it was carried into the field of education. It was one thing, the Court said, to question Sweezy, without first having shown that he had even been connected with the Communist Party, as to the contents of a university lecture he had delivered and as to his connection with a party then on the ballot in twenty-six states, and another thing to inquire into the extent of the infiltration of Communists into universities or elsewhere. The Court rejected as "a too constricted view of the nature of the investigatory process,"[74] and as not supported by the record, the contention that this particular investigation was aimed at the theoretical classroom discussion rather than at the revolutionary aspects of communism. This time the balance between the interests of the individual and those of the government was struck in favor of the latter. The prohibitions of the First Amendment were found not to have been offended.

The "Threat" Further Reduced

The third pair of cases was concerned solely with the power to investigate at the Congressional level. The issues raised in the two cases were almost identical and they were both based on the same record. They involved convictions of witnesses who refused to answer questions when, in response to summons, they testified before the House Un-American Activities Committee which was then investigating Communist infiltration into basic industries in the South and Communist Party propaganda in that part of the country. The petitioners had followed one another on the stand and they had both refused to answer questions as to Communist Party affiliation or, for that matter, any questions propounded by the Committee. In neither case did the witness base his refusal to answer on the right against self-incrimination, but rather either on the legality of the Committee to interrogate or on the pertinency of the questions. In both instances the questioning was objected to as violative of the First Amendment. The effect of the two decisions was to reaffirm *Barenblatt* v. *United States* decided two years earlier, and to further reduce the "threat" of *Watkins* v. *United* States decided four years earlier, or perhaps even to place the latter case to one side as an isolated incident.

In the first of the third pair of cases, *Wilkinson* v. *United States*,[75] the petitioner was subpoenaed soon after he arrived in Atlanta to stir opposition to the Committee which was then holding hearings there. He claimed that the sole purpose of the Committee in bringing him before it was to harass and expose him. He also raised the issue of the vagueness of Rule XI and the First Amendment. The last of these issues, that of the First Amendment, the Court disposed of rather summarily. It considered the basic questions that were raised as thoroughly canvassed in the *Barenblatt* case. All that had been said there it considered equally applicable here; "it would serve no purpose to enlarge this opinion with a paraphrased repetition of what was in that opinion thoroughly and carefully expressed,"[76] the Court held.

Attempts by Wilkinson to distinguish the two cases on the basis that he was merely participating in public discussion about the Committee and attempting to influence public opinion for its abolishment were of no avail. The fact that at the time he might have been engaged in lawful conduct could not, the Court now held, rule out an investigation of his Communist activities connected therewith. That had been settled in *Barenblatt* which established that "it is the nature of the Communist activity involved, whether the momentary conduct is legitimate or illegitimate politically, that establishes the Government's overbalancing interest."[77] The First Amendment claim was rejected as indistinguishable from that in *Barenblatt*.

Although the Court recognized now, as it had in *Watkins,* that the language of Rule XI could not be said "to state with adequate precision the subject under inquiry by a subcommittee at any given hearing," nevertheless *Watkins* provided the way around the obstacle. Quoting from that earlier decision, the Court said: "The authorizing resolution, the remarks of the chairman or members of the committee, or even the nature of the proceedings themselves, might reveal the subject under inquiry."[78] Just as in *Barenblatt*, required concreteness was found to exist among various sources such as the resolution authorizing the particular Atlanta hearing, the pattern of interrogation, statements of the Staff Director, and the Chairman at the opening of the hearing, all of which indicated a legislative purpose.

The harassment and public exposure issue was brushed aside as equally not persuasive. The prime purpose of the hearing, the Court noted, was to investigate Communist propaganda activities in the South. The fact that the petitioner might not have been summoned had he not come to Atlanta served to illustrate the very point. Moreover, the Court did not consider that it was its function to speculate as to the motivations that prompted the individual members of the committee to summon the petitioner. It was sufficient if a legislative purpose of a House of Congress was being served and, again quoting from *Watkins*, it held that motives alone would not violate an investigation instituted by one of these Houses.

In the second of the third pair of cases, *Braden* v. *United States*,[79] there was the added issue that Braden had not simply been asked whether he was or had been a Communist Party member, but whether he was a member at "the instant" he affixed his signature to a letter which urged opposition to certain bills in Congress. The petitioner claimed not only that writing such a letter was constitutionally protected, but he pointed out other legitimate activity in which he had been engaged. As a consequence, he argued that the Committee's conduct indicated a lack of proper legislative purpose and a bent on persecution of one who publicly opposed it.

Again, as in *Wilkinson*, the Court reaffirmed rather than differentiated *Barenblatt* which, it said, had not confined congressional investigatory activity to overt criminal activity nor to the Communist Party itself. Instead, it had upheld an investigation of Communist activity in education. In the present case the inquiry was directed at Communist Party propaganda in the South. The Court held: "Information as to the extent to which the Communist Party was utilizing legitimate organizations and causes in its propaganda efforts in that region was surely not constitutionally beyond the reach of the subcommittee's inquiry."[80]

There was also the added issue of the pertinency of questions asked having been left to the jury as well as the effect of reliance by the petitioner on a misunderstanding of the previous decisions of the Court. Both were resolved against the petitioner. In the case of the jury issue, not only had the petitioner not made timely objection, but *Sin-*

clair v. *United States*,[81] one of the Teapot Dome Congressional investigation contempt of Congress cases, had settled relevancy and materi-
ality as questions of law. As for a misconception of prior decisions
of the Court, that again was held foreclosed by *Sinclair* v. *United
States* in which it was held that a mistaken view of the law was not
a defense.

Four Voices in Dissent

Uphaus, Barenblatt, Wilkinson, and *Branden* were all decided by
the barest of margins. They were all five to four decisions and there
were strong, even impassioned, dissents which could very well spell
out the law should there be a shift in the favor of the present minority
of but one among nine, or even a change in the composition of the
Court in the same direction.

Perhaps most impassioned among the dissenters was Mr. Justice
Black. In his *Barenblatt* dissent he took exception to the combination
of reasons the majority relied on to justify what he considered an
infringement of the unequivocal prohibitions of the First Amendment. First, the balancing of interests, governmental versus private,
he considered an attempt to rewrite the First Amendment; second,
the notion that the right of the government to self-preservation even
entitles it to abridge First Amendment freedoms he dismissed as
resting on an unarticulated premise—"that this Nation's security hangs
upon its power to punish people because of what they think, speak
or write about, or because of those with whom they associate for
political purposes,"[82] third, the assertion that it was only Communists
that the Committee was after marked, in his judgment, "another major
step in the progressively increasing retreat from the safeguards of the
First Amendment."[83] He found no consolation in the assertion that the
Court would not allow this trend "to overwhelm us." For, he doubted
that the holding could be contained and he saw danger in it to every
group—in *Braden* even to the Negro who could be deprived by it of the
aid of whites who would speak in his behalf. Moreover, as he remarked
later in his *Wilkinson* dissent, the charge that someone is a Communist
is so common that hardly anyone in public life escapes it. Indeed, as he
noted in his later dissent, "[e]very member of this Court has, on
one occasion or another, been so designated."[84]

In *Wilkinson* Justice Black decried as a "sweeping abdication of
judicial power" the lack of concern for the motivation that prompted
the members of the congressional committee to summon the petitioners;

in *Braden* he expressed the belief that there were no longer any limits to congressional encroachment in the field of individual freedom except such as a majority of the Court might choose to set by a value-weighing case-by-case approach. In *Barenblatt* he had summed it up as follows: "Ultimately all the questions in this case really boil down to one—whether we as a people will try fearfully and futilely to preserve democracy by adopting totalitarian methods, or whether in accordance with our traditions and our Constitution we will have the confidence and courage to be free."[85]

In *Braden* Justice Black warned: "The Founders of this Nation were not then willing to trust the definition of First Amendment freedoms to Congress or this Court, nor am I now. History and the affairs of the present day show that the Founders were Right. There are grim reminders all around this world that the distance between individual liberty and firing squads is not always as far as it seems."[86] The Justice would have overruled *Barenblatt*, "its forerunners and its progeny," and returned to the language of the Bill of Rights. The new and different course the Court now followed was, in his words, "too dangerous."[87]

Even as he joined Justice Brennan's dissent in *Uphaus* v. *Wyman*, Justice Douglas made clear that he had ideas of his own on the subject. What these were he indicated in his dissents in *Wilkinson* and *Braden*.

In his *Wilkinson* dissent he noted that the Committee on Un-American Activities was authorized to investigate "the extent, character, and objects of un-American propaganda activities in the United States."[88] He considered it a dangerous leap to conclude that criticism of the Committee was within the scope of this authority. And in his opinion, that leap the Court had to take to conclude that the Committee acted within the scope of its authority in asking the questions that it did concerning Wilkinson's purpose to develop hostile sentiment toward the Committee and to bring pressure on Congress to preclude these particular hearings. That ran counter to the Justice's belief that "[c]riticism of government finds sanctuary in several portions of the First Amendment."[89] He considered it a part of free speech and as embraced by freedom of the press. But he saw even more than only these two involved here. Within the same category he placed the right to peaceable assemblies and the right to petition "for a redress of grievances." These were the reasons why he would have narrowly construed the authorizing resolution so that it would not proscribe criticism of the Committee.

In his *Braden* dissent Justice Douglas noted that in *Watkins* v.

United States the Court had decided six to one that "when First Amendment rights are threatened, the delegation of power to the Committee must be clearly revealed in its character"—that "there is no congressional power to expose for the sake of exposure." He further reviewed the holding in that case as to the extent a witness is entitled to "knowledge of the subject to which the interrogation is deemed pertinent" before he chooses whether to answer or not to answer.[90] Then he went on to review *Sweezy* v. *New Hampshire* decided on the same day as *Watkins*. As a consequence, the Justice believed that Braden was entitled to rely on both of these, especially since he had been called before the Committee in July, 1958, eleven months before the decision in *Barenblatt*, the precedent on which the majority relied as it denied Braden's claims. "If Watkins and Sweezy decided anything," declared Justice Douglas, "they decided that before inroads in the First Amendment domain may be made, some demonstrable connection with communism must first be established and the matter be plainly shown to be within the scope of the Committee's authority. Otherwise the Committee may roam at will, requiring any individual to disclose his association with any group or with any publication which is unpopular with the Committee and which it can discredit by calling it communistic."[91]

Justice Brennan wrote an extensive dissent in the *Uphaus* case and shorter dissents in the *Barenblatt* and *Wilkinson* cases. In addition, he concurred in Justice Douglas' dissent in the *Braden* case. The central thread of all of his dissents was "exposure for exposure's sake." In his *Uphaus* dissent, the more extensive of the three, he indicated that he fully appreciated "the delicacy of the judicial task of questioning the workings of a legislative investigation."[92] He was cognizant of the proper regard that there must be on the part of the judiciary for the primacy of the legislative function and for the broad scope of the investigatory power needed to carry out this function. But he was also conscious of the inescapable duty that is cast upon the judiciary of protecting the rights of speech and assembly from improper invasion whether by the Congress or state legislatures. When viewed in the light of the Constitution, he did not interpret a bare legislative authorization for an inquiry to necessarily denote a valid legislative end; nor did he consider conclusive a state court determination of the matter, although he thought it entitled to weight. Instead, he considered it the task of the Supreme Court to determine whether in fact a valid legislative end was demonstrated.

146

As Justice Brennan viewed the record in the *Uphaus* case, he could see in it nothing but exposure for exposure's sake. The emphasis of the report which culminated the first two years of the one-man committee's work was, in his words, "on individual guilt, individual near guilt, and individual questionable behavior."[93] There had been, he concluded, "overwhelmingly and predominently a roving, self-contained investigation of individual and group behavior, and behavior in a constitutionally protected area."[94] The demonstrated purpose fell short of a valid constitutional one or of private interest that could subordinate private rights. That was true, in his opinion, even if one should accept the Court's truism "that preservation of the State's existence is undoubtedly a proper purpose of legislation." The guide for the decision of this case, the Justice thought, should have been the approach taken by the Court in *N.A.A.C.P.* v. *Alabama*,[95] a case in which the Court had struck down an attempt by a state to force the N.A.A.C.P. to reveal to the state's attorney general all of its state membership and agents. The Justice recognized that, technically, a membership list was not involved in the present case, but to distinguish the two cases on that ground was, he thought, to miss the point because "if the members of the assemblage could only plead their assembly rights themselves, the very interest being safeguarded by the Constitution here could never be protected meaningfully, since to require that the guests claim this right themselves would 'result in nullification of the right at the very moment of its assertion.' "[96]

In his short, one paragraph, dissent to *Barenblatt* Justice Brennan expressed complete agreement with Justice Black that the record revealed nothing but exposure for the sake of exposure, a conclusion that he also reached in his longer *Wilkinson* dissent. In the latter he wrote: "It is particularly important that congressional committees confine themselves to the function of gathering information when their investigation begins to touch the realm of speech and opinion. On this record, I cannot help concluding that the Committee had no reasonable prospect that petitioner would answer its questions, and accordingly that the Committee's purpose could not have been the legitimate one of fact gathering. I am forced to the view that the questions asked of petitioner were therefore not within the Committee's power."[97]

The decade of the 1950's can justly be characterized as a period of search for a new standard with which to interpret the guarantees of speech and press. After the *Dennis* case, little if anything was left

147

of "clear and present danger" as Holmes and Brandeis had known it. To be sure, the phrase persisted through *Dennis,* although there it acquired a meaning that was vastly different from that which it had before. But after that it was not heard from except to be expressly rejected as not applicable in libelous utterance and obscenity cases. It disappeared even from such familiar ground as picketing, soliciting and Jehovah's Witness cases, and along with it went "preferred position" that had shared equal popularity during the prior decade. It did not figure in the Court's second encounter with the Smith Act in the *Yates* case.

Perhaps the best illustration of this search for a new standard is the course that the proposed kinship between the liberties of speech and press and legislative inquiries followed over a six year period that started in 1957 and spilled over into the next decade. In 1957 the Court required that committee authority, state as well as federal, be precisely defined in authorizing resolutions. In 1959 and again in 1961, the Court permitted a look-see at the legislative history behind authorizing resolutions for Congressional investigations to find adequate authority; with state inquiries it became a question of the balancing of interests, public versus private, which now took precedence over the nature of the mandate vested in a one-man investigating committee.

CHAPTER XII

MOTION PICTURES AND CENSORSHIP

Even before the Court had turned another corner from one decade to another in 1960 it was already evident that another change was taking place in the handling of speech and press cases. Where, ten years earlier, it had been a question of "clear and present danger" the Court gradually veered toward a "balancing of interests," public versus private. It is true that as the Court approached the end of the 1950's it was committing itself to this new theory by the barest of majorities,[1] but by the end of the decade a taut line had been drawn that did not seem likely to yield in one direction or another of itself.[2] Perhaps the best example of how this took place is the course that the law of speech and press followed in its application to the motion picture industry.

As early as 1915 the Court was confronted by an Ohio statute that established a board of censors to pass on motion pictures before they were publicly exhibited in the State. The statute required that before any could be shown they had to be adjudged "of a moral, educational or amusing and harmless character."[3] This was assailed before the Supreme Court as a violation of the freedom of speech and publication guaranteed by the Constitution of Ohio,[4] but at this early date the Court rejected any such claim: "It cannot be put out of view that the exhibition of moving pictures is a business pure and simple, originated and conducted for profit, like other spectacles, not to be regarded, nor intended to be regarded by the Ohio Constitution, we think, as part of the press of the country or as organs of public opinion. They are mere representations of events, of ideas and sentiments published and known, vivid, useful and entertaining no doubt, but, as we have said, capable of evil, having power for it, the greater because of their attractiveness and manner of exhibition."[5]

At the time of this decision *Gitlow v. New York* had not yet opened

149

the way for the application of the safeguards of the First Amendment against state as well as federal invasion through the due process clause of the Fourteenth Amendment. Nevertheless, when the question of state censorship of motion pictures came up again before the Supreme Court in 1952 in *Joseph Burstyn, Inc.* v. *Wilson,*[6] much the same arguments were advanced even though *Gitlow* had long become history and other cases had followed that further extended First Amendment freedoms into the realm of state activity. The appellees still relied heavily on the *Mutual Film* case as they sought to have a New York law upheld that authorized a censor to refuse a license should he conclude that a film was "sacriligious."[7] The capacity for evil that motion pictures were said by the Court to have in 1915 was repeated, and it was argued that the need for regulation was, if anything, greater than at the time of the earlier case. Moreover, the appellees argued that the New York law was substantially narrower than the Ohio statute since it limited the power of the licensor to refuse a license to films that were "obscene, indecent, immoral, inhuman, sacriligious, or . . . of such a character that . . . exhibitions would lead to corrupt morals or incite to crime."[8] The "big business" argument on which the Court had partly rested its 1915 decision was again advanced, and instances in which the 1915 decision had allegedly been reaffirmed were cited.

As the Court set aside the *Mutual Film* case as one no longer to be relied on, it saw no reason why motion pictures should be distinguished from books, magazines, and newspapers where a profit motive is equally present; and even if the greater capactiy for evil should be assumed, it saw no reason why this particular mode of expression should be deprived of protection and subjected to unbridled censorship. On the other hand, the Court took pains to indicate that this, in turn, did not mean absolute freedom to show any picture at any time and at any place. There could be rules as with other modes of expression, but not a statute like this one that required advance permission that amounted to "previous restraint" rather than an attempt to punish as a past offense speech or writing that falls within the permissible scope of subsequent punishment. The Court found little help in the assertion of the New York Court of Appeals that there was "nothing mysterious" about the statutory provision—that it simply meant "that no religion, as that word is understood by the ordinary, reasonable person, shall be treated with contempt, mockery, scorn and redicule."[9] The effect of this broad, all-inclusive definition was, so the Supreme Court said, to do no more than set the censor "adrift upon a boundless sea amid a myriad of conflicting currents of religious views, with no charts but those provided by the most vocal and powerful orthodoxies."[10]

Subsequent to this decision the State of New York amended its motion picture law to repair the constitutional infirmities that had been found to exist in its earlier enactment. As amended the act defined an "immoral" motion picture film as one "which portrays acts of sexual immorality, perversion or lewdness, or which expressly or impliedly presents such acts as desirable, acceptable or proper patterns of behavior."[11] This proved to be no more successful than the original act had been and a second controversy, the *Kingsley International Pictures* case,[12] arose when the Motion Picture Division of the New York Education Department refused a license for the showing of the motion picture *Lady Chatterly's Lover* until three isolated scenes, which it considered "immoral" according to the law, were deleted.

When the case reached the New York Court of Appeals, the notion that the film was obscene was explicitly rejected but the refusal of the license was nevertheless upheld on the grounds that in its entirety the picture was one that "alluringly portrays adultery as proper behavior."[13] As that court construed the statute, the legislature was found to have intended that a license be denied a motion picture if "its subject matter is adulterly presented as being right and desirable for certain people under certain circumstances."[14] However, to a unanimous Supreme Court of the United States this "struck at the very heart of constitutionally protected liberty" and it was rejected as such.[15] But even though the Supreme Court stood as one in arriving at this decision, it took six opinions for it to do so. One, written by Mr. Justice Stewart, was denominated the opinion of the Court, the other five represented the divergent views of six of the nine Justices.[16]

Although once motion pictures had been blanketed within the First and Fourteenth Amendments, the Court's initial encounter with the New York statute had been settled in terms of "previous restraint,"[17] in this second encounter with the amended version of the statute Mr. Justice Stewart did not think it necessary to reach that issue. The State's action and the attempt to justify it now represented a pure and simple misconception of the extent of Constitutional protection—a protection that is not confined to the expression of conventional ideas or those that are shared by the majority, but one that can even protect advocacy that sometimes adultery may be proper.

For support Justice Stewart turned to Justice Brandeis' concurring opinion in *Whitney* v. *California* for an apt quotation to the effect that even speech or advocacy of conduct proscribed by law is not "a justification for denying free speech where the advocacy falls short of incitement and there is nothing to indicate that the advocacy would be immediately acted on."[18] When Justice Brandeis wrote this he was elucidating on "clear and present danger" and its applicability to a state criminal syndicalism law. One can only guess whether, as Justice Stewart quoted this language, he had "clear and present danger" in mind. But whether or not he did, he apparently did not think that the effect of viewing a movie of the type proscribed by the statute would be for the assembled audience to immediately rush out and engage in a mass adulterous orgy. He found that the "inflexible command" that the New York Court attributed to the State Legislature cut "so close to the core of constitutional freedom as to make it quite needless in this case to examine the periphery."[19] Thus, he ruled out "previous restraint" and the precise question that would come up in the next motion picture censorship case:[20] whether or not the same rules must be applied to motion pictures that are applied to newspapers, books, or individual speech, despite the peculiar problems motion pictures are said to present. For the present it was enough "to reaffirm that motion pictures are within the First and Fourteenth Amendments' basic protection. *Joseph Burstyn, Inc.* v. *Wilson*, 343 U.S. 495."[21]

The opinion of the Court bore marks of compromise that sometimes must be made so that men of different minds can arrive at the same decision. It skirted around the offensive that Mr. Justice Frankfurter had mounted only two years earlier against making "previous restraint" a rule of decision; it flirted with "clear and present danger" of which Justices Black and Douglas had been ardent proponents during the earlier decade, but it did not invoke the test to the extent of provoking its chief opponent, Mr. Justice Frankfurter; it avoided the sharp five to four division of the Court that has been the hallmark of speech and press cases. In other words, while it did not entirely please everyone, it did not entirely displease anyone. All could subscribe to it in one way or another and yet be left with enough room to give vent to their own particular ideas on the subject.

While Justices Black and Douglas went along with the opinion of the Court, they nevertheless concurred and reaffirmed their view that previous restraint of any kind is unconstitutional;[22] Justices Frankfurter, Harlan and Whittaker concurred in the result but objected that it was wrong to hold the statute unconstitutional on its face—they would have confined themselves to its application to this particular film;[23] Mr. Justice Clark also concurred in the result but argued that the decision could have been based on the vagueness of the standard set by the statute. He wrote: "I need only say that the obscurity of the standard presents such a choice of difficulties that even the most experienced find themselves at dagger's point."[24]

Kinksley International Pictures was decided in an atmosphere of unity that had discordant overtones. The next case on the subject of motion picture censorship was destined to present the issue in such a manner that it was not susceptible to such unity by compromise. Furthermore, it came at the start of another decade, that of the 1960's, which the Court entered sharply divided in the area of speech and press. This was a division that had already made itself sharply felt as the Court seesawed in its treatment of the effect of speech and press on legislative inquiries. It promised to be the outstanding feature of at least the early part of the 1960's.

In 1961, two years after *Kingsley International Pictures,* the Court handed down its third motion picture censorship case. This time not only was there a change of scene—from New York to Chicago—but also a change in the basic issues presented. Now there was not the question of the validity of standards, but rather that of the very idea that a motion picture should have to be submitted to examination before it could be exhibited to the public. The case was *Times Film Corp.* v. *Chicago*[25] in which the petitioners had been refused a permit to exhibit a film known as "Don Juan" because, although they tendered a required license fee, they refused to comply with that part of the Municipal Code of Chicago, § 155-4, that called for the submission of all motion pictures for examination prior to public exhibition. They objected to this as previous restraint within the prohibitions of the First and Fourteenth Amendments. Mr. Justice Clark who had written for the Court in *Joseph Burstyn, Inc.* in which motion pictures had been freed from "unbridled censorship" and "previous restraint" within the state area, was again the spokesman. This time, however, his role may be described as one of "containment" in the sense that he wrote for the majority in a five to four decision that refused to go any further than the Court already had gone in its two most recent decisions on the subject.

As Justice Clark reviewed the cases all the way from *Gitlow* v. *New York*[26] to *Smith* v. *California*[27] he could find no instance in which the Court had held that liberty of speech is absolute or any suggestion that all previous restraint on speech is invalid. Indeed, to him *Near* v.

Minnesota, the landmark previous restraint case, indicated the exact opposite. There, Chief Justice Hughes had agreed that the principle forbidding previous restraint "is stated too broadly, if every such restraint is deemed to be prohibited. . . . [T]he protection even as to previous restraint is not absolutely unlimited. But the limitation has been recognized only in exceptional cases."[28] As the Justice proceeded through a review of the *Chaplinsky, Joseph Burstyn, Kingsley Books,* and *Smith* v. *California* cases he found nothing to support the petitioners' contention that the public exhibition of motion pictures must be allowed under any circumstances, and the state left solely with the remedy of invoking criminal process after a transgression. Indeed, chided the Justice, one of the "exceptional cases" that Chief Justice Hughes had enumerated in *Near* v. *Minnesota* was "the primary requirements of decency [that] may be enforced against obscene publications."[29] Furthermore, in *Burstyn* the Court had recognized that "capacity for evil . . . may be relevant in determining the permissible scope of community control"; that motion pictures are not "necessarily subject to the precise rules governing any other particular method of expression." Each method, the Court had said, "tends to present its own peculiar problems."[30]

Justice Clark strove mightily to confine the effect of the decision solely to motion pictures, and even as to them "only to the context of the broadside attack presented on this record."[31] But even as he did this, the taut line that now divided the Court five to four in this type case again became quite evident. Speaking for the minority of four in one of the two dissenting opinions, Chief Justice Warren went so far as to accuse the majority of arriving at the decision of the Court by interpreting cases "contrary to the intention at the time of their rendition and, in exalting the censor of motion pictures, . . . [of endangering] the First and Fourteenth Amendment rights of all others engaged in the dissemination of ideas."[32] The Chief Justice proceeded down much the same avenue that the majority had followed, but he cut a much wider swath as he made a more extended review of cases, quoted from such favorites as Milton and Blackstone, and cited numerous examples that tended to illustrate the absurd length that censorship has been carried on in the various states in the immediate past. During the course of his lengthy dissent the Chief Justice found that in *Kingsley Books, Inc.* v. *Brown* the Court had "turned a corner from the landmark opinion in *Near* and from one of the bases of the First Amendment" and that in the present decision it fell "into full retreat."[33] The Constitution itself he considered an answer to the contention that the impact of motion pictures is such that prior censorship of them is permissible. He agreed, as the Court had said in *Joseph Burstyn, Inc.* v. *Wilson,* that "each method [of expression] tends to present its own peculiar problems."[34] But in prior decisions the Court had not dealt with the context of speech—only with the conditions surrounding its delivery. Here, the Chief Justice said, the Court was using the magical phrase of *Burstyn* "to cripple a basic principle of the Constitution."[35] To him, it was the Court, not the petitioner, that made a "broadside attack."

In a shorter, less impassioned, dissent in which the Chief Justice and Mr. Justice Black concurred, Mr. Justice Douglas noted that while the problem of movie censorship is relatively new, censorship itself is ancient. Indeed, his discussion of its history started with Socrates who advocated a censor with the duty "to receive any tale of fiction which is good, and reject the bad."[36] He noted further that "[r]egimes of censorship are common in the world today,"[37] even in England where a certain vestage of it still exists in the Lord Chamberlain who presides over the stage.[38] He could imagine no more powerful a weapon of sectarian control than governmental censorship, but he saw no place for it in this country where neither is the state a secular arm of any religious school of thought, nor the church any instrument of the state. In addition, he pointed to the First Amendment and the fact that so long as it survives it deprives the censor of government support no matter how respectable his cause.

Justice Douglas' reading of *Near* v. *Minnesota* was different from that of the majority. To him it stood pure and simple for the proposition that the "chief purpose" of the First Amendment's guarantees of freedom of the press was to prevent previous restraints upon publication. He concluded his opinion with the following neat analysis of the problem: "The First Amendment was designed to enlarge, not to limit, freedom in literature and in the arts as well as in politics, economics, law, and other fields. . . . Its aim was to unlock all ideas for argument, debate, and dissemination. No more potent force in defeat of that freedom could be designed than censorship. It is a weapon that no minority or majority group, acting through government, should be allowed to wield over any of us."[39]

CHAPTER XIII

A NEW APPROACH IN THE 1960's

As the Court concluded its first full term of the 1960's it became quite evident that if the void left by the demise of "clear and present danger" was to be filled by any particular theory, that theory was to be the "balancing of interests" toward which the Court had veered at the end of the previous decade. It also became evident that if this was to be a theory that would have a lasting effect, the precarious position that it occupied as a majority doctrine at that point would have to be improved. By June, 1961, it only held its position by one vote and that could change at any time. Moreover, it had already attracted formidable opposition and considerable criticism although its history was short.[1] Nevertheless, the five to four line-up in its favor with which the Court emerged from the 1950's held in both *Scales* v. *United States*[2] in which the Court upheld the membership clause of the Smith Act, and in *Communist Party of the United States* v. *Subversive Activities Control Board*[3] in which it upheld the registration provision of the Subversive Activities Control Act.[4] However, just one week after these two cases were decided the uncertainty of this line-up was illustrated in *Deutch* v. *United States*[5] in which one Justice swung from one side to the other as the Court reversed a contempt of Congress conviction. Again the vote was five to four with Mr. Justice Stewart acting as the swing man. All three cases, *Scales, Communist Party of the United States,* and *Deutch,* also indicated the start of a trend to "tone down" First Amendment issues and even to set them to one side, if need be, to muster a majority and reach a decision.

Scales, the first of the three, had a history that covered a six-year period during which there were two convictions, one in 1955 and another in 1958, two trips to the Supreme Court,[6] one after each conviction, and one reversal pending a proposed reargument during the first trip that never took place because of *Jencks* v. *United States.*[7]

The second conviction was argued and reargued before the Supreme Court before it was finally upheld.[8] The principal issue for present purposes was whether the "membership clause" of the Smith Act was unconstitutional on its face and as applied.[9]

Although the safeguards of the First, as well as the Fifth and Sixth Amendments to the Constitution, were raised in the Petition for Certiorari and then thoroughly briefed by both parties,[10] less than one and one-half pages of the fifty-five page majority opinion were devoted to the First Amendment.[11] Indeed, with the opening statement "Little remains to be said concerning the claim that the statute infringes First Amendment Freedoms,"[12] Mr. Justice Harlan dismissed as settled in *Dennis* that the advocacy with which the Court was here concerned was not constitutionally protected speech. Moreover, although on reargument one of the five questions to which counsel were directed to address themselves was the applicability of "clear and present danger" to the membership clause, the only mention that the Court made of this in its opinion was the following brief footnote: "As both sides appear to agree that the 'clear and present danger' doctrine, as viewed and applied in Dennis, supra, pp. 508-511, also reaches the membership clause of the Smith Act, and since the petition for certiorari tenders no issue as to the method of applying it here, we do not consider either question."[13]

The Court did, however, use part of Mr. Justice Holmes' original statement of "clear and present danger,"[14] which it quoted out of context to fashion a "balancing of interests" statement for the purposes of the present case. It did this as it drew a distinction between knowing association with a technical conspiracy on the one hand, and knowing association with quasi-political parties or other groups that may embrace both legal and illegal aims on the other. While there may be a valid blanket criminal proscription of the former, a similar blanket proscription of the latter would, the Court said, mean "a real danger that legitimate political expression or association would be impaired." "[B]ut," continued the Court, "the membership clause, as here construed, does not cut deeper into the freedom of association than is necessary to deal with 'the substantive evils that Congress has a right to prevent.' *Schenck* v. *United States*, 249 U.S. 47, 52."[15] As the Court read the membership clause, it protects one who uses for legitimate aims and purposes an organization shown to engage in illegal advocacy. Such a person might "be foolish, deluded, or perhaps merely optimistic," but he lacks "the requisite specific intent 'to bring about the overthrow of the government as speedily as circumstances would permit.' "[16]

Both Justices Black and Douglas severely criticized the recently acquired test favored by the majority. Mr. Justice Black referred to its use here as a re-emphasis of "the freedom-destroying nature of the 'balancing test' presently in use by the Court to justify its refusal to apply specific constitutional protections of the Bill of Rights."[17] He rejected as unsound the suggestion that whenever this new test has been used its use has been justified because in each case abridgment of First Amendment freedoms was not direct, but rather no more than "an incident of the inferred exercise of a valid governmental function."[18] To him the current case demonstrated both the unlimited breadth and danger of the "balancing test" as he called it. The criterion of this new test he found most distasteful: "It is, rather simply whether the Government has an interest in abridging the right involved and, if so, whether that interest is of sufficient importance, in the opinion of a majority of this Court, to justify the Government's action in doing so."[19] It expressed a doctrine which he found "capable of being used to justify almost any action the Government may wish to take to suppress First Amendment freedoms."

Justice Douglas was no less adamant. While he recognized that a government has the right to move against any who take up arms against it and that constituted authority has a right of self-preservation, to him in *Scales* the Court was dealing with the legality of ideas and beliefs, not overt acts. Talk by the Court of the prevention of "dangerous behavior" and of punishing those "who work to bring about that behavior" he dismissed as a formula that "returns man to the dark days when government determined what behavior was 'dangerous' and then policed the dissidents for tell-tale signs of advocacy."[20] Addressing himself directly to the "balancing of interests" used by the majority, he wrote: "In recent years we have been departing, I think, from the theory of government expressed in the First Amendment. We have too often been 'balancing' the right of speech and association against other values in society to see if we, the judges, feel that a particular need is more important than those guaranteed by the Bill of Rights. . . . This approach, which treats the commands of the First Amendment as 'no more than admonitions of moderation' (see Hand, *The Spirit of Liberty*, p. 278), runs counter to our prior decisions. See *Lovell* v. *Griffin*, 303 U.S. 444, 450; *Murdock* v. *Pennsylvania*, 319 U.S. 105, 108; *Board of Education* v. *Barnette*, 319 U.S. 624, 639."[21]

The other issues presented by the case were equally resolved against the petitioner, some in a more lengthy but in a no more effective manner than was that of the First Amendment. Thus, the claim that § 4 (f) of the Internal Security Act of 1950[22] repealed *pro tanto* the membership clause of the Smith Act[23] was found misplaced since the clause neither proscribes membership as such in the Communist Party, nor punishes membership *per se* in an organization engaging in the proscribed advocacy. Instead, the Court construed the clause as aimed only at organizations engaged in advocacy of violent overthrow and at membership of one "knowing the purposes thereof."[24] Objections founded on the Fifth Amendment were, the Court said, met by a statute such as this one that reaches only "active" membership having guilty knowledge and interest.

The Court still recognized and held controlling the distinction drawn in *Yates*[25] between theoretical advocacy and advocacy of violence as a rule of action, "[B]ut," it continued, "when the teaching is carried out in a special vocabulary, knowledge of that vocabulary is at least relevant to an understanding of the quality and tenor of the teaching."[26] The evidence, a review of which occupied seventeen pages of the majority opinion, indicated to the Court "advocacy of action" not "sporadic" in nature—neither infrequent, remote in time, nor casual as to prevent a jury from finding the criminal advocacy fully authorized and condoned by the Party.[27]

The second case, *Communist Party of the United States, v. Subversive Activities Control Board*,[28] was a review of an order of the Subversive Activities Control Board which required the Communist Party of the United States to register according to § 7 of the Subversive Activities Control Act of 1950.[29] In effect, the case presented a host of issues, some procedural,[30] some statutory,[31] and some constitutional,[32] all of which were resolved against the petitioner in one of the longest opinions of a term of the Supreme Court which will long be remembered for verbosity.

Among the constitutional issues there was that of the First Amendment. It was raised by the Communist Party as a bar to the provisions of the Act that require the registration of individuals and the filing of information, including membership lists, by "Communist Front"[33] and "Communist Action"[34] organizations. As the Court grappled with this it had to consider several of its earlier decisions in which it had, in effect, held that registration is an impermissible form of regulation. First there was *Thomas* v. *Collins*[35] in which it had held that a paid labor organizer could not constitutionally be punished for defying a restraining order that required him to register and obtain an organizer's card before soliciting union membership; then there was *N.A.A.C.P.* v. *Alabama*[36] in which it had prevented the ouster of the N.A.A.C.P. from Alabama on the pretext that it failed to comply with the State's foreign-corporation registration act because it refused to produce membership lists and reveal its rank-and-file members; there was also *Bates* v. *Little Rock*[37] in which the Court had upset a conviction for failure to file financial statements showing the names of individual contributors, etc.; and finally there was *Shelton* v. *Tucker*[38] in which the State of Arkansas had sought to require all teachers in the State to disclose every organization that they had associated with over a five year period, but was prevented from doing so although the measure had purportedly been adopted in furtherance of the State's affective selection of teacher personnel.

Although all of these cases served to illustrate that compulsory disclosure of membership and association may violate constitutionally protected rights, they could be, and were, distinguished. "To state that individual liberties may be affected" theorized Justice Frankfurter, "is to establish the conditions for, not to arrive at the conclusion of, constitutional decision. Against the impediments which particular governmental regulation causes to entire freedom of individual action, there must be weighed the value to the public of the ends which the regulation may achieve."[39]

In other words, there had to be a "balancing of interests"—public versus private. And as Justice Frankfurter performed this delicate task, he found that the instant case differed from the *Thomas, N.A.A.C.P., Bates,* and *Shelton* cases "in the magnitude of the public interests which the registration and disclosure provisions are designed to protect and in the pertinence which registration and disclosure bear to the protection of those interests."[40] Congress, he said, had itself defined in the Act what these interests were and what threatened them. It had done this on the basis of detailed investigations and after it had made legislative findings the validity of which he did not think it the function of the courts to re-examine and reject.

The interplay between legislative findings, public interest, and individual liberty Justice Frankfurter resolved as follows: "Of course, congressional power in this sphere, as in all spheres, is limited by the First Amendment. Individual liberties fundamental to American institutions are not to be destroyed under pretext of preserving those institutions, even from the gravest external dangers. But where the problems of accommodating the exigencies of self-preservation and the values of liberty are as complex and intricate as they are in the situation described in the findings of § 2 of the Subversive Activities Control Act—when existing government is menaced by world-wide integrated movement which employs every combination of possible means, peaceful and violent, domestic and foreign, overt and clandestine, to destroy the government itself—the legislative judgment as to how that threat may best be met consistently with the safeguarding of personal freedom is not to be set aside merely because the judgment of judges would, in the first instance, have chosen other methods. Especially where Congress, in seeking to reconcile competing and urgently demanding values within our social institutions, legislates not to prohibit individuals from organizing for the effectuation of ends found to be menacing to the very existence of those institutions, but only to prescribe the conditions under which such organization is permitted, the legislative determination must be respected."[41]

To drive home his point Justice Frankfurter cited the Federal Corrupt Practices Act, the Federal Regulation of Lobbying Act, the Foreign Agents Registration Act, and the Voorhis Act of 1940, all of which require registration or disclosure designed to meet situations in which secrecy or concealment of association "has been regarded as a threat to public safety and to the effective, free functioning of our national institutions."[42]

Of the four dissents to this opinion only one, that of Mr. Justice Black, invoked the First Amendment. Indeed, even Mr. Justice Douglas, while he recognized that "the vices of registration may be not unlike those of licensing,"[43] went along with the majority of the Court in so far as the effect of the First Amendment on the bare requirement that the Communist Party register and disclose the names of its officers and directors was concerned. Just as he had once said that picketing is free speech plus,[44] so now he said that machinations such as espionage, business practices, and the formation of cells for subversion used by a foreign power to make inroads here "add additional elements to free speech just as marching up and down adds something to picketing that goes beyond free speech."[45] He chose, instead, to base his dissent on the right against self-incrimination. As he viewed the Act under scrutiny it compelled disclosure of evidence that could link the officers, directors and members of a group with crime. And even a group such as the one in question in the present case, no matter how despised it might be, he thought was entitled to be protected from this by the Constitution.

Justice Black used this occasion to again strike at the "balancing test" which he likened to the arguments used to justify the Alien and Sedition Acts of 1798. While he recognized that in this instance it was only the Communist Party that Congress sought to reach, he had no confidence that a policy of using governmental force to crush dissident groups would stop there: "The weakening of constitutional safeguards in order to suppress one obnoxious group is a technique too easily available for the suppression of other obnoxious groups to expect its abandonment when the next generally hated group appears."[46]

It should be noted, however, that even as Justice Black voiced these objections he also did not oppose registration as such. On this point the Court was unanimous in favor of constitutionality. But to the Justice, registration was not the sole issue presented. There were also the burdens that followed registration and it was to these that he took exception—to the sanctions that forced registration and then the civil disabilities, public harassment, and criminal prosecutions that he said members of the Party were subject to once they had been so identified.

Deutch v. *United States*,[47] the case in which the five to four line-up changed from one side to the other, was another contempt of Congress case. Again the issue was a criminal conviction for refusing to answer questions before a subcommittee of the House Un-American Activities Committee. This was another instance in which the petitioner testified freely before the Committee as to his own former Communist affiliations which, in his case, had taken place while he was a graduate student at Cornell University, but refused to answer questions asked about other people.[48] At the trial the Government offered as evidence of the pertinency of these questions the opening statements of the Committee Chairman at hearings covering the Albany area and at hearings aimed at Communist infiltration into labor unions.[49] Confining itself to a review of the evidence, the Supreme Cout decided the issue of pertinency against the Government and reversed the conviction.

The case is important not for what the Supreme Court had to say about First Amendment rights, but for what it did not say about them. Instead of following the approach that it had used in the *Uphaus*, *Barenblatt*, *Wilkinson*, and *Braden* cases, it explicitely refrained from deciding any question respecting the power or legislative purpose of the subcommittee, and it explicitely did not "reach the large issues stirred by the petitioner's First Amendment claims." Although the facts in the case were of the type that had earlier been considered of constitutional dimensions,[50] they were treated as presenting no more than a question of evidence. As a consequence, the minority of four that had persisted in the earlier cases[51] was now able to attract a fifth vote and shift the balance in its favor; the way was made clear for Mr. Justice Stewart to swing from one side to the other and even to write the majority opinion. Perhaps it can be said that this does not mean much since the Court was still divided five to four. The division, however, was now over an evaluation of evidence—something that could be much more flexible than a division over a highly controversial First Amendment issue. The tack that the Court took in the disposition of this case could very well be the preview of a departure from the controversial and much criticized course followed in earlier contempt of Congress cases.

OBSCENITY, LOCAL POLITICS, AND
CLEAR AND PRESENT DANGER REVISITED

On June 25, 1962, the last day of the October Term, 1961, the Supreme Court decided two speech and press cases that were all but lost in the din caused by the much discussed prayer decision.[52] The subject-matter was familiar: obscenity and contempt of court. The obscenity case, *Manuel Enterprises, Inc.* v. *Day*,[53] left intact the test set down in the *Roth* case[54] five years earlier but indicated a lack of agreement on what to do with it. The contempt of court case, *Wood* v. *Georgia*,[55] gave evidence that although "clear and present danger" had not been heard of for quite some time, it still stood in the wings and could be "dusted off" should the need for it arise.

The *Manuel Enterprises* case arose when the Postmaster General declared non-mailable certain magazines that consisted largely of nude or near-nude photographs of male models. The names and addresses of the photographers were given; there were also advertisements for the sale of nudist photographs. Although the Post Office Department ruling, which was upheld by the lower federal courts, was reversed by the Supreme Court by a vote of 6 to 1, there was anything but unanimity even among the substantial majority. Like ancient Gaul, wrote Justice Clark in dissent, they were "split into three parts."[56] Justice Harlan announced the judgment of the Court and an opinion in which Justice Stewart joined; Justice Brennan, joined by the Chief

Justice and Justice Douglas, concurred in the reversal; Justice Black concurred in the result.

To Justices Harlan and Stewart it was a mistake to assume, as the Court of Appeals had, that *Roth* established "prurient interest" appeal as the sole test of obscenity under the Comstock Act. There was also the separate element of "patent offensiveness" which the lower court had not considered—the self-demonstrating indecency of material. Both have to be proved, according to this view. Although in most instances the two elements tend to coalesce, that was not so here and the second was found lacking.

To Justice Brennan, there was more to the case than whether or not particular matter was obscene. There was also the question of the validity of the procedure that had been followed by the Post Office. Wrote Justice Brennan for himself, the Chief Justice and Justice Douglas: "We risk erosion of First Amendment liberties unless we train our vigilance upon the methods whereby obscenity is condemned no less than upon the standards whereby it is judged."[57] But even aside from the constitutional questions posed by required procedural safeguards, the federal obscenity statute that the Court had upheld in *Roth* v. *United States* was found not to be so all-inclusive as to give the Postmaster General "the power to supervise the tastes of the reading public of the country."[58] And that would be the effect of permitting this governmental official to use any process he found convenient.

Perhaps Justice Clark supplied the punch line for which the case will be remembered. He objected to the decision as one that would require the United States Post Office to be "the world's largest disseminator of smut."[59]

Wood v. *Georgia* presented an interesting study of politics at the county level. The events that led to it started during the heat of a local political campaign when a regularly impanelled grand jury was charged with the investigation of a local political situation. The jurors were given special instructions in which they were advised that in election after election there appeared to exist "an inane and inexplicable pattern of Negro bloc voting"[60] even though no racial issues were involved. They were told to inquire into "persistent rumors and accusations" of payments to Negro leaders who, it was alleged, switched to one candidate after they had endorsed another. Supposedly, these payments were accepted to cover such expenses as political advertisements, radio announcements, etc. But, commented the court, the payments actually amounted to vote purchasing since the vast majority of Negroes voted as they were told by their leaders. Reporters for all of the local news media were present in the court room at the time these instructions were given. In addition, typewritten copies of the instructions were immediately made available to the press.

The day after this took place, the petitioner, a county sheriff who was seeking reelection, issued a news release in which he questioned the action of the court as a deplorable example of race agitation. He called it "a crude attempt at judicial intimidation" or, at best, agitation for a "negro vote" issue.[61] He expressed shock at a judge "charging a Grand Jury in the style and language of a race baiting candidate for political office." Next, he addressed "An open Letter to the Bibb County Grand Jury"[62] which was made available to the jurors at his request. In it he implied that the court's charge was false and he directed attention to the county committee which he said was responsible for whatever corruption existed. One month later, the day after he was cited for contempt of court, the petitioner issued another news release in which he restated his earlier statements and asserted the truth as his defense.

In amended form, the citation for contempt alleged that the petitioner's statement "in and of itself created and presented a clear, present and imminent danger to the investigation being conducted,"[63] and to the proper administration of justice. It also alleged that the second news release presented a "clear, present and imminent danger" to the proper handling of the contempt citation. The trial court found the petitioner guilty on all counts but it neither made findings nor gave reasons for its decision.

The conviction was reversed by the Supreme Court of the United States. The Court, wrote the Chief Justice in behalf of the majority, cannot be precluded from an examination of the evidence simply by the enunciation of a "constitutionally acceptable standard" in a state court's description of the effect of conduct. He rejected as inadequate a statement, made as a matter of law but without factual support, that unless a state could punish those who expressed views on matters of great importance while they were being considered in a grand jury investigation, a clear and present danger to the administration of justice would be created. No more effective was the argument that because of his office the petitioner owed a special duty and responsibility to the court and its judges, and that because of this his right to freedom of expression had to be more severely curtailed than that of the average citizen. He had a right to speak on matters that were vital to him. Any errors in judgment or unsubstantiated opinions could be exposed, but not by punishment for contempt for the expression.

"Clear and present danger" became an issue in this case in such a manner that it was not used as an objective test with which to measure evidence as it had been earlier in *Bridges* v. *California*[64] and *Pennekamp* v. *Florida*.[65] Instead, it served as the basis for, and even to supply the terminology of, allegations in a contempt citation which the state courts adopted as conclusions of law. In effect, the Supreme Court had no choice other than to determine the issues presented in terms of "clear and present danger." For that reason, this most recent use of Mr. Justice Holmes' test is likely to do little more than increase the conjecture with which its status has been viewed since *Dennis* v. *United States*.[66] It must be noted, however, that in neither the majority nor the minority opinions was there any indication of disapproval of "clear and present danger" as there had been earlier. Perhaps this is best explained by the fact that at the moment the case was decided the ranks of the "balancers" were somewhat depleted.[67] Also, no question of national security was present.

CHAPTER XIV

SUMMARY AND CONCLUSIONS

SUMMARY

In 1921, during the course of a lecture on "The Nature of the Judicial Process," Benjamin Nathan Cardozo, then a member of the Court of Appeals of the State of New York, declared: "The great generalities of the Constitution have a content and a significance that vary from age to age."[1] He need not have confined his statement to the generalities of this document which serves as the foundation for our form of government; he could very well have extended it to some of the more specific provisions—particularly to the First Amendment and its prohibition concerning speech and press. For, couched though this is in terms that are anything but general, the meaning given to it has varied not only from age to age but even from decade to decade. From the beginning the search for the true meaning of the words "Congress shall make no law . . . abridging the freedom of speech or of the press" has followed a vacillating course that has led now to one theory and then to another. Indeed the history of this amendment to the Constitution has been one of uncertainty although it was adopted to end uncertainty.

When the Constitution was brought forth from the Federal Convention of 1787 and presented to the states for adoption, it contained no bill of right which expressly set forth and enumerated rights that were generally considered "natural." Because of this, widespread objection arose that even threatened rejection of the Constitution, and this persisted even though there was reassurance by some of the leaders of the Convention that the Constitution itself was a bill of rights. It was to allay the fears that gave rise to these objections that the First Ten Amendments to the Constitution were adopted by the First Congress and ratified by the states. In these the means were set forth to fulfill the words of the Declaration of Independence which state in the best natural law tradition: "We hold these truths to be self-evident, that all men are created equal, that they are endowed by their Creator with certain unalienable rights, that among these are Life, Liberty and the pursuit of Happiness. That to secure these rights, Governments are instituted among Men, deriving their just powers from the consent of the Governed."

The prohibition as to speech and press in the first of the Ten Amendments was the result of bitter experience which those who brought about its adoption had known intimately and against which they had rebelled. They had lived under the English law of speech and press, and they knew the nature of its consequences. They also had extensive knowledge of its history and they were aware of the theories of law and sovereignty that had permitted it to flourish. These were theories that considered the authority of government as supreme, irresistible, and absolute. Before the English Revolution of 1688 this unqualified sovereignty had been vested in the Crown, later it was vested in the authority of Parliament. It was inevitable that with such a theory prevalent any criticism of the government and of its officials should not only have been considered objectionable, but should also have been deemed to constitute a danger that had to be suppressed by every possible means and with the least possible delay. The theory of the First Amendment was to express an unqualified rejection of this experience and to assure that it would not survive in this country.

Natural rights, the secularized version of natural law, was imbedded deep enough in the faith of the Founding Fathers that it survived its role as the doctrine which had been fundamental to the struggle against arbitrary government, and it continued in this country long after it had been set to one side in Europe. It served as the basis for the American system of judicial review and it provided the principle with which to interpret the ambiguities of the Fourteenth Amendment. Indeed, its omnipresence can be felt even today as one President, the latest to be born in the nineteenth century, once made reference in a State of the Union Message to a "government based upon liberty and the God-given rights of man,"[2] and his successor, the present occupant of the office who is the first President to be born in the twentieth century, has already reaffirmed "the belief that the rights of man come not from the generosity of the state, but from the hand of God."[3] In addition, natural law continues to serve as the basis for declarations of rights in the constitutions of new states as they enter the Union.[4]

But however fundamental the natural law was to the struggle against arbitrary government,[5] and however much it may continue even today in this country as a living theory of law, in its application to speech and press it did not long survive the adoption of the Constitution and the Bill of Rights. Less than ten years after the First Congress had done its work the Alien and Sedition Acts became law. Reminiscent as these were of the English statute *De Scandalis Magnatum* of five centuries earlier, they represented an attempt to return to the concepts of law and sovereignty that had prevailed in the hated law of speech and press of England and Colonial America. The roar of resentment that ensued left unmistakable the conviction that this was not what the people at large had in mind. In our own era there has been a multiplicity of speech and press litigation as a result of the extension of the prohibitions of the First Amendment to the States through the instrumentality of the Fourteenth. This has meant not only continued, but also greatly increased, experimentation with the law of speech and press in the quest for its true meaning. First one theory has prevailed and then another, but in none has there been a return to the theories of natural rights that motivated the adoption of the Bill of Rights. And in the course of this experimentation seldom has any particular theory prevailed for more than a decade. Indeed, as every new theory has come to prevail opposition to it has developed that has provided the breeding ground for the one destined to succeed it.

The theory that prevailed in the Alien and Sedition Act trials was taken from the old English common law which prohibited any criticism of the government and which was carried over into American law by way of Blackstone's *Commentaries*, a treatise on law that gained as ready a recognition here as in England. The motivating force was the same in the Alien and Sedition Act trials as it had been in the early English common law and the statute *De Scandalis Mannatum*—fear of adverse criticism that engendered a desire to protect those in authority from its supposed evil effects.

In our own century, the twentieth, the first of the theories used in the ever-increasing number of speech and press cases was use-abuse or liberty versus license. That represented an attempt to draw a sharp line between speech and press that was considered right and speech and press that was considered wrong. It sought to place liberty on one side and licentiousness or abuse on the other. It was used in the World War I Espionage Act cases which involved either pamphlets or foreign-language newspapers that were critical of the

169

war effort. It was also used in the State Criminal Syndicalism Act cases of the 1920's.

But even as use-abuse or liberty versus license held sway another theory, Mr. Justice Holmes' "clear and present danger" test, was being developed. Although this one first gained exposition in an opinion for a unanimous Court it was, nevertheless, in the minority and concurring opinions of Justices Holmes and Brandeis in the Espionage Act and the State Criminal Syndicalism Act cases that it took shape and was made ready for a later date. However, before this later date could come to pass there was to be an interval—a decade (1930-1940)—of obscurity, and even of eclipse, for the test. This interval was the period when Charles Evans Hughes presided over the Court as Chief Justice. The major contribution of this interval to the law of speech and press was to revitalize the old English concept of "prior restraint" and make of it a "trump card" that has served the Court well ever since when nothing else has seemed applicable.

The decade from 1940 to 1950 not only saw "clear and present danger" finally achieve majority status, but also saw it extended to areas that even Holmes and Brandeis could not have envisioned. Also, civil liberties achieved a status that was frequently referred to as a "preferred position." The test that Holmes and Brandeis had used only in cases involving national security was now extended to picketing once this became recognized as a legitimate form of expression, to statutes and municipal ordinances designed to regulate the activities of Jehovah's Witnesses, to contempt of court cases, both state and federal, arising from out-of-court publications concerning pending cases, and even to enforce the right of an individual to make a provocative, challenging speech in an atmosphere of turbulence, disorder and animosity.

But again, even as "clear and present danger" reigned supreme it was not without its critic. Throughout the decade that witnessed the resurgence and extension of the test, at least one voice was consistent in dissent. In case after case Mr. Justice Frankfurter objected to what he believed to be a misconception of the origin and purpose of "clear and present danger." He insisted that it "was a literary phrase not to be distorted by being taken from its context,"[6] and that Mr. Justice Holmes had never used it "to express a technical legal doctrine or to convey a formula for adjudicating cases."[7] Soon, with a change in the personnel of the Court and the advent of a new decade, another crisis-ridden one, Mr. Justice Frankfurter had his way.

By mid-century there were indications that "clear and present danger" was about to go the way of its predecessors as the stresses and strains caused by the international Communist conspiracy increased. A strong premonition of this became evident in 1950 as the Court upheld the constitutionality of the non-Communist affidavit requirement of the Labor-Management Relations Act.[8] Here it commented on the inappropriateness of "clear and present danger" as a mechanical test to be used in every First Amendment case. One year later the Supreme Court made its most recent pronouncement in terms of the test as it upheld the Smith Act convictions of the top Communists in this country in *Dennis* v. *United States*.[9] As it did this it gave evidence that the test could no longer serve as a rule of decision. A majority was nowhere to be found that would agree on an opinion that could be considered the opinion of the Court. Moreover, although seven of the eight Justices who participated in *Dennis* subscribed to "clear and present danger" in principle, only six thought that even in principle it should be applied to this case, and of the six no more than four were with the majority. These four were together in a plurality opinion that reshaped the test and substituted "gravity of the 'evil,' discounted by its improbability"[10] for the traditional view of immediacy. The other two dissented in terms of the traditional Holmes-Brandeis exposition.

Since the *Dennis* case, the Court has entertained very much the same types of cases that it did during the prior decade—picketing, municipal ordinance and soliciting cases; Jehovah's Witness, censorship and Smith Act cases. But in none of these has "clear and present danger" played the prominent part that it once did. For more than a decade after 1951 nothing was heard of it except when it was expressly rejected as not worthy of consideration in an attempt to have it applied to libelous utterances and obscenity. Quite recently, it has appeared in one case, but not as the objective test that it once was. Instead, it supplied the terminology for a contempt of court citation which was found unsubstantiated once the conviction reached the Supreme Court.

In the place of "clear and present danger," "previous restraint" has been used on a few important occasions, but not to the extent that it can be said to have become a prevailing doctrine. There are also indications that even this time-worn doctrine may be in the process of being supplanted by a new theory of "balancing of interests," public

171

versus private, as the Court again emerges from one decade to another. But although the history of this new theory is yet short, it has already encountered formidable opposition and its future is uncertain. In addition, there appears to be a trend to "tone down" First Amendment issues and even to set them to one side, if need be, to muster a majority and reach a decision. An interesting development that started by way of dicta in 1957 has been an attempt to proclaim a kinship at both the state and Federal levels between First Amendment prohibitions (applied to the states through the Fourteenth) and the power of the legislative body to investigate. But by 1961 and the start of the persent decade, this had been reduced to no more than a "threat" as the Court has appeared to have drawn away from and distinguished its earlier pronouncement.

CONCLUSIONS

Thus, from the beginning the story of the law of speech and of the press in this country has been one of vacillation. To a considerable extent this has been due to the lack of a basic philosophy to serve as a stabilizing influence in the interpretation of the First Amendment. The premise is that this has been caused not by "insufficient data by which to determine the interests entitled to protection under it" as claimed elsewhere[11] but by a neglect of the data that is at hand, i.e., by a neglect of the natural law environment from which the Constitution and the Amendment arose, and a reluctance to place both in their proper perspective. And this has been true although it was a natural law process that served to incorporate the First Amendment into the Fourteenth, along with several of the other original Ten Amendments that comprise the Bill of Rights. On occasion this neglect has been in the form of an express rejection as when Mr. Justice Black bluntly declared in a Fifth Amendment case that an earlier decision and the natural law theory of the Constitution upon which it relied "degrade[d] the Constitutional safeguards of the Bill of Rights."[12] It has also been on a more scholarly and restrained basis as when Judge Learned Hand assumed *arguendo* "that the Consitituation and the 'Bill of Rights' neither proceed from, nor have any warrant in, the Divine Will, either as St. Thomas or Jefferson believed."[13]

No one can dispute that "there is no agreement as to the standards by which to measure the scope of the first amendment."[14] None of the tests that have prevailed at different periods during the history of the Amendment has stood the test of time for more than a decade. Furthermore, it has been asserted that the several tests are not as different from one another as they appear to be on the surface—that the difference between "liberty versus license," "clear and present danger," and the current "balancing of interests" tests is more semantical than real and that they all involve some sort of "balancing." This has been said even of such widely separated views as that expressed by Mr. Justice Holmes' "fire in a crowded theatre,"[15] statement and Mr. Justice Black's application of his "plain-language-complete-incorcorporation" doctrine.[16] Even the latter has recognized that there are some limitations to the right of free speech,[17] and in making the distinction that permits this qualification he has been accused of indulging in the very "balancing" process that he has so severely criticized.[18] But even if this is admitted for the sake of argument, the different tests have varied considerably in the amount of freedom that has been permitted under each and in their degree of flexibility.

"Liberty versus license" was quite inflexible and restrictive of speech and press while it held sway, and that eventually caused its downfall. "Clear and present danger" was more flexible, and while it prevailed the conduct of individuals could generally be fitted within its framework if the interest to be protected was private. In most of the cases in which this was done the question was whether or not an individual or a group should go to jail for committing some minor offense such as violating a state anti-picketing law, accosting a person on the street and playing a phonograph record that attacked this person's religious faith, school children refusing to salute the flag as required by state law, publishing editorials or cartoons that offended judges, some of whom were perhaps oversensitive, soliciting in areas where soliciting was not particularly welcome, or even insisting on the right to address a hostile audience in a manner that was both offensive and in bad taste. In these cases the issues were of great concern to the individuals or the groups involved—no one particularly wants to spend time in jail—but in none was there any great national interest present. "Clear and present danger" served as a good measure with which to assess the effect of the conduct of these individuals, many of whom acted in good faith and got into trouble either because their religious beliefs differed from those of the majority, because they suffered from some supposed or actual wrong, or because they encountered some overzealous local law enforcement officer. Fortunately, a liberal application of the test as it was then phrased kept

173

most of these people out of jail. However, when it became a question of the amount of leeway to be permitted any whose primary interest was to promote the interests of world communism, particularly in a time of crisis as in 1951, "clear and present danger" broke down. This became evident when no more than a plurality of four would take a chance on it in a majority opinion of the Court even if it was rephrased to substitute "probability" for "remoteness." It has not been used as a rule of decision by either a plurality or a majority of the Court since *Dennis* v. *United States*[19] in which this rephrasing appeared.

"Balancing of interests," toward which the Court had started to veer even before "clear and present danger" passed from the scene, has been described by Mr. Justice Douglas as rendering the commands of the First Amendment as "no more than admonitions of moderation."[20] Mr. Justice Black has been no less adamant in his criticism of what he has described as "the freedom-destroying nature" of this current test.[21] Its flexibility is such that it reduces speech and press to the level of every other interest and it is made to compete with these on equal terms. Moreover, it has a tendency to tip the scales against the individual, particularly in contempt of Congress cases when the Court balances "the security of the nation against the freedom of the individual litigant."[22] "Balancing" recognizes no limits except its own self-restraint; it can stop anywhere or nowhere at all. As a result, a "right" originally intended to assure that even a minority shall have the privilege of making itself heard becomes no more than a "permission." Whether this "right" is granted or denied under this test is made to depend on the one who controls the "balance."

To date the "balancing" test has never commanded the support of more than five of the nine members of the Court with one, Mr. Justice Stewart, acting as the "swing" man. Its status is, to say the least, quite precarious and the change that continues to take place in the composition of the Court could spell its doom. In fact, it has already been set to one side when Mr. Justice Stewart has chosen to desert the "balancers" and join those who oppose this form of reasoning to form a new, if but temporary, majority that appears to resolve its differences by "toning down" First Amendment issues whenever possible and treating them as questions of evidence. It may even be that this "toning down" process is gaining favor. Evidence of this appears in *Garner* v. *Louisiana*,[23] a "sit-in" case in which the petitioners, all arrested because they insisted on being served contrary to a segregation policy at a lunch counter, raised First and Fourteenth Amendment objections. Rather than decide the case on constitutional grounds, the Court chose to base its decision on whether the convictions rested upon evidence "which would support a finding that the petitioners' acts caused a disturbance of the peace."[24] The decision to reverse was unanimous with three Justices concurring, two of whom, Justices Douglas and Harlan, would have preferred to go directly to the constitutional question and dispose of it now rather than wait for another day which is bound to come.

Perhaps it would be too much to expect that even natural law, the secularized version that Jefferson and the others of his time believed in, could provide the ultimate answer. It could, however, provide a stabilizing influence and place the First and the other Amendments that comprise the Bill of Rights in their proper setting and environment. For this one need not necessarily subscribe to eighteenth century doctrine any more than one need approve the contents of legislative materials that are now so often searched to find Congressional intent. In either instance the objective is to find the meaning of words. In the case of the First Amendment, its authors had something very definite in mind when they chose the absolute terms that they did to assure the rights of speech and press. While in the broad sense these rights must be admitted to be qualified, in the narrow sense they must be recognized to encompass an area in which they were intended to be absolute. To discover the limits of this area one must consult the only data available—that which surrounded and motivated the adoption of the rights.

As the data that is available is examined, whether or not St. Thomas, the other doctors and fathers of the Church, and even Suarez, are included as a part of the line of development that extended from Zeno to Locke depends very much on the religious preference of the individual, or the lack of one, and even on environment. But whatever the position may be that is assumed in these respects, a decision for or against the early philosophers of the Church is really not as crucial as it might at first appear to be. Even among the colonists themselves opinion was anything but unanimous as to the source of the higher law that they all invoked. There were those like James Otis who thought that the law of nature was the "unchangeable will of God, the author of nature, whose laws never vary;"[25] and along with these there were the revolutionary preachers who expounded from the pulpit that government was "both the ordinance of God, and the ordinance of man; of God, in respect to his original plan, and universal providence; of man, as it is immediately the result of human prudence, wisdom concert."[26] There were also the others like John Adams and Jefferson who, while they admitted that God or a god had set things in motion, nevertheless preferred the secular doctrine of Cicero and Grotius that depended on reason rather than revelation to keep things going once they had started. But, it must be remembered, Grotius had borrowed heavily from the Scholastics and he acknowledged this debt by paying homage to Vittoria, Suarez, and others. It must also be noted that Adams, Jefferson and the others of the second group were always careful to include a reference to God in their scheme of things as they straddled and invoked both God and nature. But whatever either colonial group might consider as the source of natural law and natural rights, they all subscribed to certain basic rules of human behavior capable, it was said, of being discovered through reason, experience, and revelation. These rules were the same as Justinian's "immutable laws of good and evil" that the colonists restated as the Golden Rule that we know today. The objective was life, liberty and the pursuit of happiness with an emphasis on property. Positive law, that which man subjected himself to when he abandoned his idyllic state of nature in his search for society, had to conform to this inherited sense of right and wrong or be considered unnatural and not law at all.

However indefinite or vague this may seem today, it served both as a fighting faith for a successful revolution against arbitrary government and as the basis for a new experiment in government that sought to assure the rights of the individual. As it did the latter it set out areas with, it was assumed, well defined limits within which these rights that were considerable "natural" and "inalienable" could not be interfered with. And in so far as we are concerned today, what these limits consist of depends on whether the criterion applied is St. Thomas' admonition that man has a right to live as a human person, to perfect his moral nature, and live as a free and intelligent individual, or whether it is Justinian's "immutable laws of good and evil," the Golden Rule, or simply life, liberty, and the pursuit of happiness. In the final analysis, they all resemble each other in the sense that they are all concerned with the welfare of the individual. More significant than their contents is the idea that they were all intended to set up areas within the limits of which rights were considered absolute and not to be tampered with. Furthermore, as to speech and press, it is only in the definition of areas that the absolutes of the natural law approach differ from the absolutist ideas of such men as Justices Black and Douglas, particularly the former.

In the 1960 James Madison lecture he delivered at the New York University Law Center, Justice Black summarized his doctrine as follows: "To my way of thinking, at least, the history and language of the Constitution and the Bill of Rights, which I have discussed with you, make it plain that one of the primary purposes of the Constitution with its amendments was to withdraw from the Government *all* power to act in certain areas—*whatever the scope of these areas may be.*"[27] He left the "scope"—the limits—of the areas uncertain, and it is this uncertainty that has been used to accuse him of some sort of "balancing" without which, his accusers say, he could not put his doctrine into practice.[28]

As a practical matter, it is perhaps inevitable that the law of speech and press should change from one point to another in the manner of a pendulum which, to quote Mr. Justice Cardozo out of context, "has swung back and forth a good many times."[29] That is the unavoidable path that the collective opinion of a panel of nine men must follow as its composition changes and as it meets various situations. There is no danger so long as the pendulum remains suspended from a fixed point and the movement of the prohibition of the First Amendment as to speech and press is regulated by the natural law criteria that surrounded its adoption. There is danger if this fixed point and these criteria are ignored, and the meaning of liberty of speech and press is permitted to depend on the whims of the majority to the detriment of the minority whose rights it was intended to protect. There is also danger if the law of speech and press is artificially frozen in an inflexible position as it was for so long a time from the early law of seditious libel in England until well after the adoption of the First Amendment in this country.

Whatever one may think about a return to natural law principles as the method of approach to the meaning of the First Amendment, before it is questioned whether the Amendment is obsolete because of the impreciseness of its current interpretation[30] it should be recognized that the Amendment can hardly be said to enjoy a monopoly of this imperfection. Even the change that the Court made in 1925[31] when it suddenly held, in spite of earlier indications to the contrary,[32] that First Amendment freedoms apply to the states through the Fourteenth can scarcely be said to be unique in American legal history.

Very much the same thing has happened several times in the Court's treatment of the Commerce Clause. Thus, after it had held for more than a century that the production of goods was not commerce within the meaning of the clause,[33] the Court suddenly changed this in 1940 and wiped the slate clean of it in *United States* v. *Darby*.[34] Again, from the time of its decision in *Paul* v. *Virginia* in 1868,[35] the Court consistently held for seventy-five years that "issuing a policy of insurance [was] not a transaction of commerce."[36] In 1944 this too was changed when, in the *South-Eastern Underwriters case*,[37] the Court discarded its former position and adopted its present one that insurance is subject to regulation by Congress under the Commerce Clause. Also, the celebrated "switch in time that saved nine" in the *Washington Minimum Wage* case should not be overlooked.[38]

No more should it be considered unique to speech and press that the Fourteenth Amendment can be read with the greatest of care and yet nothing be found that indicates that there was any original intent that it be used, as it has been, to apply the First Amendment to the states. An equally exhaustive reading of the Amendment will fail in the same manner to reveal anything that could indicate any intention on the part of its framers that they were thinking about "corporations" when they were writing about "persons." Only the silver tongued oratory of a Roscoe Conkling could convince the Court of that. In the *San Mateo* case[39] he argued:

"Those who devised the Fourteenth Amendment wrought in grave sincerity. They may have builded better than they knew.

"They vitalized and energized a principle, as old and as everlasting as human rights. To some of them, the sunset of life may have given mystical lore.

"They builded, not for a day, but for all time; not for a few, or for a race, but for man. They planted in the Constitution a monumental truth, to stand four-square whatever wind might blow. That truth is but the golden rule, so entrenched as to curb the many who would do to the few as they would not have the few do to them."[40]

And, further, it should be recognized that dissenting opinions are anything but a recent innovation. They result from a habit that had its start very early in the history of the Court. In fact, the very first Supreme Court opinion to be recorded in the United States Reports is a dissenting opinion.[41] Also, before it is seriously considered that all could be solved by a new legislative approach that would discard any of that which has taken place to date so that a fresh start

178

could be made, one should pause, reconsider and meditate. For, although the Twenty-First Amendment rectified a mistake that was made a number of years earlier when it was believed that men could be legislated out of the habit of drinking by the simple device of a Constitutional amendment, the Eighteenth, it must nevertheless be recognized that even in the law it often happens that

> *The Moving Finger writes; and, having writ,*
> *Moves on: nor all your Piety nor Wit*
>   *Shall lure it back to cancel half a line.*
> *Nor all your Tears wash out a Word of it.*[42]

REFERENCES AND BIBLIOGRAPHY

CHAPTER I

REFERENCES

[1] Virginia Convention on the adoption of the Federal Constitution. See Elliot, *The Debates in the Several State Conventions on the Adoption of the Federal Constitution* (2nd ed., 1876), v. 3, p. 446.

[2] Delaware, Maryland, Massachusetts, New Hampshire, North Carolina, Pennsylvania, South Carolina and Virginia had adopted such bills of rights.

[3] James Wilson in the Pennsylvania Convention on the adoption of the Constitution. Elliot, v. 2, p. 435 *et seq.;* Farrand, *The Records of the Federal Convention of* 1787 (1911), v. 3, p. 143.

[4] Farrand, v. 2, p. 582.

[5] Farrand, *op. cit.,* v. 2, pp. 587, 588. See also Farrand, *The Framing of the Constitution* (1913), pp. 185, 186.

[6] Farrand, *The Record of the Federal Convention of 1787, op. cit.,* v. 2, pp. 587, 588, 589.

[7] *Ibid.,* v. 2, p. 334.   [8] *Ibid.,* p. 617.

[9] *Ibid.,* p. 618.   [10] *Ibid.,* p. 618.

[11] Letter written by James Madison to Thomas Jefferson, October 24, 1787. See Hunt, *Writings of James Madison* (1900-10), v. 5, pp. 17-35. See also Farrand, v. 2, pp. 135, 136.

[12] Farrand, v. 2, p. 637. See also p. 640 for a similar comment by Mason.

[13] 17 Howell's State Trials 675 (1735).

[14] *The Federalist,* Modern Library Edition (1941), pp. 558, 559.   [15] *Ibid.,* p. 560.

[16] Farrand, *Records of the Federal Convention of 1787, op. cit.,* v. 3, p. 143 *et seq.;* Elliot, v. 2, p. 435, *et seq.*

[17] Elliot, v. 2, p. 435. See also Charles Pinckney's answer before the South Carolina legislature to James Lincoln's question, "The liberty of the press was the tyrant's scourge—it was the true friend and firmest supporter of Liberty; therefore why pass it in silence" Elliot, v. 4, pp. 314-316.

[18] Jefferson to Madison, December 20, 1787. *Writings of Thomas Jefferson,* Memorial Edition (1903-4), v. 6, pp. 388, 389; Federal Edition (Ford, 1904-5), v. 5, pp. 371, 372.

[19] Jefferson to Washington, May 2, 1788. *Works of Thomas Jefferson,* Federal Edition, *op. cit.,* v. 5, p. 389.

[20] Jefferson to Madison, March 15, 1789. *Writings of Thomas Jefferson,* Memorial Edition, v. 7, p. 312.

[21] Elliot, v. 5, p. 243.   [22] *The Federalist,* nos. 10, 55.

[23] McRee, *Life and Correspondence of James Iredell* (1949), v. 2, pp. 147, 173.
[24] Article 1, Section 8.　　[25] Elliot, v. 3, p. 218.
[26] Elliot, v. 3, pp. 314-318, 445-449.　　[27] *Ibid.*, v. 3, p. 271.
[28] Elliot. For the Virginia recommendations see v. 3, pp. 657-659; for the New York ratification, v. 1, pp. 327-331; for the Maryland draft, v. 2, pp. 550-552.
[29] Elliot, v. 1, pp. 331-333.　　[30] 1 *Annals of Congress*. 432.　　[31] *Ibid.*, p. 434.
[32] *Ibid.*, p. 435.　　[33] *Ibid.*, p. 755.　　[34] *Ibid.*
[35] 1 *Annals of Congress* 778; [36] *Ibid.*, v. 2, Appendix, pp. 1984, 1985.

BIBLIOGRAPHY

Chafee, Zechariah. *How Human Rights Got Into the Constitution* (Boston, Boston University Press, 1952).

Elliot, Jonathan. *The Debates in the Several State Conventions on the Adoption of the Federal Constitution*, 2nd ed., 1876 (Philadelphia, J.B.Lippincott & Co.), 5 v.

Farrand, Max. *The Framing of the Constitution of the United States* (New Haven, Yale University Press, 1913).

Farrand, Max. ed. *The Records of the Federal Convention of 1787* (New Haven, Yale University Press, 1911-1937), 4 v.

Federalist, No. 84 (Hamilton).

Ford, Paul Leicester. *Essays on the Constitution of the United States, Published During its Discussion by the People, 1787-1788* (Brooklyn, N. Y., Historical Printing Club, 1892).

Ford, Paul Leicester, ed. *Pamphlets on the Constitution of the United States Published During its Discussion by the People, 1787-1788* (Brooklyn, N. Y., 1888).

Green, John R. "The Supreme Court, the Bill of Rights and the States," 97 *University of Pennsylvania Law Review* 608 (1948-49).

Patterson, Giles J. *Free Speech and a Free Press* (Boston, Little, Brown & Co., 1939).

Warren, Charles. *Congress, the Constitution and the Supreme Court* (Boston, Little, Brown & Co., 1935).

Warren, Charles, *The Making of the Constitution* (Boston, Little, Brown & Co., 1937).

Warren, Charles. "The New 'Liberty' Under the Fourteenth Amendment," 39 *Harvard Law Review* 431 (1925-26).

CHAPTER II

REFERENCES

[1] Russell, *A Treatise on Crimes and Misdemeanors* (2nd ed., 1826), v. 1, p. 211.
[2] 3 Edward I, c. 34 (1274).　　[3] 2 Richard II, stat. 1, c. 5 (1378).　　[4] 12 Richard II, c. 11 (1388).
[5] 1 and 2 Philip and Mary, c. 3 (1554).　　[6] 1 Elizabeth, c. 6 (1559).
[7] 3 Henry VII, c. 1 (1478). See Hallam, *Constitutional History of England* (5th ed., 1841), v. 1, pp. 35-40, v. 2, pp. 22-26.
[8] The early Roman law treated verbal insults as criminal or quasi-criminal. A private action was granted in all cases of insult. Redress was by means of a

fine proportionate to the insult. By the law of the Twelve Tables the public singing of ribald songs was a breach of the public order and was punished with death as the penalty. See *Sohm's Institutes of Roman Law,* trans. by Ledlie, 3rd ed. (1907), p. 422.

9 *De Libellis Famosis,* 3 Coke's Reports 254, 255 (Pt. 5, pp. 125a, 125b), (1605).

10 *Trial of Wm. Prynn,* 3 Howell's State Trials 561 (1632).

11 Taswell-Langmead, *English Constitutional History* (2nd ed., 1880), p. 759.

12 10 Anne, c. 19 (1711). In one form or another the stamp tax lasted until 1861.

13 3 Coke's Reports 254 (1606); Stephen, *History of Criminal Law in England, op. cit.,* v. 2, pp. 304, 305.

14 *Trial of John Udall,* 1 Howell's State Trials 1271 (1590); *Bushell's Case,* Vaughan, 135 (1670); *Trial of Richard Francklin,* 17 Howell's State Trials 625 (1731).

15 25 Edw. 3 c. 2 (1350); 26 Hen. 8, c. 13 (1534). See also *Trial of Robert Earl of Essex,* 1 Howell's State Trials 1333 (1600).

16 9 Howell's State Trials 1334 (1684).

17 14 Howell's State Trials 1095, 1127 (1704).

18 17 Howell's State Trials 625 (1731). The quotations appear at pages 658, 659. See also, *Trial of Benjamin Harris,* 7 Howell's State Trials 925 (1680); *Trial of Frances Smith,* 7 Howell's State Trials 933 (1680); *Trial of Henry Carr,* 7 Howell's State Trials 1111 (1680); *Trial of William Owen,* 18 Howell's State Trials 1203 (1752); *Case of H. S. Woodfall,* 20 Howell's State Trials 895 (1770).

19 4 Blackstone's *Commentaries* 151, 152 (published in 1759).

20 *Rex* v. *Joyce,* All England Reports (1945-2), pp. 673, 675. The court quoted from the Earl of Birkenhead's short life of Blackstone in *Fourteen English Judges* (1926), p. 203.

21 20 Howell's State Trials 895, 903 (1770).

22 21 Howell's State Trials 847, 1040 (1783-84).

23 *Trial of John Wilkes,* 19 Howell's State Trials 1075 (1770).

24 *Trial of John Stockdale,* 22 Howell's State Trials 238, 294-304 (1789); *Trial of John Almon,* 20 Howell's State Trials 803 (1770); *Trial of Woodfall,* 20 Howell's State Trials 895 (1770); *Dean of St. Asaph's Case,* 21 Howell's State Trials 847 (1783-84).

25 32 George III, c. 60 (1791).   26 22 Howell's State Trials 294-304 (1789).

27 *Rex* v. *Woodfall,* 20 Howell's State Trials 895 (1770). See also Stephen, v. 2, pp. 324, 325.

28 *Rex* v. *Shipley,* 21 Howell's State Trials 847 (1783). See again Stephen, v. 2, p. 330, *et seq.*

29 32 George III, c. 60 (1792).

30 Among other things Erskine had argued that when a plea of not guilty is entered to a bill of indictment or to an information charging a crime, the jury is entitled to enter a general verdict of guilty or not guilty and is not limited to a special verdict on the facts, the commission of which the indictment or information charges the crime to consist. 21 Howell's State Trials 847, 961, 962 (1784).

31 "the jury sworn to try the issue may give a general verdict of guilty or not guilty upon the whole matter put to issue upon such indictment or infor-

mation; and shall not be required or directed, by the court or judge before whom such indictment or information shall be tried, to find the defendant or defendants guilty, merely upon the proof of the publication by such defendant or defendants of the paper charged to be a libel, and of the sense ascribed to the same in such indictment or information."

[32] 22 Howell's State Trials 357 (1792).

[33] Dicey, *Introduction to the Study of the Law of the Constitution* (10th ed., 1959), p. 246.

[34] 6 & 7 Vict., c. 96 (1843). "And be it enacted, That on the trial of an Indictment or Information for a defamatory libel, the Defendant having pleaded such Plea as herein-after mentioned, the Truth of the Matters charged may be inquired into, but shall not amount to a defense, unless it was for the Public Benefit that the said Matters charged shall be punished."

[35] Tanner, *Tudor Constitutional Documents* (1930), p. 563; Taswell-Langmead, *English Constitutional History*, 10th ed. by Plucknett (1960), p. 316.

[36] Hansard, *Parliamentary History of England* (1806-20), v. 1, p. 862; Taswell-Langmead, p. 316.

[37] Hansard, v. 1, pp. 1326, 1327 (1621).

[38] Hansard, v. 1, pp. 1334, 1335 (19 James I, 1621); Taswell-Langmead, pp. 356-357; Hallam, v. 1, pp. 267-270.

[39] Hansard, v. 1, p. 1344 (19 James I, 1621).

[40] May, *The Law, Privileges, Proceedings and Usage of Parliament* (16th ed., 1957), p. 51.

[41] 1 William and Mary, sess. 2, c. 2 (1689). See Taswell-Langmead, pp. 449, 454, for the full text of the Bill of Rights.

[42] Michael, "Freedom of the Press Under Our Constitution," 33 *West Virginia Law Quarterly* 29, 36 (1926-27); Schuyler, *Liberty of the Press in the American Colonies Before the Revolutionary War* (1905), p. 7; Duniway, *The Development of Freedom of the Press in Massachusetts* (1906), p. 16.

[43] Quincy's Massachusetts Reports, 1761-1772, p. 266.

[44] 2 Hennings Statutes at Large [Virginia], 1619-1792 (1819-23) 517; 1 *Virginia Colonial Decisions,* edited by Barton (1909), p. 137. See also Cooley's *Constitutional Limitations* (8th ed., 1927), v. 2, p. 822; Michael, p. 36.

[45] Schuyler, p. 9; Michael, p. 37; Hudson, *Journalism in the United States from 1690 to 1872* (1873), pp. 44-49.

[46] Hudson, p. 67.

[47] 1 *Virginia Colonial Decisions* 145, 146 (Quoting from Thomas' *History of Printing,* p. 321).

[48] 17 Howell's State Trials 675 (1735).   [49] 17 Howell's State Trials 675, 699.

[50] *Ibid.,* p. 706.   [51] *Ibid.,* pp. 724, 725.

BIBLIOGRAPHY

Burdick, Charles K. *The Law of the American Constitution: its Origin and Development* (New York and London, G. P. Putnam's Sons, 1922).

Cooley, Thomas M. *A Treatise on the Constitutional Limitations Which Rest Upon the Legislative Power of the States of the American Union,* 8th ed. (Boston, Little, Brown & Co., 1927).

Dicey, Albert V. *Introduction to the Study of the Law of the Constitution,* 10th ed. (London, Macmillan, 1959).

Duniway, Clyde A. *The Development of Freedom of the Press in Massachusetts* (New York, Longmans, Green & Co., 1906).

Hudson, Frederic. *Journalism in the United States from 1690 to 1872* (New York, Harper & Bros., 1873).

May, Sir Thomas Erskine. *Treatise on the Law, Privilege, Proceedings, and Usage of Parliament,* 16th ed. (London, Butterworth, 1957).

Michael, Kenneth E. "Freedom of the Press Under Our Constitution," 53 *West Virginia Law Quarterly* 29 (1926-27).

Plucknett, Theodore F. *A Concise History of the Common Law,* 5th ed. (London, Butterworth, 1956).

Potter, Harold. *An Historical Introduction to English Law and Its Institutions,* 4th ed., by A. K. R. Kiralfy (London, Sweet & Maxwell, 1958).

Schuyler, Livingston R. *Liberty of the Press in the American Colonies Before The Revolutionary War* (New York, T. Whittaker, 1905).

Tanner, Joseph R. *Tudor Constitutional Documents, A.D. 1485-1603* with an historical commentary by J. R. Tanner (Cambridge, England, The University Press, 1930).

Taswell-Langmead, Thomas Pitt. *English Constitutional History from the Teutonic Conquest to the Present Time,* 11th ed., by Theodore F. T. Plucknett (London, Sweet & Maxwell, 1960).

Veeder, Van Vechten. "The History of the Law of Defamation," 3 *Select Essays in Anglo-American Legal History* 447 (Association of American Law Schools, 1907).

Wickwar, William H. *The Struggle for the Freedom of the Press, 1819-1932* (London, G. Allen & Unwin Ltd., 1928).

CHAPTER III

REFERENCES

[1] 3 Car. 1, c. 1 (1628). See Taswell-Langmead, *English Constitutional History* (11th ed., by Plucknett, 1960), pp. 192-193.

[2] 1 William and Mary, Sess. 2, c. 2 (1928).

[3] Coke, *The Fourth Part of the Institutes of the Laws of England,* p. 36 (published in 1644 after Coke's death).

[4] 1 Blackstone's *Commentaries* 48, 49.

[5] 1 Blackstone's *Commentaries* 162. See also Dicey, *Introduction to the Study of the Law of the Constitution* (10th ed., 1959), Chapt. 1; Haines, "The Law of Nature in State and Federal Judicial Decisions," 25 *Yale Law Journal* 617, 622, 623 (1915-1916).

[6] May, *A Treatise on the Law, Privileges, Proceedings and Usage of Parliament* (16th ed., 1957), p. 28.

[7] Milton, *Areopagitica,* 3 Harvard Classics 227.

[8] *Lord Erskine's Speeches,* collected by James Ridgway (2nd ed., 1813), v. 2, pp. 139, 140.

[9] *Areopagitica,* 3 Harvard Classics 227, 229.

References and Bibliography

[10] Michael, "Freedom of the Press Under Our Constitution," 33 *West Virginia Law Quarterly* 29, 36 (1926-27); Schroeder, *Obscene Literature and Constitutional Law* (1911), p. 214; Schroeder, "The Historical Interpretation of Freedom of Speech and of the Press," 70 *Central Law Journal* 184, 189 (1910).

[11] Cicero, *De Re Publica, De Legibus,* with an English translation by Clinton Walker Keyes (Loeb Classical Library, 1943), p. 9.

[12] Cicero, *De Re Publica,* III, xxiii (p. 211); *De Legibus,* I, vi (pp. 317-319), vii (pp. 321-323), viii (p. 325); III (p. 461).

[13] *De Legibus,* I, vi (p. 319).

[14] *De Re Publica,* I, xxv (p. 65); Carlyle, v. 1, p. 13. For the discussion of the struggle in seventeenth century England, see *infra.*

[15] *De Re Publica,* I, xxv (p. 65).   [16] *Ibid.,* III, xxxi (p. 219).

[17] Pegis, *Basic writings of St. Thomas Aquinas* (1945), v. 2, pp. 748, 750; *Selections from Three Works of Francisci Suarez,* The Classics of International Law, edited by James Brown Scott (1944), Book 2, Chapter 2.

[18] St. Augustine, *The City of God,* Chapter XV; Oates, *Basic Writings of Saint Augustine* (1948), v. 2, p. 491.

[19] 2 Pegis 743.   [20] St. Thomas quoting from Isadore, 2 Pegis 786.

[21] For a discussion of these conflicts see Carlyle, *A History of Medieval Political Theory in the West* (1953), v. 4.

[22] Pius in the second century and Callistus in the third. For further discussion of the Church's early stand on slavery see *The Catholic Encyclopedia* (1912), v. 14, pp. 36-41. See also Carlyle, v. 4, pp. 21-23.

[23] Henrici de Bracton, *De Legibus et Consuetudinibus Angliae,* edited by Sir Travers Twiss (1878-83), v. 1, pp. 13, 15, 19.   [24] *Ibid.,* p. 21.

[25] Bracton, p. 39. See also, *Select Passages from the Works of Bracton and Azo,* edited for the Selden Society by Frederick William Maitland, Publications of the Selden Society, v. 8, pp. xxx, xxxi (1895).

[26] *Trial of Sir Thomas More for High Treason,* 1 Howell's State Trials 385, 392 (1535).

[27] Holdsworth, *A History of English Law* (4th ed., 1936), v. 2, pp. 443-444. See also the dictum in *Dr. Bonham's Case,* 8 Coke's Reports 114a, 118a (1610).

[28] *Infra.*

[29] See Campbell, *Lives of the Lord Chancellors of England* (7th ed., (1878), Introduction; Pollock, *The Expansion of the Common Law* (1904), pp. 114, 115; Bryce, *Studies in History and Jurisprudence* (1901), v. 2, pp. 599, 600; Plucknett, *A Concise History of the Common Law* (5th ed., 1956), p. 675; Lawson, *The Rational Strength of English Law,* Hamlyn Lectures, 3rd series, 1951; Story, *Commentaries on Equity Jurisprudence as Administered in England and America* (14th ed., 1918), Chapt. 2.

[30] Bracton, *De Legibus et Consuetudinibus Angliae,* edited by Sir Travers Twiss (1878-83), v. 1, p. 19.

[31] d'Entreves, *Natural Law* (1951), p. 51.

[32] Hugo Grotius, *De Jure Belli Ac Pacis* (1625), The Classics of International Law, Carnegie Endowment for International Peace, v. 2, pp. 11, 13.

[33] *Ibid.,* p. 12.   [34] *Ibid.,* p. 13.   [35] *Ibid.,* p. 12.   [36] *Ibid.,* p. 14.

[37] *Ibid.,* p. 23.   [38] *Ibid.,* p. 40.

[39] Pufendorf, *De Jure Naturae et Gentium Libri Octo*, v. 2 (translation of the edition of 1688 by C. H. and W. A. Oldfather), p. 201.

[40] *Ibid.*

[41] Locke, *An Essay Concerning the Understanding, Knowledge, Opinion and Assent* (with an introduction by Benjamin Rand, 1931), pp. 19, 20.

[42] "Maiestas est summa in cives ac subditos legibusque solata potestas." *De Republica Libri Sex* (1586), Book I, Chapter VIII.

[43] Hobbes, *Leviathan* (edited with an introduction by Michael Oakeshott, 1947), Chapter 13.

[44] *Ibid.*, p. 137.

[45] Locke, *Two Treatises of Government* (with an introduction by Thomas I. Cook, 1947), Chapter II. See also, *Social Contract: Essays by Locke, Hume and Rousseau* (with an introduction by Sir Ernest Barker, 1948).

[46] Locke, p. 123 ("The Second Treatise of Civil Government").

[47] *Ibid.*, p. 207.   [48] *Ibid.*, p. 233.   [49] *Ibid.*, pp. 237, 238.   [50] Holdsworth, v. 6, pp. 282, 283.

[51] *Discourses Concerning Government* (1698).

[52] *De Iure Naturae et Gentium* (1672).

[53] *Principes du Droit Naturel* (1747).

[54] Curti, *The Growth of American Thought* (2nd ed., 1951), Chapt. 5; Cairns, *Law and the Social Sciences* (1935), p. 336; Bryce, *Studies in History and Jurisprudence* (1901), v. 2, pp. 598, 599; Haines, *The American Doctrine of Judicial Supremacy* (1959), pp. 52-59; d'Entreves, pp. 60-62.

[55] d'Entreves, Chapt. III; Bryce, pp. 597-604; Reuschlein, *Jurisprudence—Its American Prophets* (1951), pp. 1-25.

[56] *Leviathan, op. cit.,* Chapt. 14.

[57] "Second Treatise of Government," *op. cit.,* Chapt. 6,§§ 59, 63.

[58] *De Jure Naturae et Gentium*, Libri Octo (1688), p. 158.

[59] Burlamaqui, *The Principles of Natural Law* (1758), p. 2.

[60] Published in 1758.   [61] Discussed *infra.*

[62] Letter to Francis W. Gilmer, June 7, 1816, 15 *Writings of Thomas Jefferson* 23, 24, 25 (Memorial ed., *op. cit.*).

[63] Letter to John Adams, October 14, 1816, 15 *Writings of Thomas Jefferson* 76 (Memorial ed.).

[64] *Ibid.* The passage continues: "as a wise creator must have seen to be necessary in an animal destined to life in society; that every human mind feels pleasure in doing good to another; that the nonexistence of justice is not to be inferred from the fact that the same act is deemed virtuous and right in one society which is held vicious and wrong in another; because, as the circumstances and opinions of different societies vary, so the acts which may do them right or wrong vary also; for virtue does not consist in the act we do, but in the end it is to effect."

[65] Wilson's Works (edited by Andrews, 1896), v. 2, p. 103. Hamilton referred to Hobbes' doctrine as "absurd and impius." 1 *Works of Alexander Hamilton* 62 (1850-51).

[66] "A Sermon Preached in the Audience of His Excellency William Shirley, Esq. May 29, 1754," p. 2 (quoted by Becker, p. 78).

References and Bibliography

67 *Twenty Sermons Preached in the Parish of St. Philips Church, Charleston, S. C.*, (1750), pp. 59, 60.

68 Reinsch, "The English Common Law in The Early American Colonies," 1 *Select Essays in Anglo-American Legal History* (1907), 367, 377 (Quoting from Hutchinson Papers, v. 2, p. 1).

69 *Ibid.*, p. 375.

70 *The Colonial Laws of Massachusetts*, reprinted from the edition of 1672, with supplements through 1688, p. 1.

71 *Fundamental Orders of Connecticut*, 1638-39.

72 Reinsch, p. 386 (quoting from New Haven Records, I, 73).

73 1 *Virginia Colonial Decisions* 139 (1909). See Barton's Introduction.

74 *The Patriot Preachers of the American Revolution*, p. 39 (quoted by Becker, p. 75).

75 Quincy's Massachusetts Reports, p. 474.

76 See *A Source Book of American Political Theory* (edited by Benjamin F. Wright, Jr., 1929), p. 51.

77 Memorial of Boston, 1765. See Quincy's Massachusetts Reports, p. 200.

78 3 *Works of John Adams* 475 (1850-56).

79 Earlier, in 1772, Mason had argued for the freedom of the descendants of Indian women held in slavery. He contended that the act under which the original importation and sale had taken place was void for the following reason: "The laws of nature are the laws of God; whose authority can be superseded by no person on earth. A legislature must not obstruct our obedience to him from whose punishment they cannot protect us. All human constitutions which contradict his laws, we are in conscience bound to disobey." *Robin* v. *Hardaway*, Jefferson's Reports (Virginia, 1772), p. 109.

80 1 Blackstone's *Commentaries* 48, 49.

81 Wilson, "Considerations on the Nature and Extent of the Legislative Authority of the British Parliament" (1774). See *Wilson's Works, op. cit.*, v. 2, pp. 501, 507, 508.

82 *Journals of the Continental Congress* (1904-37 , v. 1, p. 108.

BIBLIOGRAPHY

Barker, Sir Ernest, ed. *Social Contract: Essays by Locke, Hume and Rousseau* (London, Oxford University Press, 1948).

Becker, Carl L. *The Declaration of Independence: a Study in the History of Political Ideas* (New York, A. A. Knopf, 1942).

Cairns, Huntington. *Legal Philosophy from Plato to Hegel* (Baltimore, Johns Hopkins Press, 1949).

Corwin, Edward S. "The Debt of American Constitutional Law to Natural Law Concepts," 25 *Notre Dame Lawyer* 258 (1949-50).

Corwin, Edward S. "The Natural Law and Constitutional Law," 3 *University of Notre Dame Natural Law Institute Proceedings, 1949.* 47.

Curti, Merle E. *Growth of American Thought*, 2nd ed., (New York, Harper, 1951).

d'Entreves, A. P. *Natural Law: an Introduction to Legal Philosophy* (London, Hutchinson's University Library, 1951).

Friedman, Wolfgang, *Legal Theory.* 4th ed., (London, Stevens, 1960).

Friedrich, Carl J., *The Philosophy of Law in Historical Perspective* (Chicago, University of Chicago Press, 1958).

Gierke, Otto Friedrich von. *Natural Law and the Theory of Society, 1500 to 1800* (Boston, Beacon Press, 1957).

Gilson, Etienne. *History of Christian Philosophy in the Middle Ages* (New York, Random House, 1955).

Haines, Charles G. "The Law of Nature in State and Federal Judicial Decisions," 25 *Yale Law Journal* 617 (1915-16).

Haines, Charles G. *The Revival of Natural Law Concepts* (Cambridge; Harvard University Press, 1930).

Lucey, Francis E. "Natural Law and the American Realism: Their Respective Contributions to a Theory of Law in a Democratic Society," 30 *Georgetown Law Journal* 493 (1941-42).

McIlwain, Charles H. *The Growth of Political Thought in the West From the Greeks to the End of the Middle Ages* (New York, The MacMillan Co., 1932).

Maritain, Jacques. *Les Droits de L'Homme et La Loi Naturelle* (New York, Editions de la Maison Francaise, inc., 1942).

Miller, John C. *Origins of the American Revolution* (Boston, Little, Brown & Co., 1943).

Padover, Saul K. *World of the Founding Fathers; Their Basic Ideas on Freedom and Self-Government* (New York, Yoseloff, 1960).

Pollock, Sir Frederick. *The Expansion of the Common Law* (London, Stevens and Sons, Ltd., 1904).

Reinsch, Paul S. "The English Common Law in the Early American Colonies," 1 *Select Essays in Anglo-American Legal History* 367 (Association of American Law Schools, 1907).

Reuschlein, Harold Gill. *Jurisprudence—Its American Prophets: a survey of taught jurisprudence* (Indianapolis, Bobbs-Merrill, 1951).

Rommen, Heinrich A. *The Natural Law,* translated by Thomas R. Hanley (St. Louis, Herder Book Co., 1949).

Sabine, George H. *A History of Political Theory, rev. ed.* (New York, H. Holt, 1959).

Stephen, Sir Leslie. *History of English Thought in the Eighteenth Century* (New York, G. P. Putnam's Sons, 1927).

Wilkin, Robert N. "Cicero and the Law of Nature," 1 *Southern Methodist University Studies in Jurisprudence* 1 (1954).

Wilkin, Robert N. *Eternal Lawyer: A Legal Biography of Cicero* (New York, MacMillan Co., 1947).

Wilkin, Robert N. "Status of Natural Law in American Jurisprudence," 2 *University of Notre Dame Natural Law Institute Proceedings, 1948,* 125.

Wright, B. F., Jr. "Natural Law in American Political Theory," 4 *Southwestern Political Science Quarterly* 202 (1923-24).

CHAPTER IV

REFERENCES

[1] Pound, *The Formative Era of American Law* (1938), pp. 102-104. See also

Pound, *New Paths of the Law* (1950), p. 14, and Pound, *Jurisprudence* (1959), v. 2, pp. 118-120.

[2] Letter, Jefferson to Madison, February 7, 1826. 12 *Writings of Thomas Jefferson* (Federal Edition, *op. cit.)* 455, 456.

[3] *Works of James Wilson* (Andrews, *op. cit.*) v. 1, pp. 92, 93.

[4] For a collection of State precedents before 1789 see Haines, *The American Doctrine of Judicial Supremacy* (1959), Chapter 5.

[5] 1 Tucker's *Blackstone* 88 (1803).   [6] 1 Cranch 137 (1803).

[7] 5 Elliot's *Debates* (*op. cit.*) 278, 279.

[8] See Locke's chapter on property in his "Second Treatise of Civil Government."

[9] 2 Dallas 304 (1795).   [10] 3 Dallas 386 (1798).   [11] *Ibid.*, pp. 387, 388.

[12] 6 Cranch 87 (1810).

[13] *Ibid.*, p. 139.   [14] *Ibid.*, p. 143.   [15] 20 Wallace 655 (1874).

[16] 20 Wallace 655, 662. The fact that the city had already paid one installment of interest was found not to have worked an estoppel.

[17] *Ibid.*, p. 663.   [18] Lowell, *Essays on Government* (1889), pp. 189, 190.

[19] *Ibid.*   [20] *Ibid.*, p. 190.   [21] Jeremy Bentham, 1748-1832. See his *Introduction to Principles of Morals and Legislation*, first published in 1789.

[22] John Austin, 1790-1859. Although his *Lectures on Jurisprudence* were published in 1832 during his lifetime, they were little noticed until they were republished after his death by his widow. See preface to the 5th ed., revised and edited by Robert Campbell (1885).

[23] Lowell, p. 190.

[24] *Monongahelia Bridge Co.* v. *U. S.*, 216 U. S. 177, 195 (1910).

[25] Holmes, "Natural Law," first published in 32 *Harvard Law Review* 40 (1918). It is reprinted in Lerner, *The Mind and Faith of Justice Holmes* (1943, 1948), pp. 394-398.

[26] *McDonald* v. *Mabee*, 243 U. S. 90, 91, 92 (1917).

[27] 169 U. S. 366 (1898).   [28] *Ibid.*, pp. 389, 390.   [29] 211 U. S. 78 (1908).

[30] 272 U. S. 312 (1926).   [31] *Ibid.*, p. 316, 317.

[32] 302 U. S. 319 (1937).   [33] *Ibid.*, p. 328.

[34] 357 U. S. 116 (1958).   [35] *Ibid.*, p. 125.   [36] *Ibid.*, p. 129.

[37] *Ibid.* (Emphasis added).

[38] See also *Rochin* v. *California,* 342 U. S. 165 (1952), the celebrated stomach pumping case, in which a narcotics conviction was reversed because the evidence was obtained by methods held violative of the Due Process Clause of the Fourteenth Amendment. Speaking through Mr. Justice Frankfurter, the majority expounded that as there conceived due process of law was not to be derided "as resort to a revival of 'natural law'." (342 U. S. 165, 171).

[39] 3 Dallas 386 (1798), cited *supra*.   [40] *Ibid.*, p. 398.

[41] See 20 Wallace 655, 699 (1874).   [42] 332 U.S. 46 (1947).   [43] 211 U.S. 78 (1908).

[44] 332 U.S. 46, 69. Perhaps Mr. Justice Black's position is explained by his belief that all of the first ten amendments to the Constitution are applicable to the states by virtue of the Fourteenth, and by his belief that there are "absolutes" in the Bill of Rights. See Black, "The Bill of Rights," 35 *New York University Law Review* 865, 866, 867 (1960).

[45] The trials are discussed in Chapter V.

BIBLIOGRAPHY

Austin, John. *Lectures in Jurisprudence,* 5th ed., rev., edited by Robert Campbell (London, J. Murray, 1885).

Bentham, Jeremy. *Introduction to Principles of Morals and Legislation* (first published in 1789).

Boudin, Louis B. "Lord Coke and the American Doctrine of Judicial Power," 6 *New York University Law Review* 223 (1928-29).

Curtis, Charles P. *Law as large as life* (New York, Simon and Schuster, 1959).

Freund, Paul A. *On Understanding the Supreme Court* (Boston, Little, Brown & Co., 1949).

Haines, Charles G. *The American Doctrine of Judicial Supremacy* (New York, Russell & Russell, 1959).

Hand, Learned. "Chief Justice Stone's Conception of the Judicial Function," 46 *Columbia Law Review* **696 (1946).**

Holmes, Oliver Wendell, Jr. "Natural Law," 32 *Harvard Law Review* 40 (1918-19).

Lowell, Abbott Lawrence. *Essays on Government* (Boston, Houghton, Mifflin and Co., 1889).

McKinnon, Harold R. "Natural Law and Positive Law," 1947 *University of Notre Dame Natural Law Institute Proceedings* 85.

Mason, Alpheus Thomas, and Beaney, William M. *The Supreme Court in a Free Society* (Englewood Cliffs, N. J., Prentice-Hall, 1959).

Plucknett, Theodore F. "Bonham's Case and Judicial Review," 40 *Harvard Law Review* 30 (1926-27).

Pound, Roscoe. *New Paths of the Law* (Lincoln, Nebraska, University of Nebraska Press, 1950).

Pound, Roscoe. *The Formative Era of American Law* (Boston, Little Brown & Co., 1938).

Pound, Roscoe. *The Spirit of the Common Law* (Boston, Marshall Jones Co., 1921).

CHAPTER V

REFERENCES

[1] Act of June 18, 1798, 1 Statutes at Large **566.** (Hereinafter cited as "Stat.")

[2] Acts of June 25 and July 6, 1798, 1 Stat. 570, 577.

[3] Act of July 14, 1798, 1 Stat. 596, 597.

[4] The Republican party which Jefferson headed is not to be confused with the present-day party of the same name.

[5] See remarks by Mr. Gallatin in the House of Representatives, 8 *Annals of Congress* 2107-2111 (5th Congress, 1797-99); also, remarks by Mr. Nicholas, pp. 2139-2144, and by Mr. Livingston, pp. 2151-2156.

[6] Letter, Hamilton to Oliver Wolcott, June 29, 1798. *See Works of Alexander Hamilton* (edited by Lodge, 1904), v. 10 p. 295.

[7] 8 *Annals of Congress* (5th Congress, 1797-99) 2093, 2094.

[8] *Ibid.,* p. 2097 *et seq.*   [9] *Ibid.,* p. 2102.

[10] Letter, Hamilton to Jonathan Bayton, *Works of Alexander Hamilton, op. cit.,* v. 10, pp. 335, 336.

References and Bibliography

[11] Elliot, *The Debates in the Several State Conventions on the Adoption of the Federal Constitution* (2nd ed., 1876), v. 4, pp. 540, 541.

[12] Elliot, v. 4, p. 529.

[13] For the answers of the states see Elliot, v. 4, pp. 532-539.

[14] Jefferson to Thomas McKean, February 19, 1803. *Works of Thomas Jefferson* (Federal Edition, 1904-5), v. 9, pp. 449, 451, 452. See also, Miller, *Crisis in Freedom: The Alien and Sedition Acts* (1951), p. 231 *et seq.*

[15] Anderson, "The Enforcement of the Alien and Sedition Laws," *American Historical Association Report, 1912.* See House Document No. 933, 63rd Congress, 2nd session, p. 120.

[16] March 3, 1801. See sec. 4 of the act cited *supra.*

[17] Wharton, *State Trials of the United States During the Administrations of Washington and Adams* (1849), p. 719.

[18] *United States* v. *Hudson,* 7 Cranch 32 (1812).

[19] He was indicted October 5, 1798, and his trial started October 7, 1798. See Wharton, p. 333.

[20] Wharton, p. 333.   [21] *Ibid.,* p. 336.   [22] *Ibid.* p. 684.

[23] *Ibid.,* p. 684.   [24] *Ibid.,* p. 685.   [25] *Ibid.,* p. 659.   [26] *Ibid.*   [27] *Ibid.,* p. 670.

[28] *Ibid.,* p. 670.   [29] *Ibid.,* p. 672.   [30] *Ibid.,* p. 676.   [31] *Ibid.,* p. 688.

[32] See Trial of Judge Chase, 14 *Annals of Congress,* 8th Congress, 2nd Session (1804-5).

[33] Letter, Jefferson to Mason, October 11, 1798, *The Works of Thomas Jefferson* (Federal Edition, *op. cit.*), v. 8, pp. 449-450; Beveridge, v. 3, p. 36.

[34] Wharton, p. 688.   [35] *Ibid.,* p. 689.   [36] *Ibid.,* p. 690.

[37] See testimony of John Mason, *Trial of Judge Chase for Impeachment,* 14 *Annals of Congress,* 8th Cong., 2nd Session (1804-5), p. 216.

[38] Testimony of James Triplett, *Trial of Judge Chase,* p. 217.

[39] Wharton, pp. 696, 697.

[40] See testimony of Gunning Bedford, Nicholas Vandyke, Archibald Hamilton, John Hall, and Samuel Moore at The Trial of Judge Chase, 14 *Annals of Congress,* 8th Congress, 2nd Session, pp. 283-291.

[41] Flanders, *The Lives and Times of the Chief Justices of the Supreme Court of the United States* (1875), v. 2, p. 47; Warren, *The Supreme Court in United States History* (1926), v. 1, p. 166, note 2.

[42] McRee, *The Life of James Iredell* (1949), v. 2, pp. 551-570.

[43] Flanders, v. 2, pp. 193-194; Brown, *The Life of Oliver Ellsworth* (1905), pp. 265, 266.

[44] Section 2 of the Act.

[45] Justice Chase in Cooper's trial, Wharton, p. 676. See also, Justice Patterson in Howell's trial, Wharton, p. 686.

[46] See Haswell's trial, Wharton, p. 685; Callender's trial, Wharton, p. 707, 708.

[47] Wharton, p. 708.

[48] Lord Mansfield in the *Dean of St. Asaph's Case,* 21 Howell's State Trials 847, 1040 (1783-84).

[49] *Trial of Gideon Henfield,* Wharton, p. 49; *Trial of Isaac Williams,* Wharton, p. 652; *Trial of Joseph Ravard,* Wharton, p. 90.

⁵⁰ 6 Stat. 802, Chapter XLV (1840); 6 Stat. 924, Chapter CXXXVI (1844); 9 Stat. 799, Chapter XXXIV (1850).

⁵¹ 205 U. S. 454 (1907).

⁵² 205 U. S. 454, 462.

⁵³ *Ibid.* But see Mr. Justice Harlan's dissent in which he registers protest to the "absence of previous restraint" theory and argues that the prohibitions of the First Amendment apply to state action through the Fourteenth. He concluded, "It is, I think, impossible to conceive of liberty as secured by the Constitution against hostile action, whether by the Nation or by the States, which does not embrace the right to enjoy free speech and the right to have a free press." 205 U. S. 454, 465.

⁵⁴ Discussed at length, *infra,* Chapter 8.

⁵⁵ 283 U. S. 697 (1931). ⁵⁶ *Ibid.,* pp. 716, 717 (amphasis added).

⁵⁷ 297 U. S. 233 (1936). ⁵⁸ *Ibid.,* pp. 248, 249.

BIBLIOGRAPHY

Anderson, "The Enforcement of the Alien and Sedition Laws," *American Histori--cal Association Report, 1912* (House Document No. 933, 63rd Con., 2nd Sess.).

Antieu, Chester J. "Judicial Delimitations of the First Amendment Freedoms," 34 *Marquette Law Review* 57 (1950-51).

Bassett, Robert C. "Freedom of the Press," 25 *Marquette Law Review* 28 (1940-41).

Carroll, Thomas F. "Freedom of Speech and of the Press in the Federalist Period: The Sedition Act," 18 *Michigan Law Review* 615 (1919-20).

Carter, John S. "Constitutional Law: Freedom of the Press: Injunction of Newspaper's Publication as a Nuisance," 17 *Cornell Law Quarterly* 126 (1931-32).

Jarrett, Lawrence. "Circulation as an Essential Element of a Free Press," 13 *St. John's Law Review* 81 (1938).

Miller, John. *Crisis in Freedom: the Alien and Sedition Acts* (Boston, Little, Brown & Co., 1951).

Peairs, C. A. "Freedom of the Press," 28 *Kentucky Law Journal* 369 (1939-40).

"Previous Restraints Upon Freedom of Speech," note, 31 *Columbia Law Review* 1148 (1931).

Warren, Charles. *A History of the American Bar* (Boston, Little, Brown & Co., 1911).

Wharton, Francis. *State Trials of the United States During the Administrations of Washington and Adams* (Philadelphia, Cary and Hart, 1849), cited as *Wharton's State Trials.*

CHAPTER VI

REFERENCES

¹ Hearings, Committee on the Judiciary, House of Representatives, 66th Congress, 2nd Session (1919-20), on S. 3317, H.R. 10650 and H.R. 12041, pp. 21, 35.

² 32 George III, c. 60 (1792), discussed *supra,* Chapter 2.

³ 27 Howell's State Trials 641, 674 (1779). See also Chafee, *Free Speech in the United States* (1946), p. 13.

⁴ *Toledo Newspaper Co.* v. *United States,* 247 U. S. 402, 419, 420 (1918).

5 *Gitlow* v. *New York*, 268 U. S. 652, 666 (1925) (emphasis added).

6 *Ibid.*, p. 667, citing 2 *Story on the Constitution* (5th ed., 1905) § 1580, p. 634.

7 247 U. S. 402 (1918), overruled by *Nye* v. *United States*, 313 U. S. 33 (1941).

8 247 U. S. 402, 419.   9 *Ibid.*, 421.

10 Act of June 15, 1917, 40 Stat. 217.

11 Act of May 16, 1918, 40 Stat. 553; repealed in 1921 to revive the 1917 act intact, 41 Stat. 1359.

12 40 Stat. 219.   13 246 Fed. 24 (C.A. 2, 1917).

14 244 Fed. 535, 540 (D. C., S. D., N. Y., 1917).   15 *Ibid.*

16 246 Fed. 24, 38 (C. A. 2, 1917).   17 249 U. S. 47 (1919).

18 *Ibid.*, 52.   19 *Ibid.*   20 249 U. S. 204 (1919).   21 *Ibid.*, p. 206.

22 *Ibid.*, 209.   23 249 U. S. 211 (1919).

24 Transcript of Record, *Eugene V. Debs* v. *United States*, case no. 714, Supreme Court of the United States, October Term 1918, p. 279.

25 250 U. S. 616 (1919).   26 251 U. S. 466 (1920).

27 252 U. S. 239 (1920).   28 255 U. S. 407 (1921).   29 *Infra*, Chapter 7.

30 For the full text of the indictment see Transcript of Record, case no. 316, Supreme Court of the United States, October Term 1919, pp. 2-15.

31 251 U. S. 466, 475.

32 *Ibid.*, 479.   33 252 U. S. 239, 244 (1920).   34 Discussed *infra*, Chapter 7.

35 *Schaefer* v. *United States*, 251 U. S. 466, 501.

36 New York Laws of 1902, Chapter 371.

37 For a collection of these see note, 84 *University of Pennsylvania Law Review* 390 (1936).

38 See *Gitlow* v. *New York*, 268 U. S. 652 (1925).

39 See *Burns* v. *Unitel States*, 274 U. S. 328, 335 (1927).   40 254 U. S. 325 (1920).

41 Chapter 463, Laws of Minnesota, approved April 20, 1917.

42 Quoted by the majority from *Frohwerk* v. *United States*, 249 U. S. 204, 206 (1919).

43 254 U. S. 325, 333.   44 268 U. S. 652 (1925).

45 New York Laws of 1902, Chapter 371.

46 268 U. S. 652, 667.   47 *Ibid.*   48 *Ibid.*, 669.

49 *Ibid.*, p. 670.   50 *Ibid.*, p. 668.

51 274 U. S. 257 (1927).   52 California Statutes, 1919, c. 188.

53 274 U. S. 328 (1927). Although the violation for which the defendant was tried and convicted took place in the Yosemite National Park, Federal property, the California law applied. By virtue of an act of Congress (Act of June 2, 1920, 41 Stat. 731), offenses committed in the park that were not prohibited by Federal law were made subject to California laws which prohibited similar offenses and provided punishment.

54 Transcript of Record, case no. 135, Supreme Court of the United States, October Term 1926, p. 68 (emphasis added).

55 274 U. S. 328, 335.   56 274 U. S. 380 (1927).   57 *Ibid.*, p. 386.   58 *Ibid.*

59 Eliel, "Freedom of Speech During and Since the Civil War," 18 *American Political Science Review* 712, 724-736 (1924); Chafee, *Free Speech in the United States* (1946), Chapter 1; Naussaman, "Free Speech in Wartime," 17 *California State Bar Journal* 109 (1942); Hanson, "The Supreme Court on

Freedom of the Press and Contempt by Publication," 27 *Cornell Law Quarterly* 165 (1941-42); *Herndon* v. *Lowry,* 301 U. S. 242, 263 (1937); *Bridges* v. *California,* 314 U. S. 252 (1941).

60 *Abrams* v. *United States,* 250 U. S. 616, 621 (1910). See also, *Pierce* v. *United States,* 252 U. S. 239, 249 (1920).

61 Mr. Justice Frankfurter concurring in *Dennis* v. *United States,* 341 U. S. 494, 540 (1951).

62 Brian, J., *Year Book,* 17 Edward IV, 2.

63 *Gompers* v. *United States,* 233 U. S. 604, 610 (1914), quoted by Mr. Justice Frankfurter, dissenting in *Bridges* v. *California,* 314 U. S. 252, 293 (1941).

64 *Ibid.*   65 *Ibid.*   66 Mr. Justice Frankfurter dissenting, *Bridges* v. *California,* 314 U. S. 252, 295.   67 *Ibid.,* p. 294.

68 Mr. Justice Black for the majority in *Bridges* v. *California,* p. 264; see also, pp. 265, 266.

69 *Ibid.,* quoting from Schofield, "Freedom of the Press in the United States," 9 *Publications of the American Sociological Society* 67, 76. See also, Radin, "Freedom of Speech and Contempt of Court," 36 *Illinois Law Review* 599 (1942).

70 See also, *Herndon* v. *Lowry,* 301 U. S. 242 (1937) in which the Court refused to apply "reasonable tendency," and *Nye* v. *United States,* 313 U. S. 33 (1941), in which the Court overruled *Toledo Newspapers* v. *United States,* 247 U. S. 402 (1918).

BIBLIOGRAPHY

Coyle, Edward L. "Limiting the Freedom of Speech by Suppressing the Advocacy of Direct Action," 4 *University of Cincinnati Law Review* 211 (1930).

Douglas, William O. *We the Judges; Studies in American and Indian Constitutional Law from Marshall to Mukherjea,* 1st ed., (Garden City, N. Y., Doubleday, 1956).

Eliel, Richard H. "Freedom of Speech During and Since the Civil War," 18 *American Political Science Review* 712 (1924).

Hanson, Elisha. "The Supreme Court on Freedom of the Press and Contempt by Publication," 27 *Cornell Law Quarterly* 165 (1942).

Mahoney, William P. "The Right of Free Speech," 15 *Notre Dame Lawyer* 241 (1939-40).

Nossaman, Walter L. "Free Speech in Wartime," 17 *California State Bar Journal* 109 (1942).

O'Brian, John Lord. "New Encroachments on Individual Freedom," 65 *Harvard Law Review* 1 (1952).

Radin, Max. "Freedom of Speech and Contempt of Court," 36 *Illinois Law Review* 599 (1941-42).

Taft, Henry W. "Freedom of Speech and the Espionage Act," 55 *American Law Review* 695 (1921).

U. S. Congress, House of Representatives, Hearings, Committee on the Judiciary, 66th Congress, 2nd Session, on S. 3317, H.R. 10650, and H.R. 12041 (1919-20).

Warner, David R. "Criminal Syndicalism," note, 14 *Nebraska Law Bulletin* 365 (1935-36).

Willis, Hugh E. "Freedom of Speech and of the Press," 4 *Indiana Law Journal* 445 (1928-29).

CHAPTER VII

REFERENCES

[1] Discussed *supra*, Chapter 6.   [2] 249 U. S. 47 (1919).   [3] See *infra*, Chapters 8 and 9.   [4] 205 U. S. 454 (1907), discussed *supra*, Chapter 5.

[5] 249 U. S. 47, 52.   [6] *Ibid.*

[7] January 24, 1918. *Pollock-Holmes Letters* (edited by Mark DeWolfe Howe, with an introduction by Sir John Pollock, 1942), v. 1, p. 258.

[8] December 1, 1925. *Pollock-Holmes Letters*, v. 2, p. 173.

[9] *Frohwerk* v. *United States*, 249 U. S. 204 (1919); *Debs* v. *United States*, 249 U. S. 211 (1919), both discussed *supra*, Chapter 6.

[10] Chafee, *Free Speech in the United States* (1946), p. 86.

[11] *Pollock-Holmes Letters*, v. 2, p. 7.   [12] *Ibid.*, p. 11.   [13] 250 U. S. 616 (1919).

[14] See Holmes' Letter to Pollock, December 14, 1919, *Pollock-Holmes Letters*, v. 2, p. 32.

[15] The facts of the case are given more in detail in the discussion of the majority opinion, *supra*, Chapter 6.

[16] 250 U. S. 616, 627.

[17] *Ibid.*, pp. 627, 628.

[18] 250 U. S. 616, 630, 631. Cf. Wiener, " 'Freedom for the Thought that we Hate'; is it a Principle of the Constitution?" 37 *American Bar Association Journal* 177 (1951).

[19] *Abrams* v. *United States*, 250 U. S. 616 (1919); *Schaefer* v. *United States*, 251 U. S. 466 (1920); *Pierce* v. *United States*, 252 U. S. 239 (1920); *Gilbert* v. *Minnesota*, 254 U. S. 325 (1920); *Gitlow* v. *New York*, 268 U. S. 652 (1925); *Whitney* v. *California*, 274 U. S. 357 (1927).

[20] The *Whitney* case.

[21] The *Abrams, Schaefer* and *Pierce* cases.

[22] The *Gilbert, Gitlow* and *Whitney* cases.

[23] The *Gilbert* case.   [24] 251 U. S. 466 (1920).   [25] *Ibid.*, 482.

[26] *Ibid.*, 483.   [27] 252 U. S. 239 (1920).

[28] See § 3 of the Act of June 15, 1917, c. 30, 40 Stat. 217, 219.

[29] 252 U. S. 239, 272.   [30] 268 U. S. 652 (1925).   [31] 274 U. S. 357 (1927).

[32] 254 U. S. 325 (1920).   [33] New York Laws of 1902, Chapter 371.

[34] 268 U. S. 652, 673.

[35] See the discussion of Holmes and Braindeis in disagreement in the section that follows.

[36] 274 U. S. 357, 375.   [37] *Ibid.*   [38] 254 U. S. 325 (1920).

[39] See Holmes' Letter to Pollock, January 23, 1920, *Pollock-Holmes Letters*, v. 2, p. 61.

[40] Mason, *Brandeis, A Free Man's Life* (1946), pp. 572-577.

[41] Sections 2 and 3 of the statute provided as follows:

"Sec. 2. Speaking by word of mouth against enlistment unlawful.—It shall be unlawful for any person in any public place, or at any meeting where more than five persons are assembled, to advocate or teach by word of mouth or otherwise that men should not enlist in the military or naval forces of the United States or the State of Minnesota.

"Sec. 3. Teaching or advocating by written or printed matters against enlistment unlawful.—It shall be unlawful for any person to teach or advocate by any written or printed matter whatsoever, or by oral speech, that the citizens of this state should not aid or assist the United States in prosecuting or carrying on war with the public enemies of the United States."

See Chapter 473, Laws of Minnesota, approved April 20, 1917.

42 See Mr. Justice Holmes' dissents in *Truax* v. *Corrigan*, 257 U. S. 312, 343 (1921); *Meyer* v. *Nebraska*, 262 U. S. 390 (1923); and *Bartels* v. *Iowa*, 262 U. S. 404, 412 (1923).

43 *Meyer* v. *Nebraska* and *Bartels* v. *Iowa*, both cited *supra*.

44 Palmer, "Hobbes, Holmes and Hitler," 31 *American Bar Association Journal* 569 (1945); Lucey, "Holmes—Liberal—Humanitarian—Believer in Democracy?" 39 *Georgetown Law Journal* 523, 545-547 (1950-51); Bernstein, "The Conservative Mr. Justice Holmes," 23 *New England Quarterly* 435, 446-451 (1950). For Mr. Justice Holmes' views on Natural Law, see his essay entitled "Natural Law," Holmes, *Collected Legal Papers* (1920), pp. 310-316; Lerner, *The Mind and Faith of Justice Holmes* (1943), pp. 394-398.

45 Holmes developed his "bad man" theory of the law in an address that he delivered in 1879. See "The Path of the Law," published in his *Collected Legal Papers*, p. 167; also, Lerner, *The Mind and Faith of Justice Holmes*, p. 71.

46 See Holmes' "Ideals and Doubts" published in Lerner, pp. 391, 393; also in *Collected Legal Papers*, pp. 303, 306.

47 Holmes, "Natural Law," Lerner, pp. 394-395; *Collected Legal Papers*, p. 310.

48 For an explanation of what he meant by "can't helps," see his "Natural Law" and his letters to Pollock, *Pollock-Holmes Letters*, v. 1, pp. 99-100, 122, 126; v. 2, pp. 251-252. See also his letters to Dr. Wu, *Holmes, Book Notices, Uncollected Letters and Papers* (1936), pp. 165, 187.

49 Letter to Pollock, April 5, 1919, *Pollock-Holmes Letters*, v. 2, p. 7.

50 *Frohwerk* v. *United States*, 249 U. S. 204 (1919); *Debs* v. *United States*, 249 U. S. 211 (1919); *Abrams* v. *United States*, 250 U. S. 616 (1919); *Schaefer* v. *United States*, 251 U. S. 468 (1920); *Pierce* v. *United States*, 252 U. S. 239 (1920); *Gilbert* v. *Minnesota*, 254 U. S. 325 (1920).

51 *Gitlow* v. *New York*.   52 *Herndon* v. *Lowry*, 301 U. S. 242 (1937).

53 *Herndon* v. *Georgia*, 295 U. S. 441 (1935).

BIBLIOGRAPHY

Biddle, Francis. *Justice Holmes, Natural Law, and the Supreme Court* (The Oliver Wendell Holmes Devise Lectures, 1960, New York, Macmillan Co., 1961).

Holmes, Oliver Wendell, Jr. *Collected Legal Papers* (New York, Harcourt, Brace and Howe, 1920).

Holmes, Oliver Wendell, Jr. "Herbert Spencer; Legislation and Empiricism," [in Shriver, Harry C., ed., *Justice Oliver Wendell Holmes: His Book Notices and Uncollected Letters and Papers* (New York, Central Book Co., 1936)].

Lerner, Max, ed. *The Mind and Faith of Justice Holmes; his Speeches, Essays, Letters and Judicial Opinions* (Boston, Little, Brown and Co., 1943).

Lucey, Francis E. "Holmes—Liberal—Humanitarian—Believer in Democracy?" 39 *Georgetown Law Journal* 523 (1950-51).

Mason, Alpheus Thomas. *Brandeis, Free Man's Life* (New York, Viking Press, 1946).

Mason, Alpheus Thomas. *Brandeis: Lawyer and Judge in the Modern State* (Princeton, Princeton University Press, 1933).

Mendelson, Wallace. "Clear and Present Danger—From Schenck to Dennis," 52 *Columbia Law Review* 313 (1952).

Palmer, Ben W. "Hobbes, Holmes and Hitler," 31 *American Bar Association Journal* 569 (1945).

Shriver, Harry C. *Justice Oliver Wendell Holmes: His Book Notices and Uncollected Letters and Papers* (New York, Central Book Co., 1936).

Wiener, Frederick B. "'Freedom for the Thought that We Hate': Is It a Principle of the Constitution?" 37 *American Bar Association Journal* 177 (1951).

CHAPTER VIII

REFERENCES

[1] "Liberty and Law," Address by Charles Evans Hughes, President of the American Bar Association, 1924-25, 11 *American Bar Association Journal* 563 (1925).

[7] Hughes, *The Supreme Court of the United States: its Foundation, Methods and Achievements, an Interpretation* (1928), pp. 165, 166.

[3] 283 U. S. 359 (1931).

[4] Penal Code of California, § 403a, in force at the time.

[5] 283 U. S. 359, 368, 369 (1931).

[6] *Ibid.*   [7] 283 U. S. 697 (1931).

[8] The pertinent parts of the statute may be found at pp. 701, 702.

[9] *Ibid.*, 707.   [10] 297 U. S. 233 (1936).

[11] Appelee's Brief, *Grosjean* v. *American Press Co.*, case no. 333, Supreme Court of the United States, October Term 1935, p. 26.

[12] 297 U. S. 233, 251.   [13] 299 U. S. 353 (1937).   [14] 299 U. S. 364, 365.

[15] Hughes, *The Supreme Court of the United States, op. cit.* pp. 165, 166.

[16] 301 U. S. 242 (1937).

[17] Hughes, *The Supreme Court of the United States, op. cit.*

[18] 299 U. S. 353 (1937), *supra.*   [19] 301 U.S. 242, 260, 261 (1937).   [20] *Ibid.*, pp. 261, 262.

[21] *Ibid.*, pp. 263, 264.   [22] 303 U. S. 444 (1938).   [23] 308 U. S. 147 (1939).

[24] 310 U. S. 296 (1940).   [25] 312 U. S. 569 (1941).   [26] 303 U. S. 444 (1938).

[27] *Schneider* v. *State (Town of Irvington)*, 308 U. S. 147 (1939); *Cantwell* v. *Connecticut*, 310 U. S. 296 (1940).

[28] 312 U. S. 569 (1941).   [29] 303 U. S. 444 (1938).

[30] 310 U. S. 88 (1940). See also, *Carlson* v. *California*, 310 U. S. 106 (1940), decided

the same day on the authority of the *Thornhill* case. Both are dscussed further in the next chapter.

31 310 U. S. 88, 101, 102.

32 283 U. S. 697 (1931), discussed *supra*.   33 This is discussed in Chapter 2.

34 4 Blackstone's *Commentaries* 151, 152.

35 21 Howell's State Trials 847, 1040 (1783-84).

36 See note, "Previous Restraints Upon Freedom of Speech," 31 *Columbia Law Review* 1148 (1931); note, "Prior Restraint—A Test of Invalidity in Free Speech Cases?" 49 *Columbia Law Review* 1001, 1006 (1949). See also, Freund, "The Supreme Court and Civil Liberties," 4 *Vanderbilt Law Review* 533, 544 (1951).

37 See in particular Chapter 11, *infra*.

BIBLIOGRAPHY

Chafee, Zechariah. *Thirty-Five Years with Freedom of Speech* (New York, Roger N. Baldwin, Civil Liberties Foundation, 1952).

Emerson, Thomas I. "The Doctrine of Prior Restraint," 20 *Law and Contemporary Problems* 648 (1955).

Freund, Paul . "The Supreme Court and Civil Liberties," 4 *Vanderbilt Law Review* 553 (1950-51).

Handel, Samuel. *Charles Evans Hughes and the Supreme Court* (New York, King's Crown Press. 1951).

Hughes, Charles Evans. "Liberty and Law," 11 *American Bar Association Journal* 563 (1925).

Hughes, Charles Evans. *The Supreme Court of the United States, its Foundation, Mechanics and Achievements, an Interpretation* (New York, Columbia University Press, 1928).

"Previous Restraints Upon Freedom of Speech," note, 31 *Columbia Law Review* 1148 (1931).

"Prior Retraint—A Test of Invalidity in Free Speech Cases?" 49 *Columbia Law Review* 1001 (1949).

Pusey, Merlo J. *Charles Evans Hughes* (New York, Macmillan, 1951), 2 v.

CHAPTER IX

REFERENCES

1 The cases decided between 1943 and 1949 in which the test is mentioned in either the majority or minority opinions, or both, are collected by Mendelson, "Clear and Present Danger—From Schenk to Dennis," 52 *Columbia Law Review* 313 (1952), footnotes 59-61, 65-69. For a list of the cases in which the phrase "preferred position" appears in Jehovah's Witnesses cases, see concurring opinion by Mr. Justice Frankfurter in *Kovacs* v. *Cooper*, 336 U. S. 77, 89, 93 (1949). See also Lusk, pp. 591-592; McKay, "The Preference for Freedom," 34 *New York University Law Review* 1182 (1959).

2 310 U. S. 88 (1940).   3 336 U. S. 490 (1949).   4 310 U. S. 88, 103 (1940).

5 State Code of Alabama of 1923, § 3448.

6 310 U. S. 88, 104.   7 *Ibid.*, pp. 104, 105.

[8] *Ibid.*, p. 105.   [9] 310 U. S. 106 (1940).   [10] *Ibid.*, p. 112.

[11] 315 U. S. 769, 776, 777 (1942).   [12] 315 U. S. 437 (1942).   [13] 320 U. S. 293 (1943).   [14] 301 U. S. 468 (1937).

[15] Wisconsin Laws, 1931, c. 376; Laws, 1935, c. 551, § 5.

[16] 312 U. S. 287 (1941).   [17] Ibid., p. 293.   [18] 312 U. S. 321 (1941).

[19] *Ibid.*, p. 325.

[20] 315 U. S. 722 (1942).   [21] 315 U. S. 769 (1942).   [22] *Ibid.*, p. 775

[23] 336 U. S. 490 (1949).

[24] *Ibid.*, 503.   [25] Missouri Revised Statutes, Annotated, § 8305 (1939).

[26] 310 U. S. 296 (1940).

[27] General Statutes of Connecticut, § 6294, as amended by § 860d of the 1937 supplement.

[28] 310 U. S. 296, 308.   [29] *Ibid.*   [30] *Ibid.*, p. 311.

[31] 319 U. S. 157 (1943).   [32] *Ibid.*, p. 163.

[33] *Jones* v. *Opelika,* 319 U. S. 103 (1943); *Murdock* v. *Pennsylvania,* 319 U. S. 105 (1943); *Follet* v. *Town of McCormick,* 321 U. S. 573 (1944).

[34] *Marsh* v. *Alabama,* 326 U. S. 501 (1946).

[35] *Murdock* v. *Pennsylvania,* 319 U. S. 105 (1943).

[36] *Follet* v. *Town of McCormick,* 321 U. S. 573, 576 (1944).

[37] *Marsh* v. *Alabama,* 326 U. S. 501 (1946).

[38] 334 U. S. 558 (1949).

[39] *Hague* v. *C.I.O.,* 307 U. S. 496 (1939); *Lovell* v. *Griffin,* 303 U. S. 444 (1938); *Cantwell* v. *Connecticut,* 310 U. S. 296 (1940).

[40] 310 U. S. 586 (1940).   [41] *Ibid.*, p. 593.   [42] *Ibid.*, pp. 594, 595.

[43] For an interesting discussion of the circumstances that surrounded Stone's *Gobitis* dissent see Mason, *Harlan Fiske Stone: Pillar of the Law* (1956), pp. 525-534. See also Curtis, *Lions Under the Throne* (1947), p. 300, *et seq.*

[44] 319 U. S. 624 (1943).   [45] 316 U. S. 584, 623-624 (1942).   [46] West Virginia Code (1941 suppl.), § 1734.

[47] 319 U. S. 624, 633.   [48] *Ibid.*, p. 634.

[49] 310 U. S. 586, 600.   [50] *Ibid.*   [51] 319 U. S. 624, 639.   [52] 310 U. S. 586, 595.

[53] The same day that the Court handed down the decision in the *Barnette* case, it also decided *Taylor* v. *Mississippi,* 319 U. S. 583 (1943), and much the same reasoning served to upset three criminal convictions. All were for violations of a Mississippi statute which made it a felony to disseminate teachings, orally or in printed form, "designed and calculated to encourage violence, sabotage, or disloyalty to the government of the United States, or the State of Mississippi"; in a like manner to disseminate teaching "which reasonably tends to create an attitude of stubborn refusal to salute, honor or respect the flag." (General Laws of Mississippi, 1942, Chapt. 178) As construed, the statute was found to make a criminal offense out of the communication of views and opinions respecting governmental policies, and of prophecies relating to the future of this and other nations. It punished the appellants although it was neither claimed nor shown that they harbored evil or sinister purposes, advocated or incited subversion, or that they "threatened any clear and present danger to our institutions or our Government." 319 U. S. 583, 589, 590.

[54] 314 U. S. 252 (1941).   [55] 328 U. S. 331 (1946).   [56] 331 U. S. 367 (1947).

57 205 U. S. 454 (1907), discussed *supra,* Chapter 5.

58 1 Stat. 73, 83.

59 See the letter written by Kent to Edward Livingston when the latter solicited Kent's criticism to a proposed Penal Code in which he, Livingston, advocated the abolition of the common law doctrine of contempts, and the substitution of a proceeding by indictment and trial by jury. 38 *American Law Review* 92, 93 (1904).

60 See Stansbury, *Report of the Trial of James H. Peck* (1833).

61 Stansbury, p. 430.

62 7 *Congressional Debates,* 21st Cong., 2nd Sess., Feb. 1, 1831, pp. 560-561.

63 4 Stat. 487, c. 98.   64 *Ibid.*

65 New Hampshire, *Tenney's Case,* 23 N. H. 162 (1851); Arkansas, *State* v *Morrill,* 16 Ark. 384 (1855).

66 247 U. S. 402 (1918).   67 *Ibid.,* pp. 418, 419, 421.   68 313 U. S. 33 (1941).

69 314 U. S. 252 (1941).

70 *Bridges* v. *California,* 314 U. S. 252, 264, quoting from Schofield, "Freedom of the Press in the United States," 9 *Publications of the American Sociological Society* 67, 76. Cf. Levy, *Legacy of Suppression; Freedom of Speech and Press in Early American History* (1960), p. 182.

71 314 U. S. 252, 261.   72 *Ibid.,* 263.   73 *Ibid.*

74 The state court decision is reported in 14 Cal. 2d 464 (1939).

75 328 U. S. 331 (1946).

76 See the citation of contempt quoted at 328 U. S. 331, 339.

77 328 U. S. 331, 334.   78 *Ibid.*   79 331 U. S. 367 (1947).

80 See appendix to the opinion of the Court starting at p. 378.

81 331 U. S. 367, 378.   82 323 U. S. 516 (1945).   83 337 U. S. 1 (1949).

84 General and Special Laws of Texas, Regular Session, 48th Legislature (1943), c. 104.

85 323 U. S. 516, 530.

86 See *Thornhill* v. *Alabama,* 310 U. S. 88, 102-103; *Senn* v. *Tile Layers Protective Union,* 301 U. S. 468, 478, quoted from by the Court.

87 310 U. S. 296, 306 (1940).   88 323 U. S. 516, 548.   89 337 U. S. 1 (1949).

90 *Ibid.,* p. 37.   91 *Ibid.,* p. 3.   92 *Ibid.,* p. 4.   93 283 U. S. 359 (1931).

94 The Illinois appellate court proceedings are reported in 332 Illinois Appellate 17, 396 Illinois Reports 41, 400 Illinois Reports 23. The ordinance appears in the Municipal Code of Chicago, 1939, sec. 193-1.

95 337 U. S. 1, 6.

96 See Mendelson, "Clear and Present Danger—From Schenk to Dennis," 52 *Columbia Law Review* 313, 320 (1952).

97 *Pennekamp* v. *Florida,* 328 U. S. 331 (1946); *Taylor* v. *Mississippi,* 319 U. S. 583 (1943).

98 Justice Jackson joined in the result, 323 U. S. 516, 544 (1945).

99 Mendelson, p. 326.

BIBLIOGRAPHY

Berns, Walter. *Freedom, Virtue and the First Amendment* (Baton Rouge,

Louisiana State University Press, 1957).

Bolan, "Freedom of Speech and the Terminello Case," 24 *St. John's Law Review* 83 (1949-50).

Burke, Richard K. "Contempt by Publication," 1 *Arkansas Law Review* 162 (1946-47).

Coleman, Edward G., and Callopy, Francis W. "The Terminello Case: An Extension or an Abuse of the Clear and Present Danger Concept?" 25 *Notre Dame Lawyer* 99 (1940-50).

Cushman, R. E. " 'Clear and Present Danger' in Free Speech Cases: A Study in Judicial Semantics," *Essays in Political Theory Presented to George H. Sabine,* edited by Milton R. Konvitz and Arthur H. Murphy (Ithaca, Cornell University Press, 1948), p. 311.

Dodd, E. Merrick. "Some State Legislatures Go to War—on Labor Unions," 29 *Iowa Law Review* 148 (1944).

Frankfurter, Felix, and Landis, James M. "Power of Congress over Procedure in Criminal Contempts in 'Inferior' Federal Courts—A Study in Separation of Powers," 37 *Harvard Law Review* 1010 (1923-24).

McKay, Robert B. "The Preference for Freedom," 34 *New York University Law Review* 1182 (1959).

Mason, Alpheus Thomas. *Harlan Fiske Stone: Pillar of the Law* (New York, Viking Press, 1956).

"Municipal Regulation of Free Speech in the Streets and Parks," note, 46 *Illinois Law Review* (1951-52).

Murphy, Walter F. "Mr. Justice Jackson, Free Speech, and the Judicial Function," 12 *Vanderbilt Law Review* 1019 (1959).

Nelles, Walter, and King, Carol W. "Contempt by Publication in the United States," 28 *Columbia Law Review* 401 (1928).

Schofield, Henry. "Freedom of the Press in the United States," 9 *Publications of the American Sociological Society* 67 (1914), published for the American Sociological Society by the University of Chicago Press.

Stansbury, Arthur J. *Report of the Trial of James H. Peck* (Boston, Hilliard, Gray and Co., 1833).

Waite, Edward F. "The Debt of Constitutional Law to Jehovah's Witnesses," 28 *Minnesota Law Review* 209 (1943-44).

Wickhem, John C. "The 'Clear and Present Danger' Test in Constitutionality of Proceedings to Punish for Contempt by Publication During Pending Cases," 1948 *Wisconsin Law Review* 125.

CHAPTER X

REFERENCES

[1] *Bridges* v. *California*, 314 U.S. 252, 295, 296 (1941).

[2] *West Virginia Board of Education* v. *Barnette*, 319 U.S. 624, 663 (1943).

[3] *Ibid.*   [4] *Pennekamp* v. *Florida*, 328 U.S. 331, 353 (1946).

[5] *Craig* v. *Harney*, 331 U.S. 367, 391 (1947).

[6] *Kovacs* v. *Cooper*, 336 U.S. 77, 96 (1949).   [7] 339 U.S. 382 (1940).

[8] 61 Stat. 136, § 9(h).

9 Brief for Appellants, *American Communications Association* v. *Douds,* case No. 10, Supreme Court of the United States, October Term, 1949, p. 58.

10 Brief for the Petitioners, *United Steelworkers of America* v. *N.L.R.B.,* case No. 13, Supreme Court of the United States, October Term, 1949, p. 34.

11 339 U.S. 382, 394.   12 *Ibid.,* p. 396.   13 *Ibid.,* p. 397.

14 340 U.S. 268 (1951).   15 340 U.S. 290 (1941).   16 340 U.S. 315 (1951).

17 340 U.S. 290, 295, 300, 301.   18 310 U.S. 296, 308 (1940).

19 Discussed *supra,* chapter 9.

20 *United States* v. *Dennis,* 341 U.S. 494 (1951).

21 183 F. 2d 201 (1950).   22 *Dennis* v. *United States,* 341 U.S. 494 (1951).

23 Hand, *The Bill of Rights* (The Oliver Wendell Holmes Lectures, Harvard, 1958), p. 59.

24 183 F. 2d 201, 207 (1950).   25 *Ibid.,* 212.   26 *Ibid.*   27 *Ibid.,* p. 213.

28 *Ibid.,* 212.   29 268 U.S. 652 (1925).

30 For a discussion of the case, see *supra,* Chapter 6.

31 183 F. 2d 201, 212.   32 341 U. S. 494, 508.   33 *Ibid.,* p. 510.

34 *Ibid.,* p. 543.   35 *Ibid.,* p. 544.   36 *Ibid.,* p. 568.   37 *Ibid.,* p. 580.

38 *Ibid.,* p. 581.   39 *Ibid.,* p. 585.   40 *Ibid.,* p. 586.

41 Chief Justice Vinson, Justices Reed, Black, Douglas, Jackson, Burton, and Minton.

42 Chief Justice Vinson, Justices Reed, Black, Douglas, Burton and Minton.

43 Chief Justice Vinson, Justices Reed, Burton and Minton.

44 See the discussion of Judge Hand's opinion, *supra.*

45 Justices Frankfurter and Jackson.

46 Justice Jackson.   47 Justice Frankfurter.

48 16 U. S. *Law Week* 3166 (1951).   49 Justices Black and Douglas.

50 *Supra,* Chapter 9.

51 See for instance, *Trial of John Udall,* 1 Howell's State Trials 1271 (1950); *Bushell's Case,* Vaughan 135 (1670); *Trial of Richard Francklin,* 17 Howell's State Trials 625 (1731). See also Holdsworth, v. 8, pp. 342, 343.

52 17 Howell's State Trials 675, 706 (1735).

53 21 Howell's State Trials 847, 961, 962 (1784).

54 32 George III, c. 60 (1792).

55 The trials are discussed in detail in Chapter V.

56 For discussions of these see Chapter VI.

57 251 U. S. 466 (1920).   58 252 U. S. 239 (1920).

59 341 U. S. 494 (1951). Discussed *supra,* Chapter X.

60 251 U. S. 466, 483.

61 *Pierce* v. *United States,* 252 U. S. 239, 250 (1920).

62 The pertinent parts of Judge Medina's charge are quoted at 341 U. S. 494, 511, 512. Compare with this the charge in *Roth* v. *United States,* 354 U. S. 476, 490 (1957), discussed *infra,* an obscenity case in which the jury was told in part: "In this case, ladies and gentlemen of the jury, you and you alone are the exclusive judges of what the common conscience of the community is, and in determining that conscience you are to consider the community as a whole, young and old, educated and uneducated, the religious and the irreligious—men, women and children."

[63] 252, U. S. 239, 250 (1920).   [64] 341 U. S. 494, 513.

[65] 247 U. S. 357, 379 (1927) (emphasis added).   [66] 341 U. S. 494, 513, 514.

[67] 251 U. S. 466, 483 (1920).   [68] 341 U. S. 494, 514.   [69] *Ibid.*, p. 587.

[70] *Yates v. United States,* 354 U. S. 298, 312 (1957); *Kingsley Books, Inc.* v. *Brown,* 354 U. S. 436, 443 (1957); *Roth* v. *United States,* 354 U. S. 476, 486 (1957), all discussed in the chapters that follow.

[71] *Beauharnais* v. *Illinois,* 343 U. S. 250, 273, 274 (1952); *Kingsley Books, Inc.* v. *Brown,* 354 U. S. 436, 447, 448 (1957); *Times Film Corp.* v. *Chicago,* 365 U. S. 43, 83 (1961), all discussed in the chapters that follow.

[72] *Yates v. United States,* 354 U. S. 298, 312 (1957).

[73] *Kingsley Books, Inc.* v. *Brown,* 354 U. S. 436, 443 (1957); *Roth* v. *United States,* 354 U. S. 476, 486 (1957).

[74] See statements by Mr. Justice Black in *Beauharnais* v. *Illinois,* 343 U. S. 273, 274, and by Mr. Justice Brennan in *Kingsley Books, Inc.* v. *Brown,* 354 U. S. 436, 447, 448.

[75] See *Scales* v. *United States,* 367 U. S. 203 (1961), in which the test merits no more than mention in a scant footnote.

[76] Chief Justice Vinson, Justices Reed, Burton and Minton were together on the plurality opinion; Mr. Justice Black joined Mr. Justice Douglas' statement in dissent on this issue.

BIBLIOGRAPHY

Antieu, Chester J. "Dennis v. United States—Precedent, Principle or Perversion?" 5 *Vanderbilt Law Review* 141 (1952).

Douglas, William O. *The Right of the People,* 1st ed. (Garden City, N. Y., Doubleday, 1958).

Gorfinkel, John A., and Mack, Julian. "Dennis v. United States and the Clear and Present Danger Rule," 39 *California Law Review* 475 (1951).

Meiklejohn, Alexander. *Free Speech and Its Relation to Self-Government,* 1st ed. (New York, Harper, 1948).

Richardson, Elliot L. "Freedom of Expression and the Function of Courts," 65 *Harvard Law Review* 1 (1951-52).

Sacks, Albert M., "Mr. Justice Frankfurter," 26 *University of Chicago Law Review* 217 (1959).

Schmandt, Henry J. "The Clear and Present Danger Doctrine: A Reappraisal in the Light of Dennis v. United States," 1 *St. Louis University Law Journal* 265 (1951).

Thomas, Helen Shirley. *Felix Frankfurter: Scholar on the Bench* (Baltimore, Johns Hopkins Press, 1960).

CHAPTER XI

REFERENCES

[1] *Beauharnais* v. *Illinois,* 343 U. S. 250 (1952).

[2] *Roth* v. *United States,* 354 U. S. 476 (1957).

[3] 341 U. S. 694 (1951).   [4] 61 Stat. 136, 141, § 8(b)(4)(A).

[5] 345 U. S. 192 (1953).

[6] Virginia Acts, Extra Session, 1947, c. 2; Virginia Code, §§ 40-68 to 40-74.

7 354 U. S. 294 (1957).   8 354 U. S. 284, 289.   9 *Ibid.*, 291.   10 *Ibid.*, p. 295.

11 345 U. S. 67 (1953).   12 345 U. S. 395 (1953).   13 345 U. S. 395, 405.

14 341 U. S. 622 (1951).

15 355 U. S. 313 (1958).   16 362 U. S. 60 (1960).   17 343 U. S. 250 (1952).

18 354 U. S. 476 (1957).   19 *Ibid.*, 514.

20 *Roth* v. *United States,* 354 U. S. 476, 483, citing *Beauharnais* v. *Illinois,* 343 U. S. 250, 266.

21 Illinois Criminal Code, § 224a; Illinois Revised Statutes, 1949, c. 38, Div. 1, § 471.

22 18 U. S. Code § 1461.   23 West's California Penal Code Ann., 1955, § 311.

24 354 U. S. 476, 486.

25 *Ibid.*, 489. See cases cited in footnote 26 of the Court's opinion.

26 354 U. S. 476, 487, 488.

27 310 U. S. 88, 101-102 (1940). Quoted at 354 U. S. 476, 488.

28 354 U. S. 476, 490.

29 New York Code of Criminal Procedure as amended in 1954, § 22-a.

30 354 U. S. 436 (1957).   31 *Ibid.*, 441.

32 354 U. S. 436, 441.   33 354 U. S. 298 (1957).   34 342 U. S. 580 (1952).

35 54 Stat 670.

36 Chief Justice Vinson, Justices Reed, Jackson and Minton.

37 Chief Justice Vinson, Justices Reed, Burton and Minton.

38 Mr. Justice Burton.

39 Chief Justice Vinson, Justices Reed, Burton and Minton in the majority; Justices Black and Douglas dissenting.

40 Justices Burton, Black and Douglas.   41 Justices Black and Douglas.

42 18 U. S. C. § 2385. [54 Stat. 670. § 2(a)(3)].

43 354 U. S. 298, 321.   44 *Ibid.*, 324.   45 28 U. S. C. § 2106.

46 Justice Black, with whom Justice Douglas joined, concurring in part and dissenting in part, 354 U. S. 298, 339.

47 Justices Brennan and Whittaker took no part in the consideration or the decision of the case.

48 Justice Burton concurred in the result, Justices Black and Douglas concurred in part and dissented in part.

49 Justice Clark.   50 354 U. S. 178 (1957).   51 2 U. S. Code, § 192.

52 345 U. S. 41 (1953).   53 354 U. S. 178, 198.

54 103 U. S. 168 (1881). See also, *McGrain* v. *Dougherty,* 273 U. S. 135 (1927), and *Sinclair* v. *United States,* 279 U. S. 263 (1928), the Teapot Dome Scandal cases.

55 354 U. S. 178, 198, 199.

56 See House Resolution 282, 75th Cong., 3rd Sess., 83 *Congressional Record* 7568, 7586, and House Resolution 5, 79th Cong., 1st Sess., 91 *Congressional Record* 10, 15. The former created the Committee and the latter made it permanent.

57 354 U. S. 234 (1957).   58 New Hampshire Laws, 1951 c. 193.

59 New Hampshire Laws, 1953, c. 307.   60 100 N. H. 103 (1956).   61 354 U. S. 234, 245.

62 Justices Black, Douglas and Brennan.   63 354 U. S. 234, 255 at 267.

64 *Uphaus* v. *Wyman,* 360 U. S. 72 (1959); *Barenblatt* v. *United States,* 360 U. S.

109 (1959); *Wilkinson* v. *United States,* 365 U. S. 399 (1961); *Braden* v. *United States,* 365 U. S. 431 (1961).

[65] 360 U. S. 72 (1959).   [66] 350 U. S. 497 (1956).

[67] 360 U. S. 72, 76.   [68] 360 U. S. 72, 81.   [69] 360 U. S. 109 (1959).

[70] See summary of petitioner's contentions, pp. 115, 116.   [71] 360 U. S. 109, 117, 121.

[72] *Ibid.,* 126, 127.   [73] *Ibid.,* 127, 128.   [74] *Ibid.,* 130.

[75] 365 U. S. 399 (1961).   [76] *Ibid.,* 414.   [77] *Ibid.*

[78] 365 U. S. 399, 407.   [79] 365 U. S. 431 (1961).

[80] 365 U. S. 431, 435.   [81] 279 U. S. 263 (1929).   [82] 360 U. S. 109, 134, at 145.

[83] *Ibid.,* 151, 152.   [84] 365 U. S. 399, 415, 419, 420.

[85] 360 U. S. 109, 134, 162.   [86] 365 U. S. 431, 445, 446.   [87] *Ibid.,* 446.

[88] 365 U. S. 399, 423 at 425.   [89] 365 U. S. 399, 425.

[90] 354 U. S. 178, 200, quoted at 365 U. S. 431, 447.

[91] 365 U. S. 431, 456, 457.   [92] 360 U. S. 72, 82.   [93] *Ibid.,* 93.   [94] *Ibid.,* 100.

[95] 357 U. S. 449 (1958).The Alabama state proceeding had been founded on a valid state statute (Alabama Code, 1940, Title 10, §§ 192-198), similar to many of other states, which required a foreign corporation to supply certain information to the state before it could engage in business there. But in its application, the state had failed to disclose a proper justification and purpose. Therefore, the Supreme Court held, "the immunity from state scrutiny of membership lists which the Association claims on behalf of its members is here so related to the right of the members to pursue their lawful private interests privately and to associate freely with others in so doing as to come within the protection of the Fourteenth Amendment." 357 U. S. 449, 466.

[96] 360 U. S. 72, 97.   [97] 365 U. S. 399, 430.

BIBLIOGRAPHY

Basil, Thomas T. "Constitutional Limitations on the Legislative Power of Investigations," 7 *Buffalo Law Review* 267 (1957-58).

Beck, Carl. *Contempt of Congress: A Study of the Prosecutions Initiated by the Committee on Un-American Activities, 1945-1957* (New Orleans, Hauser Press, 1959).

Black, Hugo L. "The Bill of Rights," 35 *New York University Law Review* 865 (1960) [James Madison Lecture, New York University School of Law, 1960].

Bradley, Lawrence J., and Marino, Joseph A. "Constitutional Law—Freedom of Speech—Obscenity 1958-1960," 35 *Notre Dame Lawyer* 537 (1960).

Crampton, Roger C. "The Supreme Court and State Power to Deal with Subversion and Loyalty," 43 *Minnesota Law Review* 1025 (1958-59).

Fleischmann, Hartly. "Watkins v. United States and Congressional Power of Investigation," 9 *Hastings Law Journal* 145 (1957-58).

Kalven, Harry, Jr. "Mr. Alexander Meiklejohn and the Barenblatt Opinion," 27 *University of Chicago Law Review* 97 (1960).

Kellett, Earl L. "Legislative Investigating Committees and the Right of Privacy," 5 *South Dakota Law Review* 97 (1960).

Konvitz, Milton R. *Fundamental Liberties of a Free People: Religion, Speech, Press, Assembly* (Ithaca, N. Y., Cornell University Press, 1957).

Landis, James M. "Constitutional Limitations on the Congressional Power of Investigations," 40 *Harvard Law Review* 153 (1926-27).

Lusk, Louis E. "The Present Status of the 'Clear and Present Danger' Test'—A Brief History and Some Observations," 45 *Kentucky Law Journal* 576 (1956-57).

Meiklejohn, Alexander. "The Barenblatt Opinion," 27 *University of Chicago Law Review* 329 (1960).

Nutting, Charles B. "Definitive Standards in Federal Obscenity Legislation," 23 *Iowa Law Review* 24 (1937-38).

Pritchett, C. Herman. "The Political Offender and the Warren Court," 38 *Boston University Law Review* 53 (1958).

Summers, Marvin. "The First Amendment as a Restraint on the Power of Congress to Investigate," 43 *Marquette Law Review* 459 (1959-60).

"Supreme Court, 1956 Term," 71 *Harvard Law Review* 83 (1947).

CHAPTER XII

References

[1] See Chapter XI, *supra.*

[2] See *Barenblatt* v. *United States,* 360 U. S. 109 (1959);*Uphaus* v. *Wyman,* 360 U. S. 72 (1959); *Wilkinson* v. *United States,* 365 U. S. 399 (1961); *Braden* v. *United States,* 365 U. S. 431 (1961).

[3] Act of April 16, 1913, 103 Ohio Laws 399. See §§ 3-5 of the act.

[4] Art. 1, § 11 of the Constitution of Ohio.   [5] 236 U. S. 230, 244 (1915).

[6] 343 U. S. 495 (1952).

[7] McKinney's New York Laws, 1947, Education Law, §§ 122, 129. See Brief of Appellees, case no. 522, Supreme Court of the United States, October Term 1951.

[8] Brief of Appellees, p. 11, 17, 18, 20-27.

[9] *Matter of Joseph Burstyn, Inc.* v. *Wilson,* 303 N. Y. 242, 258 (1951).

[10] 343 U. S. 495, 504, 505. See also the Supreme Court's one line *per curiam* opinion in *Commercial Pictures Corp.* v. *Regent of the Univ. of the State of New York,* 346 U. S. 587 (1954), in which it overturned the New York Court of Appeals' decision that the film *La Rhonde* could be banned as "immoral" and as "tend[ing] to corrupt morals."

[11] McKinney's New York Laws, 1953, Education Law, § 122 (a).

[12] *Kingsley International Pictures Corp.* v. *Regents of the Univ. of the State of New York,* 360 U. S. 684 (1959).

[13] *Matter of Kingsley International Pictures Corp.* v. *Regents of the Univ. of the State of New York,* 4 N. Y. 2d 349 (1958).

[14] *Ibid.,*   [15] 360 U. S. 684, 688.

[16] Justices Black, Frankfurter, Douglas, Clark, Harlan, and Whittaker.

[17] *Josph Burstyn, Inc.* v. *Wilson,* 343 U. S. 495 (1952). *supra.*

[18] 274 U. S. 357, 376, quoted at 360 U. S. 684 at 689.

[19] 360 U. S. 684, 689.   [20] *Times Film Corp.* v. *Chicago,* 365 U. S. 43 (1961), *infra.*

[21] 360 U. S. 684, 690.

[22] Mr. Justice Black concurred separately, 360 U. S. 684, 690, and he also joined in Mr. Justice Douglas' separate concurring opinion, 360 U. S. 684, 697.

[23] Mr. Justice Frankfurter concurred in the result, 360 U. S. 684, 691; Mr. Justice Harlan, with whom Mr. Justice Frankfurter and Mr. Justice Whittaker joined, concurred in the result, 360 U. S. 684, 702.

[24] 360 U. S. 684, 699, 701, 702.   [25] 365 U. S. 43 (1961).

[26] 268 U. S. 652 (1925).   [27] 361 U. S. 147 (1959).   [28] 283 U. S. 697, 715-716 (1931).

[29] 365 U. S. 43, 47.   [30] *Ibid.*, p. 49.   [31] *Ibid.*, p. 50.   [32] *Ibid.*, p. 51.

[33] *Ibid.*, 54.   [34] *Ibid.*, 77.   [35] *Ibid.*, 78.

[36] Plato, *Republic* (The Dialogues of Plato, Jowett trans., 1953), v. 2, pp. 221, quoted in the opinion at p. 79.

[37] 365 U. S. 43, 79.

[38] See 32 Halsbury's *Laws of England* (2nd ed., 1939), p. 68.

[39] 365 U. S. 43, 78, 84.

BIBLIOGRAPHY

"Constitutional Law—Freedom of Press—Validity of Motion Picture Licensing Statute," 58 *Michigan Law Review* 134 (1950-60).

"Constitutional Law—Freedom of Speech in Motion Pictures—Doctrine of Prior Restraint," 7 *Wayne Law Review* 589 (1961).

"Constitutional Law—Freedom of Speech—Not all Prior Restraints are Invalid," 30 *University of Cinncinnati Law Review* 386 (1961).

"Constitutional Law—Freedom of Speech—Prior Restraint on Motion Picture Exhibition," 14 *Vanderbilt Law Review* 1525 (1961).

"Constitutional Law—'Lady Chatterly's Lover'—Death to Motion Picture Censorship?" 31 *Mississippi Law Journal* 95 (1959-60).

"Constitutional Law: Motion Picture Censorship," 44 *Cornell Law Quarterly* 411 1958-59).

"Constitutional Law—Motion Picture Censorship," 26 *Brooklyn Law Review* 112 (1959-60).

"Constitutional Law—Motion Picture Censorship,"—Pre-Exhibition Licensing," 27 *Brooklyn Law Review* 343 (1961).

"Constitutional Law—Motion Pictures—Obscenity—Prior Restraint—Prior Censorship of a Motion Picture by the State is not a Violation of Free Speech and Press," 38 *University of Detroit Law Journal* 483 (1961).

"Constitutional Law—New York Statute Censoring 'Sexual Immorality' in Motion Picture Film Held Unconstitutional," 33 *Temple Law Quarterly* 242 (1959-60).

"Constitutional Law—Presumption of Constitutionality—Application to Regulation of Obscene Motion Pictures," 1961 *Wisconsin Law Review* 659 (1961).

"Constitutional Law—Prior Restraint—Administrative Censorship of Motion Pictures," 47 *Iowa Law Review* 162 (1961).

Emerson, Thomas I. "The Doctrine of Prior Restraint," 20 *Law and Contemporary Problems* 648 (1955).

Mendelson, Wallace. "Clear and Present Danger—Another Decade," 39 *Texas Law Review* 449 (1961).

Nimmer, Melville B. "The Constitutionality of Official Censorship of Motion Pictures," 25 *University of Chicago Law Review* 625 (1957-58).

CHAPTER XIII

REFERENCES

1 See Mr. Justice Black's dissents in *Barenblatt v. United States,* 360 U. S. 109, 134 (1959), and in *Braden v. United States,* 365 U. S. 431, 438 (1961), as well as both his and Mr. Justice Douglas' dissents in the *Scales* and the *Subversive Activities Control Board cases.,* discussed *infra.*

2 367 U. S. 203 (1961).   3 367 U. S. 1 (1961).   4 64 Stat. 987.

5 367 U. S. 456 (1961).

6 Certiorari was first granted in the 1955 Term of the Court, 350 U. S. 992 (1955), was first heard at the 1956 Term and was set for reargument at the 1957 Term. The first conviction was reversed on the Solicitor General's concession that Scales was entitled to at least a new trial because of the Court's intervening decision in *Jencks* v. *United States,* 353 U. S. 657 (1957). Certiorari was again granted after the second conviction in 1958, 358 U. S. 917 (1958); argument was first heard at the 1958 Term, was set for reargument at the 1959 Term, but was not reheard until the 1960 Term so that it could be heard and considered together with *Communist Party of the United States* v. *Subversive Activities Control Board.*

7 353 U. S. 657 (1957).   8 367 U. S. 203 (1961).

9 The pertinent parts of the statute are as follows:

"Whoever organizes or helps or attempts to organize any society, group, or assembly of persons who teach, advocate, or encourage the overthrow or destruction of any such government by force or violence; or becomes or is a member of, or affiliates with, any such society, group, or assembly of persons, knowing the purposes thereof—

"Shall be fined not more than $20,000 or imprisoned not more than twenty years, or both, and shall be ineligible for employment by the United States or any department or agency thereof, for the five years next following his conviction."

10 See briefs for both sides in *Scales* v. *United States,* case no. 1, October Term, 1960, Supreme Court of the United States.

11 367 U. S. 203, 228-230.   12 *Ibid.,* p. 228.   13 *Ibid.,* p. 230.

14 *Schenck* v. *United States,* 249 U. S. 47, 52 (1919), discussed *supra,* Chapter VII.

15 367 U. S. 203, 229.   16 *Ibid.,* p. 230.   17 *Ibid.,* p. 259, 261.

18 *Ibid.,* p. 261.   19 *Ibid.,* 262.   20 *Ibid.,* 262, 270.   21 *Ibid.,* pp. 270, 271.

22 64 Stat. 987.   23 18 U. S. C. § 2385.   24 367 U. S. 203, 208.

25 354 U. S. 298 (1957). See *Noto* v. *United States,* 367 U. S. 290 (1961), decided the same day as the *Scales* case, in which the record was found to present much the same infirmities as the *Yates* record. As the Court upset the conviction of Noto who had been convicted under the membership clause of the Smith Act it said: "It need hardly be said that it is upon the particular evidence in a particular record that a particular defendant must be judged, and not upon the evidence in some other record or upon what may be supposed to be the tenets of the Comumnist Party."

26 367 U. S. 203, 235   27 *Ibid.,* 230 *et seq.*   28 367 U. S. 1 (1961).

29 64 Stat. 987, amended principally by the Communist Control Act of 1954, 68 Stat. 775.

30 Based on the Board's refusal to strike certain testimony, to produce certain memoranda, and on the denial by the Court of Appeals of certain of the Party's motions.

31 The Party contended that the Board and the Court of Appeals erred in their construction of the Act and in their application of it, on the facts of the record, to the Party.

32 The registration requirements of the Act were alleged to be in the nature of a bill of attainder, to violate the provisions of the First and Fifth Amendments, to violate due process by legislative predetermination of facts. The Act was also said to be unconstitutionally vague and the Board to be so biased against the Communist Party as to deprive it of a fair hearing.

33 Defined in § 3 (3) of the Act.   34 Defined in § 3 (4) of the Act.

35 323 U. S. 516 (1945), discussed in Chapter IX.

36 357 U. S. 449 (1958).   37 361 U. S. 516 (1960).   38 364 U. S. 479 (1960).

39 367 U. S. 1, 91.

40 *Ibid.*, p. 93.   41 *Ibid.*, pp. 96, 97.   42 *Ibid.*   43 *Ibid.*, pp. 169, 170.

44 See his concurring opinion in *Bakery & Pastry Drivers & Helpers* v. *Wohl*, 315 U. S. 769, 776-777 (1942).

45 367 U. S. at 175.   46 *Ibid.*, p. 166.   47 367 U. S. 456 (1961).

48 See also *Watkins* v. *United States*, 354 U. S. 178 (1957), *Sweezy* v. *New Hampshire*, 354 U. S. 234 (1957), *Uphaus* v. *Wyman*, 360 U. S. 72 (1959), discussed *supra*, Chapter XI.

49 The petitioner had been subpoenaed to appear before the subcommittee in Albany but, at the request of his counsel, it was agreed that he would appear before the subcommittee three days later in Washington, D. C.

50 The *Uphaus, Barenblatt, Wilkinson* and *Braden* cases, cited *supra*.

51 The Chief Justice, Justices Black, Douglas, and Brennan.

52 *Engel* v. *Vitale*, 370 U. S. 421 (1962).   53 370 U.S.478(1962).

54 *Roth* v. *United States*, 354 U. S. 476 (1957).   55 370 U. S. 375 (1962).

56 370 U. S. 478, 519.   57 370 U. S. 478, 497.

58 See *Hennegan* v. *Esquire, Inc.*, 327 U. S. 146, 156 (1946).

59 370 U. S. 478, 519.

60 See Transcript of Record, Supreme Court of the United States, case No. 369, October Term, 1961, p. 6.

61 *Ibid.*, p. 12.   62 *Ibid.*, pp. 17-19.   63 *Ibid.*, pp. 42-44.

64 314 U. S. 252 (1941).   65 328 U. S. 331 (1946).

66 341 U. S. 494 (1951).

67 Mr. Justice Frankfurter, the archenemy of "clear and present danger," did not participate in the decision of the case because of illness and Mr. Justice Whittaker had retired.

BIBLIOGRAPHY

"Constitutional Law—Communist Party Membership—Criminal Convictions Upheld," 33 *Mississippi Law Journal* 131 (1961).

"Constitutional Law—Due Process of Law—Self Incrimination Privilege—Membership in the Communist Party Held to be Criminal Offense—Communist Party Required to Register with the Attorney General," 37 *Notre Dame Lawyer* 239 (1961).

"Constitutional Law—Freedom of Association and Right Against Self Incrimination Under First and Fifth Amendments—An Order that the Communist Party Register in Accordance with the Subversive Activities Control Act is not Unconstitutional," 23 *University of Pittsburgh Law Review* 237 (1961).

"Constitutional Law—Subversive Activities Control Act—Sufficiency of Evidence —Mandatory Registration of the Communist Party Constitutional," 29 *Albany Law Review* 95 (1962).

Hand, Learned. *The Spirit of Liberty, 2nd ed., enlarged* (New York, Knopf, 1953).

Lockhart, William B., and McClure, Robert C. "Censorship of Obscenity: The Developing Constitutional Standards," 45 *Minnesota Law Review* 5 (1960).

Murray, John Courtney. *We Hold These Truths* (New York, Sheed and Ward, 1960).

Paul, James C. N., and Schwartz, Murray L. *Federal Censorship; Obscenity in the Mail* (N. Y., The Free Press of Glencoe, Inc., 1961).

CHAPTER XIV

REFERENCES

[1] Cardozo, *The Nature of the Judicial Process.* See Hall, editor, *Selected Writings of Benjamin Nathan Cardozo* (1947), p. 111.

[2] President Dwight D. Eisenhower, Annual Message on the State of the Union delivered to the Congress, January 9, 1959. See House Document 1, 86th Congress, 1st Session. See also, 105 *Congressional Record* 359, 362 (1959).

[3] President John F. Kennedy, Inaugural Address, January 20, 1961. 107 *Congressional Record* 970 (1961) [daily pagination].

[4] See the Constitution of the State of Alaska agreed to by the Delegates of the People of Alaska, February 5, 1956.

[5] See address delivered by the late Robert H. Jackson, Associate Justice, Supreme Court of the United States, before the annual meeting of the Canadian Bar Association, February 19, 1944, Toronto, Canada, 90 *Congressional Record* A1172 (1944).

[6] *Pennekamp* v. *Florida,* 328 U. S. 331, 353 (1946).   [7] *Ibid.*

[8] *American Communications Ass'n* v. *Douds,* 339 U. S. 382 (1950).

[9] 341 U. S. 494 (1951).

[10] See Judge Hand's original exposition of this in *United States* v. *Dennis,* 183 F. 2d 201, 212 (C. A. 2, 1950).

[11] Nutting, "Is the First Amendment Obsolete?" 30 *The George Washington Law Review* 167, 171 (1961).

[12] *Adamson* v. *California,* 332 U. S. 46, 70 (1947).

[13] Hand, *The Bill of Rights* (1958), p. 2.   [14] Nutting, p. 171.

[15] *Schenck* v. *United States,* 249 U. S. 47, 52 (1919).

[16] Nutting, p. 172.

[17] See, for instance, his opinion for a unanimous Court in *Giboney* v. *Empire*

Storage & Ice Co., 336 U. S. 490 (1949), and his dissenting opinion in *Konigsburg* v. *State Bar of California*, 366 U. S. 36, 64 (1961).

18 Nutting, p. 173. See also Charles L. Black, Jr., "Mr. Justice Black, the Supreme Court, and the Bill of Rights," *Harpers*, February, 1961, pp. 63, 65; Mendelson, *Justices Black and Frankfurter: Conflict in the Court* (1961), the entire tenor of which appears to be an indictment of Mr. Justice Black and a glorification of Mr. Justice Frankfurter. One should not read the book without also reading James Clayton's book review of it that appeared in *The Washington Post* for January 15, 1961. Mr. Clayton not only makes the point that the treatment accorded Mr. Justice Black's judicial philosophy is lopsided and unfair while Mr. Justice Frankfurter's philosophy is depicted as so perfect that no one should question it, but he also asserts that it might have been worthwhile for the publisher to make the reader aware of the fact that Mr. Mendelson once worked for Mr. Justice Frankfurter in Washington. He could have noted this, wrote Mr. Clayton, in the descriptive material about Mendelson. For a different type review of the book see that by Professor Dixon, 30 *Fordham Law Review* 214 (1961), in which Professor Mendelson's reaction is said to be "both sharp and profound" and the result "a powerful work."

19 341 U. S. 394 (1951).

20 *Scales* v. *United States*, 367 U. S. 203, 270, 271 (1951).

21 *Ibid.*, p. 261.

22 1962 James Madison Lecture delivered at The New York University Law Center, February 1, 1962, by Mr. Chief Justice Earl Warren.

23 368 U. S. 157 (1961).   24 *Ibid.*, pp. 163, 164.

25 Otis, *The Rights of the British Colonies Asserted and Proved* (1765), p. 8.

26 "A Sermon Preached in the Audience of His Excellency William Shirley, Esq., May 29, 1754," by Jonathan Mayhew. See also a sermon preached by the Reverend Samuel Quincy in which he maintained that the knowledge of God by light and nature taught that God "has endowed us with Reason and Understanding (Faculties which Brutes have not) on purpose to contemplate his Beauty and Glory, and to keep our inferior Appetites in due Subjection to his Laws, written in our Hearts." *Twenty Sermons Preached in the Parish of St. Philips Church, Charleston, S. C.* (1750), pp. 59, 60.

27 35 *New York University Law Review* 865, 874, 875 (1960) [emphasis added].

28 See Nutting, cited *supra*, Mendelson, cited *supra*. Also Dixon, 30 *Fordham Law Review* 214, 217, footnote 18.

29 See Hall, editor, *Selected Writings of Benjamin Nathan Cardozo* (1947), p. 200.

30 Nutting, "Is the First Amendment Obsolete?" cited *supra*.

31 *Gitlow* v. *New York*, 268 U. S. 652 (1925).

32 See *Prudential Ins. Co. of America* v. *Cheek*, 259 U. S. 530 (1922). See also Mr. Justice Holmes' opinion in *Patterson* v. *Colorado* in which the Court left "undecided the question whether there is to be found in the Fourteenth Amendment a prohibition similar to that in the First." 205 U. S. 454, 462 (1907).

33 Among the later cases see *Kidd* v. *Pearson*, 128 U. S. 1 (1888); *United States* v. *Knight*, 156 U. S. 1 (1895); *Capital City Dairy Co.* v. *Ohio*, 183 U. S. 238

(1902); *United Mine Workers* v. *Coronado Coal Co.,* 259 U. S. 344 (1922); *Hammer* v. *Dagenhart,* 247 U. S. 251 (1918).

34 312 U. S. 100 (1940).   35 8 Wallace 68 (1868).   36 *Ibid.,* p. 138.
37 322 U. S. 533 (1944).

38 *West Coast Hotel Co.* v. *Parrish,* 300 U. S. 379 (1937).

39 *San Mateo County* v. *Southern Pacific Rairoad Co.,* 116 U. S. 138 (1885). Although argument on the case took place in December, 1882, consideration of the case was differed by stipulation of the parties and it was finally dismissed in 1885.

40 Oral argument on behalf of Defendant by Roscoe Conkling, case no. 106, October Term 1883, p. 34. See also Brief for Defendant by S. W. Sanderson, pp. 28-55.

41 *Georgia* v. *Braislford,* 2 Dallas 402, 405 (1792).

42 *Rubaiyat of Omar Khayyam,* Fitzerald translation, 5th ed., verse 71.

BIBLIOGRAPHY

Black, Charles L., Jr., "Mr. Justice Black, the Supreme Court, and the Bill of Rights," *Harpers,* February, 1961.

Cardozo, Benjamin Nathan. *The Nature of the Judicial Process* [Hall, Margaret E., *Selected Writings of Benjamin Nathan Cardozo* (New York, Fallon Publications, 1949)].

Clayton, James. Book Review of Mendelson's *Justices Black and Frankfurter: Conflict in the Court* (1961), *The Washington Post,* January 15, 1961.

Dixon, Robert Galloway, Jr. Book review of *Justices Black and Frankfurter: Conflict in the Court,* by Wallace Mendelson (Chicago, University of Chicago Press, 1961), 30 *Fordham Law Review* 214 (1961).

Dixon, Robert Calloway, Jr. Book review of *Shall We Amend the Fifth Amendment?* by Lewis Mayers (New York, Harper Brothers, 1959), 9 *Journal of Public Law* 214 (1960).

Fairman, Charles, and Morrison, Stanley. "Does the Fourteenth Amendment Incorporate the Bill of Rights?" 2 *Stanford Law Review* 5, 140 (1940-50).

Graham, Howard Jay. "The 'Conspiracy Theory' of the Fourteenth Amendment," 47 *Yale Law Journal* 371 (1937-39), 48 *Yale Law Journal* 171 (1938-39).

Hand, Learned. *The Bill of Rights.* Oliver Wendell Holmes Lectures, Harvard, 1958 (Cambridge, Harvard University Press, 1958).

Jackson, Robert H. An address delivered before the annual meeting of the Canadian Bar Association, February 19, 1944, at Toronto, Canada, 90 *Congressional Record* A1172 (1944).

Meiklejohn, Alexander. "The First Amendment is an Absolute," *1961 The Supreme Court Review* 245.

Mendelson, Wallace. *Justices Black and Frankfurter: Conflict in the Court.* (Chicago, University of Chicago Press, 1961).

Nutting, Charles B. "Is the First Amendment Obsolete?" 30 *The George Washington Law Review* 167 (1961-62).

"The Supreme Court, 1960 Term," 75 *Harvard Law Review* 40 (1961).

Warren, Earl. 1962 James Madison Lecture delivered at The New York University Law Center, February 1, 1962, by Mr. Chief Justice Earl Warren. [See "The Bill of Rights and The Military," 37 *New York University Law Review* 181 (1962)].

212

TABLE OF CASES

214

INDEX

(See also Table of Cases)

218

219